LOSING DAD

PARANOID SCHIZOPHRENIA:
A FAMILY'S SEARCH FOR HOPE

AMANDA LAPERA

ADAMO PRESS

Aliso Viejo, Calif.

Publisher's Cataloging-in-Publication
(Provided by Quality Books, Inc.)

LaPera, Amanda.
    Losing Dad : paranoid schizophrenia : a family's search for hope / Amanda LaPera. -- First edition.
    pages cm
    Includes bibliographical references.
    LCCN 2013916680
    ISBN 978-0-9897037-2-7
    ISBN 978-0-9897037-3-4 (pbk.)

    1. Paranoid schizophrenia--Popular works.
    2. Paranoid schizophrenics--Family relationships.
    3. Anosognosia--Popular works.   I. Title.

RC514.L37 2013   616.89'8
                          QBI13-600166

For Dad,
With love

A portion of the proceeds from the sale of this book are donated to NAMI-OC, an affiliate of the National Alliance on Mental Illness

To contact Amanda LaPera, and for information on her books and speaking schedule, go to www.amandalapera.com. You may also contact her through the publisher's website www.adamopress.com.

CONTENTS

PART THREE: CATACLYSM

FOREWORD

by Dr. Xavier Amador

SCHIZOPHRENIA, SCHIZOAFFECTIVE AND BIPOLAR DISORDER are biological brain disorders. One half of all persons diagnosed with these disorders suffer from a symptom that leaves them unaware they are ill and at odds with most everyone that is trying to help them. If you didn't think you had a disease, would you take medication for it? From the time he was first diagnosed with schizophrenia and for the next two decades, this is what my brother Henry experienced. He knew he was not ill and all of us that loved him were equally certain he was and desperately needed treatment. This unawareness symptom—called anosognosia—and my naive response to it—trying to educate Henry about an illness he was certain he did not have—led to seven years of conflict between two brothers who had always been close, respectful and trusting.

Early in my career as a clinical psychologist, in the mid-1980's, I worked extensively evaluating neurological patients. I could not help but notice the similarities between the neurological syndrome called *anosognosia* (i.e., unawareness of deficits, symptoms, or signs of illness) and poor insight in persons with serious mental illness. Patients with anosognosia will frequently give strange reasons—what neurologists call *confabulations*—to explain any observations that contradict their beliefs that they are not ill. For example, one man I evaluated had been in a car accident and had suffered a serious brain injury, leaving him paralyzed on the left side of his body. When I asked him if he could raise his left arm, he said he could, but was unable to do so. Even though his arm lay motionless, he still believed he could raise it. When asked for an explanation he said, "You've done something to my arm, tied it down in some way." Such was his certainty that nothing was changed and all was well with him.

There is now abundant research that links severe and persistent unawareness of having schizophrenia, bipolar and related disorders to functional and structural abnormalities in the brain, usually involving frontal lobes. Some people, unfortunately, still believe that severe and persistent problems with insight are only a consequence of "denial" (i.e. a coping mechanism) despite scientific consensus to the contrary. When I was asked to co-chair the text revision of the "Schizophrenia and Related Disorders" section of the DSM-IV-TR, together with my co-chair we called on experts in the field to review the scientific literature and draft descriptions of the disorder that reflected scientific consensus, not merely personal opinion. Here is what they found:

Associated Features and Disorders

"A majority of individuals with Schizophrenia have poor insight regarding the fact that they have a psychotic illness. Evidence suggests that poor insight is a manifestation of the illness itself rather than a coping strategy…comparable to the lack of awareness of neurological deficits seen in stroke, termed anosognosia." American Psychiatric Association Press, 2000. Page 304

A word about how I met the author of *Losing Dad*. In response to my experiences trying to help my brother and countless others with serious mental illness who had anosognosia, I developed—over many years of trial and error—the Listen-Empathize-Agree-Partner® (LEAP®) communication program. Eventually, this led to the creation of The LEAP® Institute and the training of tens of thousands of family caregivers, health care professionals and even law enforcement and corrections officers in a form of communication that builds bridges to persons suffering alone with these illnesses. Amanda LaPera was among those eager to learn a different way of interacting and communicating with her father who was suffering from mental illness.

She first approached me after going through a similar struggle with her father, who displayed an unusual case of late-onset severe mental illness. At the time, she did not know about the LEAP strategy. Her father's dramatic transformation and subsequent hallucinations and paranoia, created a distance between him and his loved ones. Like my brother, her father displayed "poor insight" into his illness and refused treatment. He cycled through involuntary mental hospitalizations before cutting contact with his loved ones and ending up homeless. This tragic reality, unfortunately, is one lived by too many other families.

As I had done, Amanda LaPera found help with the National Alliance on Mental Illness (NAMI), the largest grassroots organization dedicated to helping those affected by mental illness. I encourage all family members, worldwide, who are struggling with a mentally ill relative to investigate and become involved with a family advocacy group (like NAMI in the US) for many reasons, not the least of which is to feel less alone and more supported in their quest to better the life of their mentally ill relative. I have learned much from NAMI and similar foreign organizations that have followed its example. I have found great comfort in knowing not only that there are many other families like mine but also that there are forces at work to change mental health laws, fund research, and improve treatments.

Amanda LaPera gives a human face to mental illness. Her book, *Losing Dad, Paranoid Schizophrenia: A Family's Search for Hope* allows people who have not directly experienced the effects of a severe mental illness get a realistic glimpse into the emotions and feelings of a family in crisis. Those who have a loved one with a severe mental illness can relate to her family's story and gain a better understanding of this shared experience. As a reader, you become a member of her family.

What impresses me most about her book, *Losing Dad*, is the honesty and compassion she uses to expose how severe mental illness affects an entire family – children, spouses, and parents. The research and interviews that went into the writing of this book add a level of authenticity that allows the unbelievable to be believable. Beautifully woven between the facts are the feelings. She shows that behind every severe mental illness there is a human being and an often untold tale of despair and oftentimes hope. Rather than try to paint over her past, she unapologetically opens up to her readers about words and actions she cannot take back. I highly recommend *Losing Dad* both as an educational tool and as a heartfelt tale.

I am grateful to her for choosing to share her experience. And I admire and share the hope she inspires when she says, "it is not too late for others."

Xavier Amador, Ph.D.
Founder, LEAP Institute
Author, *I am Not Sick, I Don't Need Help!* (Vida Press 2012)
www.LEAPinstitute.org

LOSING DAD

PARANOID SCHIZOPHRENIA:
A FAMILY'S SEARCH FOR HOPE

INTRODUCTION

LIKE A MASTER COMPUTER, the brain controls everything, but when it malfunctions there is no system reset, no disk recovery, no memory restore.

Joseph† graduated from college in Illinois, bought a house in California, and raised a family in the suburbs. By all accounts his life seemed normal. And it was, until he got the news: cancer.

After a successful operation with a good prognosis, a routine procedure went awry. Doctors rushed him into emergency surgery and, for the second time in a week, put him under general anesthesia. When he was released, everything changed.

Joseph descended into psychosis, extreme paranoia, and grandiose delusions.

Within a couple of years, he did the unthinkable. He embarked on a trip involving four continents, thirty countries, and thirteen wives. Joseph gave up everything along the way: his career, his finances, and his family. He was purportedly arrested in Israel, preached to the Mafioso in Italy, and hailed as a prophet in Africa. Penniless, he returned to America where he had run-ins with drug dealers and prostitutes.

This true story follows one man's bizarre journey through mental illness.

He is not a faceless stranger living on the streets.

He is my father.

†Many names throughout this book have been changed to protect the privacy of the individuals involved.

1

CHAPTER ONE

MAY 2000: THE CALL

MY THREE-AND-A-HALF-YEAR-OLD son threw a tantrum in the store. By the end of the difficult shopping trip, Justin helped his single mom bring in the groceries. I put the milk cartons in the refrigerator and hoisted the rest of the plastic bags onto the kitchen counter. When I reached for the bananas, the flashing red light on the answering machine caught my attention. I hit play.

"Sunday May 28, 2000. You have one new message." The machine clicked.

"Amanda."

I didn't recognize the voice.

"It's Dad. Sorry I missed you, but I'll call back at six o'clock your time in California. That's six o'clock Pacific Time. I pray to our Lord Jesus Christ you will be there to answer the phone. Give praise to God and Jesus, our Lord and Savior. There, it's done. God will have you there to answer the phone. In His name I pray." Beep.

Stunned, I hit replay. I hadn't spoken with nor seen Dad in over a year. Eight months had passed since he abandoned my stepmom Hilda in West Virginia. Several months had passed since he mysteriously showed up at my sister's house before disappearing again. Like my sister and brother, I had tried to push all thoughts of Dad from my head.

While Dad's message repeated, I thought about the Bible he mailed me on November 22, 1999, and the random letter he sent me from the Hotel

3

Tivoli Lisboa in Portugal in March of 2000, with the neatly folded pieces of extremely soft facial tissue. I ran to my bedroom to find the letter, which was in the file cabinet under the file labeled Dad. Handwritten in black ink, in tiny print, on a small sheet of hotel stationary, the note read:

Sunday, March 26, 2000

Dear Amanda,

    I hope you and Justin are in good health and the grace of God is keeping your hearts and minds in peace through our Lord and risen Savior, Christ Jesus, the only begotten Son of God.

    Since the last time I wrote, I've been many places. In 10 or more countries, preaching and teaching the Kingdom of God and witnessing for Jesus. I now tell them 4 things are needed: 1. Believe with all your mind, strength, heart & soul & confess (to yourself) with your lips "I believe Jesus Christ is the Son of God" 2. <u>Complete</u> submersion (any Pentecostal church) in water in the name of the Father & of the Son and of the Holy Ghost (Sprinkling not enough) 3. #1 & more than anyone else: I love you, God and Jesus! 4. Love everyone else as Christ has (& does) love us.

    *After Bulgaria (My last wife) I left Bulgaria. Now, #1 – No smoking, #2 – No alcohol (due to my stomach, although one beer in Germany was OK – in moderation) #3 – No affection with a woman (or husband) who isn't your wife (husband) – In fact, Paul says in 1 COR 7:1 "It is good for a man not to touch a woman." From Bulgaria, I went to Turkey (Istanbul→ Izmir→ Bodrum→ Antalya→ Istanbul). How beautiful is Turkey by the Hand of God through Jesus. I did free Greek dancing for customers in both Istanbul (upscale dinner/night club) & in Sofia, Bulgaria (Sheraton & a Greek "taverna" =café). Turkey→ Sofia→ Bucharest, Romania (all this for Jesus/God, of course, <u>not</u> <u>my</u> glory!) (God forbid I should do otherwise!)→Thessaloniki, Greece→ Skopje, Macedonia→ Thessaloniki→ Athens→ Frankfurt, Germany→ Stuttgart, Germany→ Italy (Milan→ Venice→ Bologna→ Rome→ Naples). On a train from Bologna to Rome, after<u> conversing with an Algerian Muslim who spoke English & wished to improve his German,</u> **He** <u>asked for (& I gave with great joy) a "New Testament" written in English, German, and French! (Thank you, Jesus! Praise the Lord! Glory to God in the highest! Bless his Holy Name, Forever & Ever! Amen!</u> To Sicily (From Palermo to Catania→ "Mafia Capital," <u>I ministered to the taxi</u>*

driver, a low-level Mafioso (Or Mafioso Family son)! Then, the Malta (oldest architecture in world – St. Paul stopped there & started a church) → Spain (Barcelona→ Madrid) → I'm now is Lisboa, Portugal!

Amanda, the <3 softest and <3 most durable "Kleenex" I've had are these 2 pieces from a kiosk in Istanbul, Turkey!!! One is for <3 you <3 & one for <3 Justin <3 !!! Tell him to say "thank you, God" and "thank you, Jesus" as he always should when receiving any blessing (anything good is from God). As in meal time the grace of our Lord Jesus Christ be with your Spirit, Yours in Christ, Love, Peace, Joyful Anticipation for Jesus!

Dad (Grandpa)

I looked up at the clock: 4:30 P.M.

Justin grabbed my skirt. "Mommy, I wanna watch TV."

Normally, I would've encouraged a book or a toy. Not now. I flipped on the television, popped a cartoon movie into the VCR, and sat Justin on the couch. He asked for a drink. I concocted an odd mix of chocolate and strawberry milk, grabbed a bowl of Cheerios and handed them to him. I replayed the message a third time then speed-dialed my stepmom Hilda, whom my Dad had abandoned in West Virginia the year before.

"Hallo." When Hilda had emigrated from Argentina, her accent came with her. Born in Bolivia and raised in Argentina, Hilda chose to stay in the United States after meeting my Dad fifteen years ago. "What is going on with my little Amandy?"

"I'm so glad you're home."

"Uh-oh, what is the matter?"

"Dad called," I said, "and he's going to call back in about an hour. What should I do?"

"Ai-yi-yi." Hilda paused. "Please *listen* to me. He *needs* help. He is not well. You *have* to get him help. He needs to be at a hospital."

"Yes, but I don't know where he is."

"Well, dear, see if you can find out. Call me back. Oh, Amandy, if you only knew."

Justin whimpered.

"I've got to go," I said. "I promise I'll call you back tonight."

"It doesn't matter how late. You know I'll be up."

After ending the call, and in between entertaining Justin, I phoned my sister and my brother. Before I knew it, the clock read: 5:45 P.M. Even though I had a cordless phone, I sat next to it and waited.

The minute hand jerked forward onto precisely 6:00 P.M. The phone rang. I checked the caller ID, but the number came up as unavailable. My heart raced. I let it ring again before cradling the receiver against my cheek. I took a deep breath.

"Hello," I managed to say calmly.

"Amanda?" the voice hesitated.

"Dad? Is it really you?"

"That's a silly question. Who else would it be? God instructed me to call you."

Not expecting that response, I asked, "Where are you?"

"I'm on the streets, doing God's work as he has commanded me to do."

"Okay, but what State are you in?"

"Who said I was still in America?"

Again, he caught me off-guard. I took another deep breath. "Well, where are you?"

"That's not important."

I couldn't risk him hanging up, so I didn't push. "Are you okay? I mean we've all been worried about you, me and Hilda and—"

"I don't want to hear that devil's name."

"Your wife's name?"

"She's not my wife anymore."

I tossed his answer around in my head for a moment. How could that be? I could've sworn they were still married before he took her from California, crossed the country, and left her in West Virginia.

He continued in a stern voice, "Don't worry about it. It's not any of your business." His tone softened. "I've had over ten wives already."

I nearly choked. "What? How's that possible? You've only been married three times." I counted my sister's mom, my brother's and my mom, and my stepmom. Yes, only three.

"I've been married by God. My fourth wife was a 59 year old Filipina prostitute in Amman, Jordan."

I grabbed a paper and pen and scribbled notes.

"My fifth wife was in Cairo, Egypt; she was a very dark-skinned, large Bantu African from Sudan and was 30 years old. We spent two nights together. My sixth wife was in Bucharest, Romania. She was a gypsy woman, maybe about 35 years old. She had two children: a 15 year old daughter and a 7 year old son. The seventh was a 22 year-old Bulgarian prostitute. I proposed marriage to her at a night club in Sofia on February 9th, but she wanted 100 US dollars. At least I kissed her lips twice. I chose a wife for only 100 US dollars from a "menu"—in my hotel—but, she was not my wife….had a devil in her…not me. My eighth and ninth wives were both from Senegal, West Africa. My last wife, the tenth one, was from the Ivory Coast. I need a woman badly, but absolutely no sex before marriage…holding hands, hugging, and face or lip kissing is okay."

What the hell? I didn't think Dad was capable of sexual relations after his prostate surgery, so this information baffled me. Was he sleeping with these women?

"Dad, where did you meet them?"

"I just told you where they were each from. I've been to over thirty countries so far and over fifty cities. I've spent over $60,000 spreading the word of God. This was not for me, you understand. It's to spread the word of our Lord."

"Which countries have you been to?"

"Hmm, let me think. First, I went to Amman, Jordan, then to Tel Aviv, Israel, then back to Jordan, then Cairo, Egypt. After that, I went to Romania, Bulgaria, and then to Turkey. That's where I did a Greek folk-dance at the Sheraton for free. After Turkey, I went back to Romania, on to Greece, Macedonia, and then to Germany. That's where I had rindwurst, which is a beef sausage, with sauerkraut, and a dark blend, the *best* Pilsner beer I ever had. Then, I went to Italy and to Spain and Portugal. Oh, I sent you a letter from Portugal, did you receive it?"

"Yes, yes, I did." My hand cramped.

Through the phone, I could sense Dad smile. "Wasn't that the softest tissue ever?"

"Yes, the tissue was really soft."

"Well, after Portugal, I went to Morocco, to Casablanca. In West Africa, I went to Dakar, Ivory Coast, Sierra Leone, and Gambia. After that, God sent me to Paris, France, then to North Germany, to Austria, Hungary, and to Poland….that's where I was in Warsaw and Gdansk. Then I went to Copenhagen where I went to Tivoli Gardens. Next, God commanded me to Oslo, Norway, Amsterdam, Holland, then back to Oslo, Bergen, Trakiso, Lakso. Then I went from Stockholm, Sweden to Finland and then back to Stockholm."

"How on Earth did you afford to go to all of those places?"

"God provides for me," he said. "God and his angels have delivered a message to me for you. How would you like it if you and little Justin flew out here and joined me on the streets in spreading the word of God?"

"Uh, no thank you." I searched for a decent excuse. "I'm still trying to finish college." I wouldn't finish my bachelor's degree until December.

"Amanda, college is not important," he said.

I did a double take. This statement ran contrary to everything he had ever taught me. "But it will sure help me get a real job to pay the rent."

"Forget the treasures of this world for the treasures of the next."

Dad was floating above any earthly reality.

This was nonsensical. Dad had informed me I was going to college before I even knew what college meant, and now was discounting the value of an education and a roof over my head.

"Okay, that's great, but I have a small child to support. Remember your grandson Justin? Rent's expensive."

"You're only worried because you're not yet saved. You cannot be saved until you are baptized under the water and accept Jesus as your Lord and Savior."

"Are you forgetting I was already baptized?"

"The Catholic Church doesn't count. Their doctrine is incorrect. I am the only one with the true doctrine of Christ. God has made me a prophet."

Stunned, my jaw dropped as he finished.

"But I can't blame you for being taught incorrectly. It's partially my fault and I will take the blame. You see, the Catholic Church doesn't do it right.

The only real way is a full body immersion under the water. Only then can you be saved."

A wild and crazy idea popped into my head. Without thinking, I blurted out, "Well, how do I get saved?"

"I can baptize you. God has granted me that power. I have already saved people. I have even brought an animal back from the dead."

"What are you talking about?"

"Back in 1999, Shadow had tried to eat a little animal, but I brought it back to life because God works through me. I can save you and Justin if you are honestly ready and willing to accept God into your hearts. I can baptize you both."

"Where would you baptize us?"

"Oh, anywhere. The location is unimportant. The ocean, a river, a lake, anywhere—"

"What about my apartment pool?"

Giddy with excitement, Dad took the bait. "Yes. Yes, I can do that. You can have Keith come too."

"I don't know about Keith." I didn't think my brother had recovered from being traumatized by Dad. "I'll have to ask him. So, when can we be baptized?"

"How about next weekend? I can be there next weekend. Oh, praise the Lord Jesus. In His name, I give thanks and praise."

"Do you need my address?" He had never been to my apartment. The last time Dad came to visit me—he had taken Justin for the weekend—I was still living with my Mom.

I shared the information with him then he abruptly had to go, complaining his calling card would run out any second. We said our good-byes and hung up. I sat by the phone and stared across the room at Justin leafing through the pages of his favorite book.

I felt a twinge of guilt for what I was planning to do.

CHAPTER TWO

JUNE 2000: THE CONSPIRACY

OVER THE NEXT COUPLE days leading up to the weekend, I made phone calls and created plans. Whenever I questioned my intentions, I talked to Hilda for emotional support. I consulted the police department, the county mental hospital, and a local support group for the National Alliance on Mental Illness (NAMI). I'd been informed the police department could come take Dad against his wishes to the mental hospital for only two valid reasons. He either had to be an immediate danger to himself—as he had been during his previous three sanitarium admittances—or he had to be an immediate danger to others.

I figured as soon as he learned of my true intentions, he would probably meet criteria number two. I made arrangements for Justin to be elsewhere, if needed, at a moment's notice. I made one last call to both the police department and the mental hospital. Tiring of my hypothetical situations, they reassured me they would help if my scenarios played out as I imagined.

Friday came and I cleaned house. Saturday, I woke up early and rehearsed my speech. Sunday, I paced anxiously. When would he be there?

Monday came and I had to go back to work and college. I was confused. Hilda was disappointed. My sister Jackie was upset. My brother Keith merely said, "Oh, well."

Tuesday and Wednesday came and went.

Tired from a long day, I opened the mailbox on Thursday to find a post card addressed to me and Keith. It read:

Monday, May 29, 2000

Dear Amanda and Keith,

I am not going back to the USA. God warned me in a dream that my enemies are setting a trap for me.

I stopped reading and, in disbelief, dialed Hilda's number. She would never believe this one.

"Hallo?"

"Hilda? It's me." I glanced back at the postcard.

"Did you hear from your dad?"

"Well, I just got a postcard."

"Me, too."

"What does yours say?"

"Hold on, just a minute." Hilda set the phone down, but quickly returned. "It's dated Monday, May 29, 2000 from Stockholm, Sweden, postmarked on May 30th."

"Mine, too. That's the day after I spoke to him on the phone."

"Yes, dear, I know. Let me read it to you." She cleared her throat. "*'Hi! From Stockholm, Sweden from Joseph, a servant of God and of the Lord Jesus Christ, the Risen Savior and Son of God. This is for Amanda.'* He underlined your name and wrote down your phone number, but the last four digits are wrong.

"Anyway, then he wrote:

'Tell her three things: #1) God warned me in a dream not to go back to USA because my enemies are setting a trap for me. It may be. I'll go up north of Arctic Circle (nice weather now, always light) to travel nomadically with the Sami people (Lappland) and looking for a reindeer named Cupid. Could spend the rest of time with God and Jesus? The will of God – maybe to another country (probably tomorrow) as my work appears done in Scandinavia → you all will hear from me no more! #2) Amanda, Keith...all of you must (suggest Assembly of God) ASAP reconfess Jesus as Son of God and get baptized in Name of Father & Son & Holy Ghost by complete immersion under the water. Repent of sins, submit to God, love God #1 & thy neighbor as Christ has loved you & you love yourself. #3) Tell Amanda to READ following, King James

Authorized version Jeremiah 1:17-19➔ *Luke 18:28-30* ➔ *Hosea 4:13* ➔ *Psalms 35, 40, 41, and 64!!!*

Getting a new wife and making babies (have a new Life) ➔ *God made covenant with me via rainbow & then a double rainbow!! My God is an awesome God!!! Thank you Jesus! Praise the Lord! Glory to God! Bless His Holy Name forever & ever! Amen.*

"Well, Amandy." Hilda chuckled. "Daddy's crazy. What can we do? Nothing."

"I don't know what to say. He wrote the same part to me about the dream of his enemies plotting against him. That's so strange. Do you think he knew what we were up to?"

"I don't know, dear. We'll see what happens." She paused. "Daddy's been sending me postcards from all around the world."

"Really? I only got tissue paper from Portugal or Turkey or something."

"At least that's something. I get postcards from Bulgaria, Turkey, Italy, Germany, Malta, and so many other places. He tells me about his other wives…stupid prostitutes."

"I'm sorry, Hilda. You shouldn't have to hear about that. He doesn't know what he's doing. He's not in his right mind."

"I know. But I wish I could do something. He was such a wonderful husband and dad. It's so sad."

"Don't worry about it tonight. We'll just wait and see what happens next." I couldn't imagine being in her place, stranded by myself clear across the country in West Virginia.

"Yes, we'll just wait and see."

It would be two years before I'd hear from Dad again.

Over the next several months, I couldn't help but dwell on this rare contact with Dad. It was as if another man now occupied his body and mind. Things hadn't always been like that, though. Dad used to be normal. Before his mental illness struck, I had nothing but fond memories of him and of our fun family weekends and annual road trips.

No symptoms hinted to Dad's impending mental decline.

But there is one thing that does stand out, the beginning of our troubles, Dad's cancer. That was four years earlier, back in 1996.

PART ONE
DIAGNOSIS & SURGERY

CHAPTER THREE
BEFORE DAD'S DISAPPEARANCE

AUGUST 1996: TREATMENT

DAD SNUGGLED CLOSE TO Hilda to process his new reality. A month earlier, they had celebrated his 53rd birthday.

"I'm scared," he said. "How can it be cancer? I've always taken good care of my health." He removed his gold-framed glasses, leaned his head into her chest and put his arms around her petite body.

"It'll be okay." Hilda ran her fingers through his thinning brown hair, past his blue eyes, and along cheeks which were creamy white against her bronzed complexion. His too-pale-to-tan skin was a trait passed down from his Ashkenazi Jewish ancestors.

"I don't want surgery," he said.

"But your doctors said you need it."

"You know I hate needles," he said. "What if they screw up? How many people come out worse than when they go in?"

"What about that hospital your friends told us about? The one in Mexico. They use holistic methods and natural medicines and have a high success rate with cancer."

"It's not cheap, but it's worth looking into."

"It's going to be all right." She squeezed his hand. "I love you."

"I love you, too." He tucked her short black hair behind her ears and nuzzled his head against her neck.

Dad and Hilda drove from San Bernardino County down to Tijuana, Mexico to discuss his options with the medical staff. After they crossed the border, they were greeted by numerous drug stores advertising cheap drug prices. Along the city streets, they encountered young peddlers pushing handmade bracelets and packets of gum, all laid neatly across blankets on the sidewalks. Leaving the sewage stench of downtown, they arrived at their destination, the alternative medical center. The doctors there professed whole-body healing and an antioxidant rich diet.

When he felt ready to commit to the treatment plan, Dad phoned his father John for advice.

"No, don't do it," my grandpa said. "It's definitely not a good idea. There aren't any competent doctors down there. They're not properly educated and trained."

"But I've heard many success stories. When Hilda and I went there, everything they said made a lot of sense. The doctors are smart. They've had extensive training, much of it done in the States. They just choose to work with holistic methods."

"Mexico is dirty. It's not sanitary. You're going to open yourself up to problems like other diseases and then it'll be too late to get treatment here. They'll make you sicker with their hokey medicine."

"I know people who've been cured there. I don't want surgery."

"I understand you're scared, but you need to listen to your doctor before it's too late. Trust modern medicine. Don't trust those people in Mexico. Get treatment here."

"Well, at least I'm going to get a second and third opinion."

"That's a smart idea. But if they agree, ultimately you should trust your physician."

Overwhelmed after visits to other doctors, Dad scheduled the surgery. On August 19, 1996, he drove to the hospital with Hilda and my fifteen year-old brother Keith. Their pastor from church met them there.

In the final moments before surgery, Dad probed Hilda's eyes. One word escaped from his lips, "Jackie?" the name of my older sister.

"She asked me to call her as soon as you're out." Hilda planted a kiss on his clammy forehead and stroked his cheek, still smooth from the morning's shave.

Their pastor turned to my teenaged brother, nudged him on the shoulder, and whispered, "You can give your dad a hug and kiss."

Keith did so then slunk behind, hiding beneath his long brown bangs

Hilda kissed my dad again and released him from her arms.

Dad and the nurses disappeared down the hallway.

Later, a doctor entered the waiting room and approached Hilda.

"How is he?" Hilda asked.

"Your husband did just fine. He's being brought up to his room and should be coming to in a few minutes."

Hilda and Keith found him asleep in a hospital bed.

When he opened his eyes, he glanced around the room until his eyes met Hilda's. He smiled at her before dozing off again.

Days later, while Dad was still in the hospital recovering, doctors came into his room to remove the catheter, a routine procedure.

Medical instruments in hand, the doctor got to work.

Dad winced.

The doctor's face blanched. He pushed a button that brought several people. They scurried about and thrust papers into Dad's face. Dad penned his signature.

Sides of the hospital bed raised and locked in place. The wheel mechanisms released.

Dad asked the anesthesiologist, "What's happening?"

"I'm going to give you a general anesthetic. When was the last time you ate?"

Teary-eyed, Dad reached for the doctor. "Help me, why does it hurt?"

"The catheter splintered."

Fluorescent lights blurred overhead. The room grew dark. Dad closed his eyes.

"How does something like that happen?" Hilda said. "And why wasn't I notified?"

"I'm sorry, ma'am," the nurse said. "There wasn't time. Don't worry. He's fine."

"Fine? How can you say he's fine? How could the doctor have screwed that up?"

After Dad recovered from this second procedure, Hilda took him home.

The man who left the hospital was not the same one who had entered. But we didn't know it yet, and neither did he.

CHAPTER FOUR

SUMMER 1996: HARD CHANGES

JACKIE PULLED HER THICK dark curls into a ponytail and hung up the phone after a difficult conversation with Dad. He had laid a major guilt trip on her. "Jackie, why didn't you visit me at the hospital? I could've died," she remembered the words as abrasive as sandpaper.

"But, I didn't think the surgery was a big deal. I didn't realize," she had replied. Naïve Jackie felt like a failure. Our dad, who only last month had confided his inner fears to her, was disappointed, which she couldn't bear.

She slumped to the carpet, engulfed in tears.

Her boyfriend Neil arrived to pick her up for a camping trip. Half a foot taller than she, Neil had brown hair, a broad chest, and a stocky stance, lingering evidence of his football days. He wrapped his arms around her while tears streaming from her brown eyes burned into his chest, leaving a trail of black mascara across his white shirt.

For Dad and Hilda, the alluring warmth of the San Diego sun and sand and the refreshing breeze blowing in off the Pacific Ocean were bonuses for visiting Jackie. After recovering from his surgery, Dad and Hilda took the trek down from San Bernardino to take Jackie and Neil to dinner. As they made their way under neon signs and over the red carpets laid out to welcome patrons, a cacophony of music and boisterous laughter spilled out from clubs and restaurants. The foursome turned a corner, welcomed by the sea breeze coming in off the coast of upscale La Jolla. Serenity was quickly displaced by the noises rising again as they approached their destination, the Hard Rock Café. Once inside, they encountered a noisy restaurant with a long wait.

By the time their table was ready, hunger bit at their bellies. Seated under photos of the Rolling Stones and Aerosmith, they slid into the booth. Metallica then Bon Jovi blared out of the speakers above their table. They had to shout out their orders to the server.

Weighty topics of Dad's surgery and the subsequent surgical mishap hung heavily over their heads during dinner. Initially, a guitar solo had obscured their conversation. Later, the ensuing silence was deafening. Neil brought up baseball.

Dad, always talkative anyway, erratically drove the conversation in a million different directions. So much so, the others found it nearly impossible to keep up. Even the spacey guitars in Led Zeppelin's "Kashmir" couldn't keep pace with his random ideas and jarring thoughts.

Dad joined Neil in a round of beers.

Jackie leaned close to Hilda. "Dad's drinking? Is he trying to relate to Neil?"

Hilda shrugged.

The tattooed arm of a busboy reached across them and cleared the table. Dad's voice progressively grew louder and louder as the music softened to Guns N' Roses' "November Rain."

Dad insisted on paying, as he usually did. With his hands under the table, he discreetly counted out the money for the tab, plus a modest tip, and left it under the bill.

Momentarily hard-of-hearing from the loud music, they headed outside to finish their discussion on the sidewalk. In front of the restaurant, couples strolled by, hand-in-hand. An older man sat hunched over on a bus stop bench, reading the newspaper. A few kids bounded at their parents' heels and entered the crosswalk.

Dad stopped mid-sentence, turned away, and focused his flitting attention on every single passerby. "Hello, it's a nice evening, isn't it?" he asked the couple to his right.

They nodded.

"Heading out to dinner tonight? What type of food are you looking for?" he asked to another on his left.

They shrugged.

Turning to the man at the bus stop, he cracked a few jokes to his captive audience, "You know that reminds me of this joke. There was a priest, a rabbi, and a minister on a boat."

The gentleman on the bench, engrossed in the headlines, pretended not to notice.

Dad finished the joke and chuckled aloud.

"Joseph, what, what are you doing?" Hilda asked.

"Shush. I'm connecting to these people."

"No, you're out of touch," Jackie said. "Didn't you notice their reactions?"

He didn't seem to hear a word she said.

Jackie searched for the full moon she swore must be up there somewhere to explain his erratic behavior. She shook her head. No moon.

Dad continued jumping from one person to another. Helpless to do much about him, the strangers' polite nodding were merely meant to placate him.

Jackie turned to Hilda and to Neil. How to handle the situation?

"Dad, leave them alone," Jackie said. "I'm tired. Let's go home."

Dad recited another joke as Hilda and Jackie each grabbed an arm and led him back to the car.

CHAPTER FIVE

LATE SUMMER 1996: MIXED RESULTS

AFTER A FEW UNEVENTFUL days, Hilda tried to get back into her regular routine. Gingerly patting and brushing dirt from her worn gardening gloves, she set them down next to the potting soil. Her roses and bushes needed almost daily love and attention.

She stood up and wiped her hands on her pants. The sun had warmed her bones and relieved the arthritis which she had begun to feel at the age of fifty-three. The pain wasn't too bad, so she hadn't seen the doctor for it yet. Because of Dad's cancer, Hilda felt she had seen enough doctors these past couple of months.

With a slap to her thigh, she ushered her two poodles in the front door after her. They raced around her feet—Shadow and Star had far more energy than she.

No sooner had the latch clicked than the phone rang.

"This is Dr. Sarjin's office. Joseph's blood work is in. The doctor wants to schedule an appointment to go over the results."

Dad and Hilda sat side-by-side in the waiting room. She thumbed through a magazine. He paced, wearing a trail in the carpet in front of her.

She glanced up at him. "Dear, come have a seat."

He sat down next to her and fidgeted. "So, do you think the cancer is still there?"

"I'm sure it's gone."

"But you don't know. They already screwed up once with the catheter."

"And they fixed it."

"Maybe they made the mistake on purpose. You know, get more money from the insurance company."

"I don't think so." She reached for his hand.

He pulled away. "You wouldn't know. They do it all the time. I know these things. You don't know." He stood and commenced pacing.

"Joseph?" a nurse in a blue jumpsuit called out.

"Let's go." Hilda hooked her arm in his.

While waiting for the doctor to come into the patient treatment room, Dad began his rant again. "Nobody cares here. They all want you to get sicker, screw with you a little bit more, better for business that way."

"That's nonsense." Hilda settled into a padded chair. With the magazine in her hand, she flipped from page to page and back again. Now she didn't bother to read anything and instead let the black and white print swirl into the full-page color ads.

The doctor entered, set a medical chart on the counter top, sat on the revolving stool, and slid up to Dad's side.

"I've got good news," the doctor said. "I have the results here from the lab and your surgeon's notes. Your PSA count is normal. That means the cancer is gone."

Hilda breathed a sigh of relief.

"So, how are you doing?" the doctor asked. "Are you feeling better now?"

"I don't know. I have these pains. And there's the incontinence problem."

"Unfortunately incontinence is a bit of a problem for most men after this procedure. It isn't permanent and there are things we can do—"

"I wouldn't let anyone touch me again."

The doctor skimmed the nurse's notes. "It looks like you have elevated blood pressure."

"And why would that be?"

"You do sound a bit stressed."

"Of course I am. People have been following me. And well, there are other things. Things aren't right. I don't feel good."

"Ai-yi-yi." Hilda shook her head. "This isn't right, Joseph."

The doctor tilted his head and studied Dad's face for a moment before turning to Hilda. "What do you mean, when you say things aren't right?"

"I don't know," she said. "It's the truth, you hear him. Listen to what he's saying. He's driving me nuts at home, all this crazy talk about this and—"

"I am not." Dad narrowed his eyes.

The doctor wrote a note on the chart and turned again to Hilda. "What do you mean specifically?"

"He says that man's doing this, she's doing that. He never said these things before, accusing people, making up stuff. It's in his head."

Dad raised his voice. "It's not in my head."

"Okay," the doctor cleared his throat, "I'm going to give you a couple of prescriptions."

"For what?"

"It should help with the paranoia your wife is noticing."

"I'm not paranoid. People are following me."

The doctor scribbled on his notepad. "I recommend you start attending a cancer support group. My nurse will get you a flier with the meeting dates and times—"

"I don't need counseling."

"Joseph, listen to me. It's of the utmost importance you take this seriously and attend this prostate cancer support group."

"Why? You yourself said the cancer's gone."

"Look, men go through different reactions after this surgery—some think they aren't men anymore. Some come to feel they have lost a part of their manhood. Many develop suicidal tendencies, and some even do end up committing suicide. We don't want to see you suffer like this, so, in my professional opinion—I can't stress this enough—you need to talk to others who have shared this same experience. It will greatly decrease your recovery time from this anxiety, depression, and paranoia."

"I don't need to talk to anyone."

"I'm signing you up for the prostate cancer survivors' support group." The doctor separated the prescription order from the pad and handed it to Hilda. "This is an anti-anxiety medication which should help alleviate his symptoms. I want you to schedule an individual appointment with a psychologist as soon as possible and a follow up appointment with me. I'd like to see you back here in a couple of weeks."

Nearly a month and a half later, Hilda pleaded with my dad. "You've only attended the support group two or three times. The doctor said you need to go."

"It's a waste of time and not helpful in the least bit."

"*Piggito*, you're also not taking your medications."

"Those damn drugs have too many side effects. You know how sleepy and out of it they make me. I can't live like that, like my mind is in a fog all the time."

"We've been to several doctors now. We've tried several different prescriptions. They'll all have some side effects. You have to deal with it."

"Why? They don't help me."

"Of course they don't help you when you only take them once in awhile."

"What the hell do I need those drugs for, anyway?"

"You know what they're for, the paranoia, depression, anxiety—"

"None of which I have." He stormed out of the kitchen.

She watched his shadow fade down the hallway. Her chest and throat tightened as she held back tears.

CHAPTER SIX

EARLY AUTUMN 1996: GOING BACK

PHYSICALLY, DAD HAD RECOVERED from the cancer surgery. He no longer had to have Hilda and Keith help him with a urine bag. He returned to his routine of cycling on his stationary bike while watching a sports game on TV. Hilda, a licensed hair stylist, permed his short brown hair into curls, which gave the illusion of more hair. He got dressed every day in a polo shirt, Dockers slacks, and belt, like he used to.

His doctor suggested he return to work, so Dad went back to programming computers in the glass tower in Pasadena where he had spent his days for the last seventeen years.

Soon after returning to work, Dad began to have difficulty sleeping. His psychiatrist prescribed sleeping pills, along with another round of psychiatric drugs.

At the office, Dad stared at the rows of code on his computer monitor. His eyes grew heavy. The numbers and letters blurred. The computer screen swayed and went black.

He looked around. He was back forty years, sitting at the Cubs game in Chicago with his father, the crisp air rushing by their faces, the crowd ruckus fading into the distance.

"Sure can't beat these hot dogs, piled high with mustard, relish, onions, and kraut," Grandpa said while leaning forward to get another big bite.

Dad smiled. He knew it wouldn't matter whether their team won or lost, so long as he and his father were together.

"If the pitcher strikes out one more batter in this inning, the teams switch sides. Are you listening to me, Joey?"

"Yes, I always listen to you. Can we go to a museum next week?"

Grandpa's eyes lit up. "Which one?"

"The one you like, the Field Museum. It's my favorite too."

"If your mom lets us."

"Why wouldn't she?" With his parents still married, and he being an only child, it didn't make sense.

Dad's elbow slipped off the edge of the desk. He almost smacked his face onto the keyboard. He rubbed his eyes.

The cursor on his monitor blinked for his attention. After a stretch, he started to type again, but left work early to avoid falling asleep on the road.

During the drive home, he turned on his car radio. "Without a dream in my heart, without a love of my own," blared out of the speakers.

He upped the volume. Dad had been eighteen in 1961 when he first heard *The Marcels* sing "Blue Moon" on Chicago's WLS on the AM dial. It sure wasn't the classical music his mom adored.

Together, Dad and I listened to "Blue Moon" on his 8-track when I was a young child. Besides singing in the car, we enjoyed doing so many other things. We planned vacations. I navigated during our road trips. We stayed up all night playing blackjack or chess, talking about life and the universe. Dad, Hilda, Jackie, Keith, and I sprawled across the couches, watching videos and eating ice cream with Magic Shell or fruit salad with Cool Whip.

Those days have passed. My sister and I grew up and moved out on our own. When the bank foreclosed on our mom's house, Keith moved in with Dad and Hilda a few months before Dad's surgery in the summer of 1996.

Keith didn't enjoy playing ball with Dad like I used to. Instead, he spent all day playing video games. This irked Dad who believed nothing felt the same as being outdoors—feeling the heavy Louisville Slugger in your arms. He always reminded me to point the label down, so the bat wouldn't crack.

"Elbows out, bend your knees," he'd say. "Keep your eye on the ball. Choke up on the bat."

While we played, Dad told me about his childhood in Lincolnwood, north of Chicago, where he used to play ball with his cousins and his father, and how he once hit a ball on top of the school's roof.

Dad chuckled when he told me how he and the other kids discovered the apartment building's heating coal doubled as sidewalk chalk. The groundskeeper caught them red-handed and chased them off. Fortunately, the kids could run fast.

I loved hearing his stories.

CHAPTER SEVEN

AUTUMN 1996: PARANOIA

ALTHOUGH HAPPY TO HAVE Keith living with him, Dad worried my brother wasn't adjusting well to the move. Keith didn't keep his shoes out of the living room, or his bed made, or his bathroom clean. He ditched school, didn't do his homework, and lied about it.

Morning light streamed in through the curtains. Keith, a thin teen with long sandy bangs hanging over his eyes, awakened. He sat up and stretched, but jerked back at the sight of Dad, standing still at the foot of the bed. Keith hadn't heard him enter.

"Yeah?" Keith asked.

Dad narrowed his eyes.

"What?" Keith asked.

Dad maintained a rigid posture and stared at him.

"What's going on?"

Dad scowled, shook his head, and retreated.

Dinner was quiet, other than the occasional, "Can you pass the salt and pepper?"

"Thanks for dinner, Hilda." Keith pushed in his chair, put his dishes in the sink, and left for the bathroom.

Before my brother could shut the bathroom door, Dad blocked it with his foot. "Leave the door open."

"What do you mean?" Keith asked.

"I said, leave . . . the . . . door . . . open. You are not to close the doors when you go in the bathroom. You are not to close your bedroom door, either. Do you understand me?"

"But why?"

"Are you doing drugs?"

"No way. What are you talking about?"

"Do as I say. Leave the door open."

Dad walked away in finality. Keith shut the door in defiance.

Dad studied the Bible. He attended church with Hilda on a more regular basis. Keith opted to stay home. Dad made note.

One morning after church, Hilda said, "*Piggito*, you need to stop worrying about everything. You weren't like this before. Your behavior is erratic."

"Me?" Dad said. "I'm not the one bringing people over to cleanse our home of whatever demons you think have found their way in. These metaphysical spiritual and sage housecleaning rituals aren't going to purify our house. And I don't know what you're talking about. What erratic behaviors?"

"You keep making up stories about people, about our neighbors. You're paranoid."

"I'm not paranoid. Other people are acting strange, not me. This is ridiculous."

Hilda reached for his hand.

He pushed her away.

When the voices started, Dad didn't know where else to turn, so he hid in a corner of his bedroom floor and phoned me, his middle child.

"Don't tell anyone about this," he said. "They won't understand."

"I won't," I said. "What's going on?"

"People are watching me. The neighbors, the FBI, they're all in on it."

Quiet for a moment, I didn't believe I heard him correctly. Sitting in the college library doing homework, I glanced around.

"Listen, I know these things." He lowered his voice. "Do you believe me?"

"Yes, I believe you," I said, "but what do you know and how do you know it?"

"They tell me."

"Who tells you?" I kept my voice down, so as to not disturb other students.

"I don't know… They do, angels maybe, but they're warning me."

I dropped my pencil and leaned my elbows on the table. "Warning you of what?"

"I can't say." His voice quivered. "I have to go now before they find out."

"Who finds out? What?"

He hung up.

I rubbed my eyes. I considered phoning him back, but convinced myself I must have misunderstood. Nevertheless, even at eighteen, I couldn't help but feel something was amiss. Yet, without any knowledge of mental illness, I felt too ashamed to tell anyone my dad was hearing voices. I figured maybe the voices would go away like a cold or maybe he was making it up. Ultimately, I decided if Dad mentioned hallucinations again, I would say something. I could call Hilda or Jackie. I thought for a moment. Instead of doing anything, I returned my attention to my studies.

One evening after dinner, Keith entered his bedroom. He groped around in the darkness for the light switch. As his fingertips brushed the textured wall, he was shushed.

Trying to make out the silhouette, Keith walked toward the window where he found Dad frozen in place, gripping the draperies shut and peeking out at the street.

"What's going on?" Keith asked.

"Quiet." He motioned for my brother to come closer. "See those two people?"

Keith's eyes had to adjust to the darkness before he could discern the moving figures at the end of the opposite side of the street. The streetlight revealed an older couple taking a stroll.

"Yeah?" Keith asked.

"They're spying on us."

"What are you talking about?"

"Shhh, whisper, they're listening. This is the second time they've walked by our house. We're being spied on."

Keith glanced from Dad's solemn face back to the old man and woman. Holding hands, the couple trudged along the curving sidewalk. A few moments later, they had passed by without so much as taking a single look at the house.

"Dad, what's going on?"

He pointed at a car driving by. "See that car? It keeps driving by. We're in deeper trouble than I thought. A lot of the neighbors are in on it, if not all. Scary, isn't it? You know what else? The FBI's involved."

"I'm going to bed now." Keith shifted his weight to his other leg.

"No, no…listen…they're out there….Okay, if you're going to sleep, listen for them, okay? The neighbors are conspiring with the FBI. I don't know why yet. It's not safe anymore."

"You're crazy. No one's spying on us."

"Yes, yes, they are."

Every morning thereafter, Dad stood watch at the end of Keith's bed. As soon as Keith woke up, he'd hear Dad say, "I know what you're up to."

Keith never responded, only clutched his blanket until Dad left the room.

Soon Dad would also add, "Are you trying to kill me?"

Keith never acknowledged these accusations. Nor did he mention it to anyone.

CHAPTER EIGHT

OCTOBER 1996: HALLOWEEN

O<small>N</small> H<small>ALLOWEEN</small> <small>EVE</small> <small>IN</small> 1996, Dad and Hilda planned to spend the evening home alone, handing out candy to the costumed trick-or-treaters. Keith had gone to a Halloween party.

After pacing back and forth across the living room, Dad shut off the porch light.

"Something bad is going to happen." He embraced Hilda. Even at 5'5", he still towered over her 4'10" frame. "Keith's going to do something to us tonight. We need to leave."

"Dear, nothing's going to happen," she said. "Just relax."

"No, it's not safe here." He put on a sweater. "Let's go for a ride."

Worn out by resisting his constant irrational arguments, Hilda indulged him. She thought, perhaps we can take a drive, get out of the house, and he can relax a bit.

Dad headed straight for the freeway onramp.

The car shook from the sudden gunning of gasoline.

He glanced behind his shoulder and moved left across three consecutive lanes to the fast lane. He adjusted the rearview mirror, pushed the accelerator down as far as it could go and swerved two lanes to the right.

Vrrrroomm, the engine roared. Their seats vibrated from the high speed.

Hilda's eyes opened wide. She had never been more frightened.

He changed lanes. The tires roared while the car passed over the Botts' Dots. He urged the car faster and faster.

"Joseph, stop it. Let's go back home."

"I will not go back to the house. It's not safe there. Keith's going to hurt us tonight." He continued to speed and swerve lane to lane.

"Keith is at a Halloween party. It's all right." Her chest heaved, her throat tightened. "I'll jump out if you don't go back to the house." She pushed with her shoulder to open the door a crack to let him know she meant it.

The force of the wind made a screaming sound.

"I can't. We're being followed." He kept his sight glued on the road in front of him. Every few seconds he glanced through the rear window, so often he seemed more preoccupied with what might be coming from behind than potential dangers ahead.

The speeding car drifted to the right.

Hilda gasped for air. "This is ridiculous. Please stop." She shuddered and slammed the door shut, surrounding them in relative quiet.

He straightened out the car's wayward course.

"We're not safe!" he screamed. "Ke-eith?" he said, his voice rising in pitch, spoken as though my brother were in the back seat.

"Joseph, please...please...take me home." She clasped her hands together in prayer, rocking back and forth.

"We can't go back."

"Please . . . Joseph." Her voice was hardly distinguishable between her sobs. "Please . . . Oh God. Oh God. Oh God, help me. Please . . . Joseph, take me home now. I swear to God I'll jump out." She gripped the door handle again, preparing to follow through on her threat.

After a few more tense exchanges, his tone softened. He looked over at her. She was hunched over in hysterics. "Hilda, please stop crying . . . . I'm sorry. I'll take you home. Please . . . stop crying."

The car decelerated, the engine's whine disappeared into a quiet purr.

An eternity seemed to pass before he pulled into the garage and turned off the ignition.

"Oh, *Piggito*, I was so scared." She grabbed his shoulders and embraced him.

Dad shut the garage door and led them into their dark house. Once inside, he locked and double-locked the doors. His wild eyes searched the room.

He grabbed Hilda's shoulders and whirled her around.

"We aren't safe here," he said. "We have to leave again."

"Nothing is going to happen."

"Fine, if you're not going, I'm leaving."

Hilda watched him throw clothing into a small suitcase. He kissed her goodbye and rushed out the door. She collapsed onto the couch.

Dad told me parts and Hilda parts of what happened next, at least through his eyes. We pieced his story together.

Dad closed the garage door, hopped back into his car, and turned his head to check the backseat. Empty. He locked the doors and shifted into reverse. While the car rolled down the driveway, he flipped on his headlights. After backing out, he moved the stick shift into first gear, and paused along the curb for a moment.

He scanned the street in both directions. Nobody was out there, no one he could see. But bushes and trees everywhere aided his enemies, blanketed them in darkness. He edged the car forward, inching along the winding residential road.

The headlights revealed movement. He hit the brakes, bringing the car to a sharp halt. He squinted into the distance.

There again. A shadowy mass darted across the street. He gripped the steering wheel in his cold hands. Where had it gone?

He waited. Nothing was out there. But he hadn't imagined it.

He felt for the door lock. His forefinger pushed down on the metal tab, already down as far as it would go. His pulse sped faster than he could count.

Keith was coming for him.

The idling engine awaited his command. What to do? Go or stay?

He rolled down his window just a crack to hear the sounds outside. The purring of the motor was louder now. A cool breeze brushed through his hair.

The headlights formed a tunnel of light, illuminating a triangular patch on the pavement. Out of the corner of his eye, he discerned whatever or whoever was getting closer. He rolled the window up.

Keith was coming for him. Or he was sending his messenger—his Agent of Death. Predestined to face it, Dad felt powerless.

Out of nowhere, it came. His headlights caught demon eyes which reflected back a ghoulish illumination. The figure disappeared into the bushes to the right side of the curb, coming closer.

Dad slammed his foot on the gas and the clutch. He struggled with the shifter, momentarily forgetting how to get into second gear. The car stalled.

A pit bull lunged from behind a tree, its eyes glowing red. He had been sent for.

Get the hell out of there.

He came to his senses long enough to get the car to move. He gunned the engine. The tires screeched. He roared through the neighborhood.

Catching all green lights and a few yellows, he drove in a roundabout way toward the freeway. His head pounded to the beat of his heart. His temples throbbed in pain.

Keith won't get me tonight. That's right, not tonight.

The green freeway sign reading "West" was a welcome sight. He swerved into the right lane in preparation for his escape. A red pick-up truck became visible in his rearview mirror.

He focused on the onramp and guided the car up to the right. Lights flashed in his side mirror. Why was the truck following him?

He stomped on the gas pedal with all his might. The speedometer needle, 60…65…70… The truck's white lights faded to small glowing dots.

He let up on the gas. Soon the car was in pace with the few other vehicles out this late at night. His breathing slowed and his pulse leveled off.

The fan circulated the air throughout the small sedan. He adjusted the vent to blow along his cheek, which helped to calm his nerves.

Bright lights of Los Angeles appeared in the distance.

In his rearview mirror, he noticed a pair of headlights growing bigger and brighter by the second. He stared ahead. Light reflecting in his mirrors blinded him. His entire car shone as bright as day. His body tensed.

Keith was after him again.

He prepared to accelerate again. The light disappeared, plunging him back into darkness. To the left, a black and white police car sped by. After it passed, it transitioned back into his lane. The cop car's red tail lights disappeared into the distance ahead.

So the police were in on it, too?

Have to get off the freeway now. People are after me…the cars…the police…can't trust anyone anymore.

At the next exit, he swerved to the right and veered off the freeway. He rolled through the stop sign, made a left under the freeway and re-entered the highway, this time heading east.

I'll lose that cop. Bet he didn't expect me to change directions.

Every car seemed to hover around his, one car in front, one behind, one to each side. He was boxed in, trapped. He tapped his brakes and the vehicles conspiring against him sped up and regrouped in front of his car. A black pick-up truck darted into the lane behind him.

Quick, swerve into the other lane. Slow down. Okay, pull off the freeway here, it's dark off this exit. Hurry, before they catch up.

The truck didn't exit.

I lost him. Good thing I can still outsmart them yet, turn right…half a mile…turn left…it's dark over here. Where am I?

It doesn't matter, as long as they don't find me.

There weren't any houses off the exit, no signs of life. He drove down the two lane highway. A few dirt roads led off in various directions. There weren't any cars, no sounds other than the car's motor and his heart.

The tires kicked up dirt as he drove behind some bushy trees.

With the car hidden, he took a final look at the clock, only a few more hours before daybreak. Ignition off, lights off, doors locked, everything went silent.

Why am I always being followed? What did I do to deserve this? Why me?

Exhausted, he fell asleep.

When the sun rose, Dad tried to open his eyelids but fell back into a deep slumber.

The sun beat down on the metal. He wiped his eyes and waited for his vision to come back into focus. He glanced at his watch. He was late for work.

With his excellent sense of direction, he retraced his way to the freeway. The entrance sign blurred past his window, civilization up ahead.

He pulled into the parking garage underneath his office building.

The elevator groaned its way up.

They say it's all nonsense. Everyone tells me I'm making it all up, but why?

Because they are conspiring against me, they're all in on it. They've gotten to Keith. Maybe the FBI convinced him, or the neighbors, or all of them.

Is Hilda in on it?

No, I don't think so, but you can never be sure of anything anymore.

There was Mike. There was his best friend, Minh. And there were Larry and Pat, his co-workers whom he'd known for years.

Do they have any idea what I'm going through?

Probably not, look at them joking around.

Are those genuine smiles or are they in on it, too?

Don't be ridiculous. I'm safe here.

I am only safe here. I can't go home. They are at home, the FBI, Keith, the neighbors, I know all about them.

Do my co-workers know about the conspiracy?

No, they're on my side.

Are they blind to what's been going on?

Stop it now, they're my friends.

Yes, that's true…

They need to know.

CHAPTER NINE

NOVEMBER 1, 1996: ABSURDITY

HILDA SAT WORRYING ON the couch. Keith came home after midnight from the Halloween party.

"You still awake?" he asked.

"Oh, I couldn't sleep," she said. "How was the party?"

"Okay, I guess. Is there anything wrong?"

"No, no, you go to bed."

She didn't want to worry him, to tell him Dad was missing.

Hilda looked at the clock and closed her eyes. Her body jerked awake. She looked at the clock again until her eyes shut. The cycle continued all night.

1:00 AM . . . nothing.

3:00 AM . . . nothing.

5:00 AM . . . nothing.

She called the police; they didn't have record of anything concerning her husband. They suggested she check with the traffic division for reports of accidents. She called, but nothing had been reported. She called local hospitals, but no one by his name had been admitted.

What am I going to do? Where am I going to look for him?

When Keith awoke the next morning, Hilda broke the news of Dad's disappearance.

"Don't worry so much," Keith said. "He probably went to visit Jackie."

He left for school. Hilda flopped on the couch, almost catatonic.

By late morning, she had called the police station another three times before the dispatcher performed a reality check.

"Look, ma'am, I understand you are worried and upset, but there is nothing the police department can do at this point," said the dispatcher. "If he doesn't show up by tomorrow, you can call us back and file a Missing Persons report. Then we can send an officer out to your house to assist you."

"You don't understand," Hilda said. "My husband is not mentally okay. He's very sick right now and needs help. I have to find him."

"Ma'am, has your husband threatened to harm you?"

"No," Hilda said. "But you don't—"

"Ma'am, has your husband threatened to harm anyone else?"

"No, he hasn't, but—"

"Has your husband threatened to harm himself?"

"No."

"Well, ma'am, you'll have to call us back tomorrow."

"But he thinks his son is trying to kill him."

The dispatcher paused. "Has your son threatened bodily harm against you or your husband?"

"No, but my husband is crazy and thinks his son will attack him." She was doing her best to keep the police station on the phone. She knew they were probably busy, but she needed to maintain some connection, any connection with another human being willing to listen.

"I'm sorry to say this to you ma'am, but being crazy isn't a crime."

"It's easy for you to say. I don't know if he's even alive right now or if something else happened."

"If we discover something has happened to your husband, the police *will* notify you."

Hilda, choked up with tears, sniffled into the phone.

The dispatcher continued, "If you don't hear from your husband by tomorrow, call us back and file a Missing Persons report."

"Okay." Hilda took deep breaths. She regained her sense of equilibrium. "Thank you." Her voice steadied.

The stress over her husband's absence became suffocating. A wave of exhaustion poured over her as she lay across the couch.

Her poodles jumped up beside her. Star curled up at her feet. Shadow lay along her side, resting his front paws and wet nose across her arm. Soft ringlets of fur brushed against her skin. Hilda shut her eyes and let the world around her fade away.

After 2 PM, the phone rang. The sounds blurred into her dreams before she awakened. She jumped off the couch and ran into the kitchen. Her pulse quickened.

Picking up the phone, she cringed, fearing the police might be calling…they must have found his body somewhere.

"Hilda?" a female on the other end asked.

"Yes?" She couldn't stop it. The horrible news was coming. A bomb was going to drop.

"It's Jane, from your husband's office. You need to pick up Joseph immediately."

"What? He's alive! He's there? Oh thank God. Is he okay?" The words flew out in a flurry. A mixture of emotions permeated Hilda's thoughts—relief, fear, and frustration.

"Yes, yes," Jane said. "I mean no, he's not well. Something's wrong. He's saying crazy things. We're really concerned. We didn't know whether to call you or the doctor or—"

"What happened?"

"I don't know. I've never seen him like this before. We're all really worried. We didn't know what else to do besides call you. If you can't come get him, we'll have to call the paramedics. Joseph told us to tell you not to come alone, because he's worried somebody's going to kill you on the freeway. We're keeping him in a closed office for now. In fact, he doesn't want to leave that room."

"You're not making any sense. What happened to him? What time did he get there? Has he eaten anything? Did he drive there? Has he been awake all night?" She tried to prepare for the worst.

"Hilda, *he* isn't making any sense. He's saying he can't go home…that *they* are after him. Whom he is referring to isn't even clear. He just keeps repeating he's not safe…that he's only safe here."

Hilda broke down in tears.

Jane took a deep breath. "Look, I've known your husband for years. I don't know what to make of it. He's not well. We've already called his doctor. He needs to get to the hospital."

Enveloped in a shroud of shock, Hilda and her friend Esther's husband, Mario—whom Hilda didn't remember phoning for help—drove to Dad's work. From there, they decided Hilda would drive Dad to the hospital in her car and Mario would follow in Dad's car.

Most of the time, Hilda avoided driving on the freeways because she didn't feel comfortable traveling at high speeds. Tension and stress would overcome her because of how rushed everyone was on the road. Today, she didn't notice.

They arrived in Pasadena in the late afternoon.

She took a deep breath. Mario wrapped his arm around her shoulders in support. They waited for the elevator doors to open to deliver them to Hell.

The situation was worse than his co-worker had led her to believe. Dad was covered in mud—his hair speckled with it, his shoes caked with chunks of it. Dried mud sprinkled from his sweater and slacks with every movement. He looked bizarrely out of place among the cherry wood desks, framed motivational pictures, and planters of greenery.

He shrank in fear at the sight of Hilda and latched onto her a moment later, embracing her so tightly she gasped for air.

He leaned in and said, "You have to protect me . . . got to keep me safe . . . keep them away. They're close . . . really close. They're coming after me." Tears flooded his eyes.

Hilda didn't know how to respond; she had never in her wildest dreams thought she would be confronted by anyone in a mental state such as this. She ran her fingers through his hair. What could she do but pray to God to save him?

Dad's boss, Mike, Jane, whom Hilda had spoken to on the phone, and his best friend, Minh, stood by in silence. A combination of horror and sorrow washed over their faces.

Hilda and Mario grasped Dad's dirty arms and walked him toward the elevator.

Dad's glazed eyes twitched and scanned the room.

Mike tiptoed up to Hilda and whispered, "Call me when you get to the hospital." He rested his hand on her shoulder for a moment.

In the parking garage, Dad reached for the keys from Hilda's hand.

"No," Hilda said. "I have to drive."

"No, I'm going to drive in case someone's following us. You won't know what to do or how to handle that."

Hilda didn't argue, gave him the keys and got into the passenger seat. She turned to him. "What in God's name is wrong with you? Where were you?"

"I was being followed."

"By who, Dear?"

"I don't know . . . people . . . cars . . . a couple of police cars, too…a red pickup truck…maybe the FBI? I dunno. Last night, I had to pull off the freeway. Thank God I was able to ditch them. Oh, Hilda, I was so scared, and you weren't with me."

"Where did you spend the night?"

"I had to hide in the car behind some bushes to stay safe, and then I drove over here. I didn't know where else to go."

On the freeway, Hilda remained silent for awhile and watched him drive.

He pushed the door lock down and looked at the cars around them.

"Watch out," he said. "We're being followed."

"That's ridiculous, no one is following us." Tears streamed down her cheeks. "Only Mario is behind us."

"Yes, they are. Why can't you see that? Are you naïve?" He glanced at every passing car.

She shook her head. "We need to go to the hospital right now."

"Please, Hilda, no. I'm so tired. I've been driving all night. I'm hungry. Let's eat something. Let me go home and sleep first." He possessed a wild look in his eyes—like a trapped animal watching the cage door close in front of him.

"We need to go to the hospital." She focused on the road, not wanting to feel his pain.

"Hilda, love, please don't. I promise if you just let me go home and sleep, we can go tomorrow. I promise. Please, not now. Please."

She couldn't handle his pleas for mercy. "Do you promise me, honestly promise you'll go tomorrow?" No sooner had the words escaped her tongue than she regretted giving in.

"Yes, I promise you."

His eyelids were getting heavy and his head kept drooping forward. About to fall asleep, he told her he couldn't keep driving. He spotted a diner and exited the freeway

Mario parked next to them, and once outside, he told Hilda he couldn't stay. Mario had to drop off their car at their house, pick up his car, and go to work.

After lunch, Hilda decided to drive and Dad seemed too tired to object.

At home, she paused for awhile before coming around to the passenger side to wake him. As she opened his car door, crumbs of dirt tumbled onto the concrete.

Before he stepped out, she wiped away her tears with her sleeve.

CHAPTER TEN

NOVEMBER 2, 1996: TRANSPORTATION

THE SUN ROSE OVER the majestic San Bernardino Mountains, which were wine-dark purple against the muted light of dawn. A dim glow filled the bedroom. Shadows faded until the wooden bed frame displayed its rosy grains.

Hilda stared at Dad's head resting on his pillow. She studied his face wanting to believe everything was back to normal like it had been only four months ago. She could believe it too, if it weren't for his muddy shoes and dirty clothes lying on the floor of the garage in front of the washing machine.

Slipping out from under the covers, she left him undisturbed. She tip-toed to the kitchen and busied herself preparing breakfast.

She hadn't gone to work at the beauty salon in several days. Thank goodness her employer was sympathetic. How much longer this lenience would last was anyone's guess.

She sipped her *maté* [Argentinean tea] and peered out the kitchen window at her garden. Her colorful azaleas and roses were still in bloom, thanks in part to the mellow autumn weather in Southern California.

Her thoughts were interrupted when Dad came and took his seat at the table.

Hilda placed a plate of eggs and semi-burnt toast—as he liked it—in front of him, along with apple jelly and orange juice. She sat alongside him and nibbled on a piece of toast.

"Do I have an appointment with the doctor?" Dad asked.

"Yes, I called to reschedule the appointment we missed last night."

"I didn't realize I had an appointment last night."

"Your work called the hospital and the doctors were expecting us. I told them you were too tired and we would come this morning instead."

"Oh," he said as if they were discussing just another routine doctor's appointment. In fact, that's how he seemed to think of it, just another appointment of which he had had so many lately, the surgeon, psychologists, and psychiatrists. What did he have to show for it all? Impotence—drugs to treat that; anxiety—drugs to treat that; and insomnia, which he had to rely on drugs to relieve.

At the hospital, Dad went behind closed doors with the doctor. His company had already sent over a detailed report of his behavior, but because of patient privacy laws, Hilda wasn't allowed to view them.

She sat alone in the waiting room. She folded her sweater, laid it neatly across her lap, twisted her gold bracelet watch around her wrist, and became lost in thought.

I wonder which medicine they'll try this time. I don't know what to do with him anymore. Aren't these doctors supposed to know what they're doing?

She'd never known anyone with these problems, and held on to the belief that, like any cold or flu, this "disease" just had to run its course. She worried, maybe she did something wrong. Maybe one of the medicines the doctors prescribed was causing weird side effects.

This is all because of the general anesthetic was administered twice within a short time period. She felt there was no other explanation.

Dad's personality had changed after those surgeries. He was never like this before, not in the least bit. She cursed the surgeon for the medical mishap and her HMO for hiring inept professionals. They had created this problem, and she expected them to fix it.

Whatever medication they would be sending home with him this time had better work. Or she might have no other choice than to find a good attorney and sue the doctor, the hospital, and the insurance company.

Maybe she could get the money to hire someone to fix her husband. Hilda stroked the soft cashmere of her sweater.

A doctor came out and approached her. "Are you Hilda, Joseph's wife?"

"Yes."

"I'd like to speak with you for a moment. Please come with me."

She followed him into another room where they each took a seat. Her stomach fluttered.

The doctor explained the diagnosis. "Your husband has paranoid schizophrenia. It's uncommon for this type of severe mental illness to develop at his age, fifty-three. Typically, symptoms show up when a person is in their teens or early twenties. You've never noticed anything before?"

She shook her head. "Only after his surgery."

He continued explaining what Hilda had already suspected to be true. "Your husband suffers from extreme paranoia. The irony with paranoia is although it's one of the simplest conditions to treat with medicine, it's the most difficult to treat, because of the inability of the patient to trust the doctor treating them, or to even believe that there is a problem needing treatment to begin with. Joseph also suffers from delusions. The paranoid schizophrenia, anxiety, and depression are serious and definitely need to be treated, even though he's refusing treatment."

Hilda's stomach sank to the floor. She took a moment to gather her thoughts. "Is he going to get better?"

"Depends on him. If he follows the treatment, he will."

"What treatment? What can we do?"

"We want to transport him to a mental hospital in Chino for further evaluation and treatment. Is that okay with you?"

"Yes." She cleared a lump from her throat. "He needs help. What do I need to do?"

"You'll need to go to Chino to fill out some paperwork."

The doctor returned Hilda to the waiting room. She sat and awaited additional instructions. Through the window, she watched clouds floating across the sky.

A ruckus broke out in the hospital entryway. Paramedics rushed a patient out the double doors—an unusual sight since most patients were taken in. The gurney jerked from side to side. The paramedics exited through the automatic doors.

Hilda dropped her sweater when she recognized the gold metal-rimmed glasses over those pale blue eyes. She knew the creamy white flesh of those brow wrinkles and the thin brown wisps of hair she had cut year after year.

Dad immediately recognized her as well. Lifting his head inches off the pillow, he twisted and struggled against the tight nylon straps pinning him down. His face contorted. He shrieked. "Please, Hilda, don't let them take me! I'm okay, I'll be okay! Hilda! Please don't let them take me!" He tried to stretch his arms out to her but could only lift his fingertips, repeating his calls for help.

The paramedics wheeled him into an ambulance. Hilda followed.

Tears streamed down Dad's face as he continued another round of frantic screams. "Please! Please, Hilda! Don't let them take me! I don't want to go! Please stop them! Don't let them take me!"

Hilda began to hyperventilate.

"Are you his wife?" one paramedic asked while the other secured Dad inside the ambulance.

Hilda nodded.

"We're transporting him to Chino Mental Hospital. They're going to admit him for treatment."

Her voice quivered. "Where do I have to go?"

"I'll give you directions, but you can just drive your car and follow us."

Dad's persistent pleas continued.

Hilda crouched inside, gave him a kiss and stroked his face. "It'll be okay, dear. Everything's going to be okay. I'm going to see you in a little bit. Don't worry."

Crying, Dad tilted his head back toward her with a look of abandonment—like a helpless child beaten by his parents and left to fend for himself.

Hilda climbed out. She gazed down at the paramedic's white shoes. The ambulance door slammed shut. Dad's moans pierced her heart.

PART TWO
NOTICEABLE CHANGES

CHAPTER ELEVEN

NOVEMBER 1996: VISITATIONS

"MY HUSBAND JOSEPH WAS just taken here," Hilda said. "The doctor said I needed to fill out paperwork."

One of the two women behind the reception's desk handed her a clipboard and stack of papers.

Hilda wrote in his name, birth date, address, phone number…now they wanted insurance information? She stared at the white space. He filled out financial forms. Social security number? She couldn't remember. She did the best she could and returned the clipboard. She never felt so lost and confused. This whole saga felt surreal. She wanted nothing more than to have her old husband back in her arms, like old times.

"You won't be able to see your husband today," the receptionist explained, "but you can see him tomorrow. Let me explain the visiting rules. You cannot bring any children. There is a one hour limit per day during the set visiting hours. You can visit him in the visiting room or the common areas. Here, you'll need to bring this every day." She handed Hilda what looked like a credit card. "This is your security tag. It's how you get into the secured patient area. Scan this at the security door and push the button."

Hilda stared at the card in her hand.

The next day, Hilda returned as instructed and scanned the card. The door separating the lobby from the patient area opened. At first she hadn't noticed anything special about these double doors, but as she passed through them, she saw how thick they were. Each had a little window like an armored truck. She hadn't gone more than five steps when a loud click echoed behind. Scared, she turned; the waiting room was hidden behind the steel door. She was trapped on this side.

Hilda stopped at the sign for the visiting room. Inside were a TV, some tables and chairs, and a beverage center with coffee, teas, and sodas. She sank into a chair and waited.

Dad appeared in the doorway, dressed in street clothes. He moved across the room and gave her a kiss. "I love you." His eyes and mouth drooped. In a low voice, he said, "I'm sorry I'm here."

Hilda didn't respond.

He asked rounds of questions. "How are the dogs? How's the house?" She gave him brief answers. Then he asked, "How long am I going to be here?"

"That depends on you. You've got to do what the doctors say and take the medication."

"Yes, I'll do whatever they tell me to do."

She raised an eyebrow and hugged him. She wished he was being honest, but doubted it. She missed their nightly routine of snuggling together on the couch watching TV, of spending the weekends folk-dancing with friends, of renting movies on Friday nights and eating grapes or ice cream together. Sure they argued occasionally, but in comparison to this moment, life had been perfect. She had pictured growing old together, traveling the world together, and visiting grandkids together. But now here he was, locked up in a mental hospital. She squeezed her eyes shut and faked a smile. She needed to be strong, strong enough for them both.

Leaving the hospital, Hilda observed the countless trees and bushes adorning the well-manicured landscaping. She remarked at the irony of the hospital's serene surroundings as she drove away in stunned silence.

Each time Hilda visited Dad, he complained about the medication's side effects, the headaches, the stomachaches. On occasion, the nurses agreed one drug or another was bad for him, because it made him vomit. After 2-3 days on each medication, they'd change it. Not that it mattered, since he wasn't really swallowing the pills. Hilda could do nothing about that.

She was told she'd have to talk to the social workers before he was released, but anytime she did speak with the social workers or the nurses, they said he was doing better. They insisted he would continue to get better, as long as he kept taking his medication.

Either they didn't care or didn't know Dad wasn't really taking the meds. He was getting good at faking them out.

One evening after visiting him, Hilda came home and saw the answering machine light blinking. She pressed play.

"Good afternoon, this is ---- High School calling regarding your son, Keith. He was absent from periods five and six after lunch again today. This seems to be another unexcused absence. Please call the attendance office at your earliest convenience to schedule a parent meeting. We need to—"

She pressed stop before the message had time to finish.

Keith had spent the weekend at our mom's apartment in Orange County. On Sunday afternoon, he called Hilda to let her know he was ready to be picked up.

"No," Hilda said. "I'm not coming."

"Why not?" he asked.

"I'm kicking you out. I can't take you and your father right now. With him in the hospital, and your problems at school, it's just too much for me to handle."

"Are you serious? What am I supposed to do?"

"Well, you're just going to have to stay with your mother. I'm sorry, Keith. You know I love you, but I can't deal with everything right now."

Keith had felt invincible until that moment. He hadn't thought about the consequences of his actions. What about the few friends he had finally made at his new high school?

That night, Keith went to sleep on a blanket on Mom's bedroom floor as he would continue to do for the next eight months. He also would not be in school for the next three weeks until Mom could figure out what to do with him.

Hilda sat down at the kitchen table, the empty kitchen table.

She drank her tea and stared out the window at her backyard. The grass needed mowing. Dad usually mowed the lawn, but in his absence it went uncared for. The rose buds that had burst forth last week in full blooms of lavender, red, and pink were now limp. The white, yellow, and peach petals had browned at the edges. They needed to be plucked or cut to encourage new growth.

The poodles barked to be let out, stirring Hilda from her thoughts.

"Since I'm up already, I might as well tend to my flowers." She set down her drink, put on her garden shoes, and grabbed the shears and gloves. At least tending her garden, trimming her bushes into animal shapes, and coaxing new life from the earth invigorated her. But she would give it all up—the trees, roses, and shrubs—to have her old husband back.

A court order extended Dad's involuntary stay to two weeks, at which point his case would be up for another review. The social workers had hinted to Hilda that, because of insurance company restrictions, Dad wouldn't be kept much longer unless his condition dramatically worsened.

Hilda tried to preserve his dignity by washing his clothes at home. She followed him down the hallway to his room to get his laundry.

The bare room contained little more than a small circular table, a wastebasket, and a ceiling fluorescent light. Sunshine filtered in through the bars in the windows.

A nurse entered.

"Good afternoon," she said. "Joseph, are you ready to take your medication?"

He glared at her.

The nurse dropped a few pills into his open palm and handed him a cup of water.

He placed the pills on his tongue, and closed his mouth.

"Drink up," she said.

He brought the water to his lips and took a sip. He crumbled the paper cup and tossed it into the trashcan. As soon as the nurse left, Dad got up and quietly closed the door. He took a tissue, spit the medicine out into it, and dumped the wad into the trash.

"You see?" He sat down on the bed and whispered, "They're trying to poison me. I need to get out of here. Can't you get me out?"

Hilda scooted her chair closer to his bed and lightly caressed his face. His pale complexion, a trait passed down from his Ashkenazi Jewish ancestors, was in sharp contrast to her bronze skin.

"I miss you," she said. She longed for her husband, but wasn't sure if the person in front of her was that person. She knew he wasn't any better than when he had been admitted. She knew she had to say something to the nurses about the medicine; this wasn't the first time she had watched him spit out the drugs. She wanted him to get better, but without the medicine, she felt it wouldn't happen.

Hilda intertwined her fingers with his. He chatted about his morning. He told her how difficult it was to speak with the other patients, who often didn't make sense. He said he watched TV and slept most of the time.

Dad's voice trailed off. He closed his eyes. Whatever medication the nurses had gotten him to swallow caused him to be tired. Or maybe the combination of depression, anxiety, and the medication was knocking him out.

Hilda kissed his hand, as she had done every day for the past thirteen years. Whenever they drove anywhere, they held hands in the car. They would take turns planting a kiss on the back of each other's hand. If he irritated her, she would nibble on the edge of his palm until he complained and apologized.

She smiled at these fond memories, glanced at her watch, and knew their visiting hour was over. With a heavy heart, she got up, kissed him again, and left him asleep.

The next morning, as soon as Hilda cleared security, she headed straight to the nurses' station. She motioned to a nurse.

"What can I do for you?" the nurse asked.

Hilda spoke in a hushed tone. "My husband Joseph has been spitting out his medication."

"Really? I've given him his morning meds the last two days and watched him swallow them."

"He's only swallowing the water. He's been hiding the pills under his tongue and spitting them into the trash the moment you leave the room. Don't you check for this?"

"Yes, well, sometimes they fool us. We can't catch them all the time. I'll be more careful with him from now on. Don't worry—I'll put a note in his chart for the evening nurses, too."

Hilda's heart filled with fear and remorse for having violated her husband's trust. "Please, don't tell him I said anything. I don't want him to know I told you."

"Don't worry, I won't," the nurse said. "I'll be in there in a bit to give him his morning dosage."

Hilda hung her head and entered Dad's room. She handed him his clean clothes and gave him a kiss.

His face lit up. "My little Ducky, I've missed you."

He hadn't called her that in months. Hilda choked up with tears and couldn't respond.

He embraced her in a tight hug. He had been having good days and bad days. Today seemed like a good day. Maybe he might get better after all. Nothing could make her happier.

Moments later, the nurse came in with some pills in one paper cup and water in another. She gave them both to my dad and stood back waiting for him to swallow, which he did.

"Can you open your mouth for me?" the nurse asked. "I need you to lift up your tongue."

He gave her a death stare as he complied. As he lifted his tongue, two damp pills were exposed from their hiding spot.

"You need to swallow your medicine," the nurse said. "Drink some more water."

Dad glared first at the nurse then back at Hilda. He drank the rest of the water and swallowed the pills.

Hilda stared at the floor.

"Lift up your tongue . . . thank you." The nurse turned in her white shoes and left.

Dad lay down, grunted, and turned his back to Hilda. "Just leave. I don't want to talk to you." He closed his eyes.

She reached for him but he swatted her hand away. Her chin quivered. She paused a moment before picking up her purse. She opened her mouth to speak, but couldn't, and left his room without saying good-bye.

The next day, Hilda drove to Chino, only to be told her husband refused to see her. She wept the entire drive home and alternated between cursing God and praying to him for help.

Hilda was relieved when Dad allowed her to visit him again. He was even being pleasant. She told him she kicked Keith out of the house. He stared at her blankly and didn't respond.

Instead, they chatted about his day.

Before she left, Dad handed Hilda his wedding band. "Here, take this home. Because of water retention, they had to use soap to remove it."

She stared at the gold ring, the symbol of their love and commitment, lying in her palm. Her stomach hurt. In their twelve years of marriage, he had never taken it off before.

Dad never put his wedding ring on again.

CHAPTER TWELVE

NOVEMBER 1996: GETTING OUT

THE MENTAL HOSPITAL HAD a courtyard for the patients' enjoyment. Hilda convinced Dad to go outside. Because of the cool autumn breeze, she handed him a jacket. Arm-in-arm, they walked down the hallway.

At the end of the hallway was a great-room with couches, chairs, and tables. Patients, most in street clothes, sat around quietly. While some appeared to talk to themselves, many watched television.

"Won't it be nice to see our grandson Justin for Thanksgiving?" Hilda asked, referring to my baby boy, their first grandchild. "We've haven't seen him since he was born last month. And it's been awhile since the kids have been together at our house."

"Mmm-hmm." He stared at the ground.

"Amanda's taking a few months off to be with Justin. She's going back to college for the spring semester and said she's still on track to earn her degree in four years. Even though it's too bad she got pregnant, at least she's taking responsibility. Aren't you proud of her?"

"Mmm-hmm."

She nudged him in the side. "Keith started high school near his mom. I think he stopped ditching school. Isn't that good news?"

"Mmm-hmm."

"Joseph, are you listening to me?"

"Yes, dear."

She sighed, stopped talking, and walked with him towards the back door, about thirty feet ahead. A glass panel lined both sides of the door, with barred windows next to the panels.

"Dear," he said, "do you mind if we sit for a bit here in the TV room? I'm so tired."

Hiding her disappointment, because she felt the fresh air would do him some good, she agreed. They sat down on a couch and snuggled close.

A tall slender girl, of no more than eighteen years of age, with long straggly blonde hair came running past them at full speed. The strange young woman ran from one end of the TV room to the other. She burst through the glass panel, shattering it to pieces. Scratched and bleeding, she did not stop but continued running outside. The glass had merely slowed her down. A loud alarm shrieked and employees ran to and fro herding the patients back into their rooms. The hospital went into lockdown. The staff secured all doors. They shooed out the visitors.

Hilda hardly had time to kiss Dad good-bye when a nurse took him by his arm and yelled at her. "You need to leave immediately!"

The next day, Hilda arrived for her visitation. Walking through the security door, she couldn't help but wonder what had become of the poor girl from the day before.

The heavy metal doors clacked shut behind her. She walked to the nurse's station where she asked to speak with Gary, the social worker coordinating Dad's care.

Once she opened the door, she found Gary at his gray metal hospital-issue desk filling out some paperwork. He looked up and acknowledged her. "Hello there, what can I do for you?"

She sat down across from him. "How's the treatment going? How's my husband?"

"Well, while Joseph's been here, we've continually changed his medication because he keeps complaining about side effects." He pulled a file out of the mound of paperwork on his desk and read through the latest notes.

"Yes, I know that already. How much longer does my husband need to be here?"

"Well, the doctor wrote down here that he can be released this Friday."

"But he doesn't seem any better to me. I want to speak with the doctor." She came to hear something new, but only seemed to be getting the same regurgitated responses.

Gary picked up the phone and dialed an extension. "I have Joseph's wife, Hilda, here in my office and she'd like to discuss his care and prognosis with you." He drew his attention back to a pile of papers on his desk and sorted them into a number of smaller stacks.

The office door opened. A tall man with a full head of gray hair entered.

"Doctor McKinley," the man said. "How can I help you?"

"I need to know Doctor, will my husband . . . ." She stopped mid-sentence. "He doesn't seem to be getting better."

"It's going okay; he's going to be okay. In fact, he'll be able to go home at the end of this week, but he has to take his medication. If he takes it, he'll be all right." Dr. McKinley almost sounded as if he were convincing himself of this truth.

"But what if he's not? Will he be kept here longer?"

"As it turns out," Gary said, "your insurance company isn't willing to pay for any additional days of inpatient mental health care beyond the initial fourteen. So his release date is set for the end of the week."

Dr. McKinley seemed to carefully choose his words. "I really believe he'll be fine as long as he takes his medication."

Intuitively, Hilda felt this scenario was highly unlikely. Ever since Dad had been diagnosed with paranoid schizophrenia, he had being refusing care.

"If there's a problem, and he won't take his medication, what do I do?" She felt there was something Dr. McKinley and Gary were not saying, but couldn't tell for sure.

"Call his psychiatrist, or if he can't help you, you can always call us," the doctor said.

She shook her head and went to go visit Dad, which seemed a better use of her time. Besides, she was determined to get him outside for some fresh air.

He agreed to join her for a walk. They held hands and walked toward the patio door.

Hilda looked around for evidence recounting the horrific event from the previous day. No glass shards remained. The window panel had been replaced as if the incident never happened. That struck her as more than a bit eerie.

Fences divided the courtyard from the free world. Ignoring the curled barbed wire on top, she led him onto the grass. The trees, still full of lush green leaves, surrounded them.

"During autumn, I sure do miss Chicago," Dad said. "Well, not necessarily the freezing cold wind blowing in off of the lake, but for the way the whole landscape changes with every season unlike here, where it's basically summer weather all the time. Oh, Hilda, the changing colors of the fall are really something, the blazing reds, yellows, and oranges, the colors on the leaves are always so bright as they began to fall from the trees."

She smiled. He sounded normal for once. "Yes, dear, I remember visiting Chicago with you in the fall. It was beautiful. Remember when we took the kids there?"

He stared off into the distance. "Y'know, California really doesn't come close to Chicago right about now. I mean, I do love the mountains here, Illinois is so flat, so the mountains here are definitely magnificent, but the leaves, the colors of the seasons, I miss that."

"We can go back and visit if you'd like." She squeezed his hand. Anything was worth a try, anything to bring her beloved *Piggito* back to her.

"Mmm, maybe." He hung his head. "I'm tired, dear. I need to take a nap."

He always seemed tired and a little off-kilter. She brought him back inside. Remembering she had a dental appointment, she kissed him good-bye.

Although Hilda had always been a private woman with her thoughts, feelings, and life, something caused her to open up while lying on the reclined dental chair under the bright spotlight. All it took was for her long-time family dentist to ask, "Good to see you again. How are you? How's Joseph?"

He held the mirror and scraping tool up to her mouth and almost inserted them, when—before she knew it—she blurted out the story. The dentist, eyebrows raised, leaned back on his stool and listened.

"I think the anesthesia caused this," she said. "He was put under it twice in one week and he's never been the same since."

"I'd have to agree with you. I've known you and your husband for years. This is one of the most bizarre things I've ever heard. Perhaps the anesthesia from his cancer surgery may have altered the chemicals in his brain. You said something about an alternative hospital in Tijuana?"

"That is where he should have gone for treatment in the first place. We have friends who were successfully treated there."

The rest of the cleaning and exam was done in mutual silence. On her way out, the dentist requested she keep him posted. She agreed. And now she had an idea what she could do next.

Thursday came and went. Friday, the day of his release from the hospital, finally arrived.

Dad grabbed hold of Hilda as soon as she walked into the hospital room and gave her a kiss. "I love you, my little Ducky."

Hopeful the worst was behind them, she kissed him back. "I love you too, my Monkey."

Once in the car, he fell asleep from the rocking motion. She didn't mind, though. He was coming home.

Although she wished she didn't have to, Hilda continued to work five days a week at the beauty salon cutting and coloring hair. Every evening when she came home, she discovered Dad had locked all the doors, closed all the windows and curtains, and slept all day.

A week later, she confronted him. "I'm worried you sleep all day. It's not healthy."

"I'm fine." He sounded groggy.

"What about that hospital in Mexico?" she asked. "Shouldn't we at least call? Don't you think?"

"All right, go ahead and call them. See what options they suggest for me being so damn tired all the time."

Hilda spoke to the receptionist in Spanish, relating the situation to her. "*¿Puede ayudar?*" Hilda pleaded for help. "*Por favor. Es urgente. Necesitamos tu ayuda. José no está bien mentalmente.*"

The answer on the other end of the phone was along the lines of: "The doctors told him he would be okay without the surgery, but you two didn't listen to us. We promised you but you didn't want to believe in us. His body is intoxicated. If he comes down here and stays for one week in our hospital, we can give him a treatment to get rid of all the chemicals in his body. We can cleanse his body through nutrition, all-natural foods, fruits and vegetables, natural medication, herbs, absolutely no fast food."

She and Dad agreed to give it a try. This time he wouldn't call my grandparents for advice. In fact, my grandparents had no idea what had been happening with Dad's mental health. They preferred to live in denial. After all, they were in Chicago, anyway. What could they possibly do for him?

CHAPTER THIRTEEN

NOVEMBER 1996: THANKSGIVING

A WEEK WENT BY. Hilda had made the four-hour round-trip drive down to Mexico on her own several times. At last Dad's treatment was completed and he was ready to come home. She led him out to the parking lot, into the bright sunshine.

"Hilda, would you like me to drive home?" he cheerfully offered.

She grinned at the life force she saw glowing again in him. She wished to maintain this precarious balance of sanity, so she declined. "No thank you, dear. You rest. I'll drive. I don't mind at all."

Dad reached over and surprised her with a kiss on the lips before he got into the car. He chatted about the patients he had met and also how kind and knowledgeable the staff had been. This time he did not fall asleep during the ride home. They talked about plans for Thanksgiving, less than a week away.

After his return from Mexico, Dad didn't mention a single word about Keith or the FBI or anyone else plotting to kill him. Hilda chose not to remind him of his ungrounded fears.

She invited all of us kids, Keith, Jackie and her boyfriend Neil, and me and my one-month-old newborn, to celebrate the Thanksgiving holiday with dinner at their house.

I was excited, but tentative. Dad and Hilda hadn't seen Justin since his birth in mid October. At the hospital, when Dad held my son and smiled for the photos, his eyes seemed glossy. Usually talkative, Dad stayed relatively silent. I was saddened to realize my dad had become like a stranger since his surgery. Not the bright eyed, animated, intellectually playful person I remembered.

Jackie hadn't seen Dad since his birthday in July, when he had just received his cancer diagnosis. During the birthday festivities, he had held a private conversation with my sister, expressing his fear of death. He wanted her to know he was proud of her, no matter what happened to him.

At the beginning of Thanksgiving week, Hilda returned to work at the request of her clients. She made arrangements to go in late so she could accompany Dad to his back-to-back follow-up appointments with his psychiatrist and psychologist. Hilda sat in the same waiting room where she had witnessed Dad's forced transportation about three weeks prior.

Not trying to be superstitious, Hilda chose a seat in the waiting room as far away as possible from where she sat the last time. She balanced her checkbook, trying to get her mind off the haunting memories. Calculating the balance required her concentration, since finances was a task Dad previously handled with utter efficiency.

Every few minutes, Hilda glanced up at the doorway in fear she would see Dad strapped on a gurney screaming. But it didn't happen. Instead, he walked toward her of his own free will with a prescription in hand and a triumphant smile across his face.

She stood up. "So it went well, dear?"

"They said I should be fine. I only need to fill these prescriptions and take them on a regular basis. Now, I warned them that if they caused the same side effects as the other stuff, I would stop taking them ASAP. But they assured me these were milder. They refilled the sleeping pills, too. The fatigue's still an issue because I'm having trouble falling asleep at night, but, of course, it's not as bad as before I went down to TJ."

She nodded and together they walked to the pharmacy, holding hands. She felt things were going to be better.

After taking him home, Hilda drove to work. On the way, she reminded herself to go grocery shopping after work for the rest of their Thanksgiving dinner. The turkey was defrosting in the refrigerator. All she needed was a pie crust and pecans because Dad had agreed to make his famous pecan pie—thoughts of which were already making her mouth water. In the afternoon, before leaving the beauty shop, she called home to check on him.

"Hi, dear," she said. "How are things going?"

"Fine. I just came in from taking the dogs for a walk. Why, what's going on? Is something wrong?"

She quickly made up an excuse for calling. "Oh, nothing. I'm going to pick up some pecans and pie crust on the way home. Do we need anything else from the store?"

"We're almost out of tuna fish and apple jelly. I can go shopping tomorrow for them."

"No, no, it's fine. I'll pick some up. It's not a problem." She didn't want him to strain himself in any way, to risk losing any of the progress he had achieved in Mexico. Thinking about the appointments earlier in the day, she asked, "Did you start the medication yet?"

"Yes."

Although Dad's mental state improved after his first weekend home from Mexico, he relapsed the day after beginning his new medication. Hilda came home from work to find him asleep on the couch. Shadow and Star whimpered by the door to be let out. She opened up the curtains, allowing the final minutes of sunlight to stream into the house.

After he woke up, they ate dinner in relative quiet. His mannerisms made Hilda feel uneasy. He seemed groggy and agitated at the same time. She cleared the table while he sat, staring off into the distance. She wanted so desperately to shake him out of it. She reflected on the first few days since their return from Mexico.

Had he really been better? Or was she just viewing him through wishful rosy lenses?

She put on her nightgown and turned toward the bed. It was empty. Where was he?

In the living room, she found him lying on the couch, fast asleep.

She nudged him on the shoulder, softly calling out to him, "Dear, it's time to go to bed. C'mon, wake up, dear."

He grunted and sat up.

Lifting up the sleeve of his terry cloth robe, she took his hand and guided him down the hallway.

"All right." He moaned softly.

"Did you take a sleeping pill?"

He mumbled. "Yeah."

"Why?" After closing their bedroom door, she tried to help him remove his robe.

He jerked away from her, reached into his robe pocket, and pulled out three orange pill bottles. He gripped them tightly.

Upon seeing this, she again asked, "Why did you take a sleeping pill?"

"I haven't been sleeping well for awhile now." He shoved the pill bottles back into his pocket, dropped the robe onto the floor, and slipped into bed.

"But you've been sleeping all day," she said.

He didn't reply.

Hilda watched him for a moment before turning out the lights. She cuddled up to him, but he was out cold.

Wednesday passed in the same manner as Tuesday, much to Hilda's dismay. After coming home from work, she thought ahead of all the cooking she would be doing the next morning. Perhaps a hot shower might melt her troubles away. Steam filled the bathroom. She closed her eyes. The rush of warm water pelted all thoughts from her mind and rinsed them down the drain.

She inhaled one final cleansing breath and turned off the water. Dressed in her robe, she walked out to stand in front of the L-shaped double vanity counters, glancing at her reflections in both mirrors. She paused and examined her expression. She looked tired. Still, she was thankful to be in a state of relaxation. She dragged the brush through her midnight-black hair, applying pressure to massage her scalp as she ran the brush through again. Satisfied, she changed into her nightgown and turned towards the king size bed calling to her.

Dad wasn't there, again. Hilda took a deep breath. She would probably have to wake him up from the couch, and he would probably be too tired to snuggle with her. She walked down the dark hallway into the living room. The curtains were drawn and the doors locked, as they had been all day. A crystal table lamp next to the window cast a dim light over the room.

He was asleep on the couch, sitting upright. His robe was slightly open, exposing his pajama pants and white t-shirt. His arms rested along his sides, his head tilted back against the cushions.

At least he could have lain down to be more comfortable.

"C'mon, Joseph," she called out to him. "Let's go to bed now."

He must not have heard her in his sleep, since he did not stir. She reached out for his left hand to pull him up. He didn't respond to her light tugging, so she let go. His hand fell limp to his side.

She tapped him on the shoulder and repeated her request, "Joseph, wake up. Let's go to bed now."

He didn't move an inch. She figured he must be really tired.

Inches from his ear, she yelled, "Joseph, get up! Get up! Get up!" Her hot breath bounced off of his skin. He didn't make the slightest movement.

Hilda's stomach sank. Her heart raced. She hyperventilated. She grabbed his shoulders and shook him. His body slouched over to the side. Three orange pill bottles slipped from his right hand onto the floor.

She shrieked and picked them up. At least they weren't empty. One by one she opened them. She couldn't be sure, but they seemed emptier than they should have been. She dropped the bottles and raced to her bathroom. He had another set of prescriptions in the medicine cabinet. In a panic, she fumbled with the child-proof caps. Pills from his old medications were missing, too. She couldn't focus on the small writing on the labels, but knew one was his anti-anxiety medication and one was his sleeping pills. She raced to the kitchen. Reaching for the phone, she stopped herself.

Too embarrassed to call for help—she might be worrying over nothing—she ran back to shake him awake.

"Huh?" He grunted. "Wha…what?" he mumbled.

Hilda threw on some clothes and started the car. She darted back inside and tried once again to wake him.

Another minute passed. With strength she didn't know she possessed, she pulled his arm and raised him to a semi-standing position. The weight of his body almost toppled her. She wrapped one arm around him and locked her hands together.

"Uh . . . ur . . . ." his voice trailed off into incomprehensible blabber.

Hilda tightened her grip and thrust her weight forward. She grunted under the tremendous burden. "Joseph!" She screamed, drew in another breath and pulled him a few feet forward.

"Uh? Huh?" he murmured.

Pausing, she squeezed her muscles together to shift his body in front of her. She dragged him. His head bobbed against hers. She bent her knees, took a deep breath, and yanked him toward the door.

Oblivious to the pain, she struggled with the dead weight. Almost there. With a final thrust, she tackled him into the passenger seat. He moaned.

Tears raced down her face while she drove, but no one could console her.

The hospital came into view. She pulled to the curb and ran inside the emergency room entrance.

Panting, she yelled to the receptionist, "My husband's in the car."

Two orderlies raced outside and loaded Dad onto a gurney.

They admitted him immediately.

The emergency room doctor ran several tests on Dad. They concluded he had overdosed, but hadn't ingested enough to require stomach pumping. They decided to wait it out until he regained consciousness. Hilda kept a vigilant watch at his bedside until he began to stir later in the morning. When he blinked, a flood of emotions overtook her.

After the nurses took Dad for further testing, Hilda found the nearest pay phone. She left a message on the answering machine at her sister's house and at my mom's house.

She phoned Jackie who answered.

"Your daddy is in the hospital again." Hilda had decided not to explain the details to us right away. Instead, she kept the conversation short. "He's okay. But, we aren't going to have dinner at the house today. Maybe we can postpone Thanksgiving for a couple of weeks or something. I don't know right now. I'm sorry, dear. I'll call you soon to explain."

"What happened?" Jackie asked. "I don't understand. I thought he just got out of the hospital and he was in TJ. Did something go wrong in Mexico? Should I drive up there?"

"No, don't drive here. Your daddy is going to be okay." Hilda paused. The nurses wheeled Dad down the hallway. "I'm sorry, dear, I have to go."

The doctor re-examined my dad who wouldn't say much and didn't seem to remember, or admit to, his actions the preceding night. The doctors decided to transport him back to the mental hospital in Chino for what would likely be two more weeks of involuntary confinement.

Hilda felt she had no more tears to cry and kissed him good bye. She promised to see him either later that day or early in the morning. She couldn't muster the energy to go with him.

This time, when the paramedics wheeled him outside to the ambulance, Dad didn't protest or yell for Hilda. He only closed his eyes.

CHAPTER FOURTEEN

NOVEMBER 1996: DROWNING

Friday morning, Hilda awoke to the ringing phone.

"Hilda? *Soy yo, Marisol.*" Her sister sounded alarmed. "I got your message late last night. I was having Thanksgiving dinner at my daughter's in-laws' house. *¿Que pasó?* Is Joseph all right?"

"*No lo sé*, Marisol. I don't know what I'm going to do about him." Hilda sank onto the stool next to the chair and rubbed dried tears from her eyes. She had on the same clothes she threw on for the trip to the hospital. She must have been too tired to change.

"I'll be there as soon as I can and I'll stay through the weekend."

"No, no I'm okay." Hilda lied. She wanted to be alone in her depression. "Don't worry about me. I'm fine."

"I've already got a bag packed in the car. I'll leave in a few minutes." Marisol hung up before Hilda could argue.

Hilda grabbed a clean glass out of the dishwasher, which hadn't been unloaded. She didn't feel like using the stool to put everything up into the cabinets. Dad usually did that.

Opening the refrigerator for juice, she was greeted by the large defrosted turkey, far too much food for her alone. Besides, it only served as a reminder of the family gathering that had never taken place. She dragged the trash bin towards the refrigerator. In a wild frenzy, she purged the fridge and countertop of any remnants of Thanksgiving. The turkey, which would have fed all of us along with leftovers for us to take home, landed with a loud thud in the trashcan. Spotting the cranberry sauce, the sweet topping she enjoyed so much, she tossed it on top of the bird. Red sauce splattered against the sides of the trash bag. She saw the pecans and pie crust on the counter from the pie he never made, and slammed those into the trash. Smells of the cranberries and pecans mixed with the raw meat, making her nauseated. Pulling the drawstring tight, she heaved the heavy trash bag outside.

Hilda scrubbed her hands clean, went back to her room and before she knew it, was fast asleep. Sleep was so much easier than dealing with the pain.

Small in stature like her sister, Marisol also sported a short haircut. She wore more foundation, eye shadow, and blush than her sister, and her wrinkles gave her face a permanent smile. She gave Hilda a hug and busied herself cleaning house and making small talk.

"Should we go visit Joseph?" Marisol asked. She too, had a lingering accent, which made her voice high-pitched.

"Today, I want to go to the hospital to visit him alone." Hilda appreciated her sister's concern. When Hilda came to America, Marisol showed her around and encouraged her to date, which is how she met my dad. Marisol was the witness at their Las Vegas wedding. When Marisol divorced her husband and was left as a single mom raising a teen-aged girl, Hilda had been there for support. They had a tight bond. They could stay up for hours laughing and chatting, alternating between English and Spanish sometimes in the same sentence.

Friday and Saturday's hospital visits went much the same as before. Dad was tired. Hilda got him outside for a few minutes before they retreated back into the TV room to watch some mindless television. After a hug and a kiss, their time was up. The days passed by in a blur.

On Sunday morning, Marisol's last day with her sister, Hilda decided to bring her along to visit Dad. While they ate breakfast, Hilda tried to prepare her sister for what she would see at the mental hospital.

Marisol poured juice into two glasses. "I've been an in-home caretaker for years. I know what to expect." Marisol and Hilda both had worked for rich families in Beverly Hills, doing housework or caring for children. Now, Marisol focused her time on caring for the elderly, her kind spirit well-suited for the job.

"Uh-uh," Hilda said, "I don't think so. You'll be surprised. This is much different from the people you've cared for. These patients are out of their minds."

"We'll see," Marisol said.

Hilda led her sister past the security checkpoint. Marisol jumped at the sound of the heavy metal doors slamming shut behind them. Hilda laughed remembering how it took her nearly two weeks to become accustomed to hearing that sound, and Marisol giggled, seemingly out of nervous embarrassment.

With her sister in tow, Hilda turned another corner and entered the TV room.

Minutes later, Dad appeared. He smiled weakly at Hilda. Apparently in a medicated daze, his eyes had that faraway look which had become all too familiar. He eventually noticed his sister-in-law and mustered up the energy to say, "Hi, Marisol."

He sat next to Hilda. She tried to embrace him. He allowed her do so, but only limply responded. He seemed glad she was there, but didn't smile.

"How are you, dear?" Hilda asked. "I've been so worried about you."

"They're trying to kill me," he whispered into her ear.

She closed her eyes, trying to squeeze those words out of her mind, that horrible, untrue allegation. "Joseph, dear, I love you. But I don't think anyone's trying to kill you, *Piggito*."

She hoped he would believe her, but knew he wouldn't. Or couldn't. She didn't know which.

She wondered if her darling husband had actually attempted suicide. Was her beloved husband really in a mental institution, again? Did he just make another paranoid accusation? She flickered between denial and depression.

Dad pulled away. "I have to go to the bathroom."

She stood up, giving him room to leave.

He shuffled across the floor toward the restroom.

Hilda sat back down and leaned over to her sister. "Oh, Marisol," she said. "I don't know what I'm going to do. Did you hear him?"

"Yes." Because the room was so quiet, Marisol had indeed heard the words. She changed the subject. "How are the kids doing?"

"They don't really know. Obviously I had to cancel the Thanksgiving plans."

"How's Amanda's baby Justin doing? Isn't he a month old? I haven't seen him yet."

"I haven't seen him since he was born. Amanda was supposed to come over on Thursday, but now I don't know when I'll see her or the baby. They won't let her visit her daddy. The nurses said seeing her daddy here could be so upsetting it would spoil her breast milk. Not that I blame the nurses, I don't want the kids to see their daddy this way."

"My grandson just turned two months." Marisol beamed. "He's so big already. My daughter says she can start sending baby clothes for Justin. Her son's already outgrowing the size three months clothing. Can you believe that?"

"Joseph's been in there awhile now. Should I go and check on him?"

"I'm sure he's fine. Go talk to the nurses if you're concerned."

Without waiting to hear another word, Hilda approached the nurses' station. She recognized a nurse. "Excuse me."

"Yes?" the nurse said. "What can I do for you?"

"My husband went to the bathroom awhile ago, but he hasn't come out. Should someone go and check on him?" Hilda felt a bit ridiculous, since she was probably getting all worked up over nothing.

"You can, ma'am," the nurse said. "There aren't any locks on the bathroom doors. You're welcome to check on him anytime you like. If you need anything, push the call button in the restroom."

In the TV room, Marisol sat, tapping her foot. Hilda turned towards the bathroom door and knocked lightly.

No response.

She turned the door handle and the hollow wooden door swung open. Dad wasn't sitting on the toilet. Kneeling on the floor, he was bent over a white trash can. He wasn't moving.

Hilda gasped. In what felt like slow motion she tip-toed across the white tiled bathroom floor and peered over his back. The trash pail was full of water. His head was submerged. She tried to scream, but couldn't. She spun around. Next to the toilet, a sign on the wall read: Press for Help. Her fist slammed on the call button.

She turned back around. "Joseph!" she screamed. "Stop it!"

A nurse's voice rang out, "How can I help you?"

"Help!" Hilda yelled. "My husband's trying to kill himself! His head's underwater."

Nurses rushed into the bathroom and dragged him out. His thin brown hair was darkened from the water, which dripped down his face onto his soaked shirt. He coughed and spat. While attending to him, the nurses directed Hilda to return to the waiting room. Hilda and Marisol sat together.

In a hushed voice, Marisol said, "I don't know what to say, Hilda. I'm so sorry this is happening to him. He's a good man and neither of you deserve this."

"It's so sad. He's a lovely person, an intelligent man, everything was for his children. He always cared about his kids. He's such a wonderful person, a wonderful man, a wonderful husband. He is the greatest person in my life. I've never met anyone like him, such an honest soul. He's the only one I ever really loved. I did something wrong." She choked up and sobbed.

Marisol took Hilda's arm and spun her around. "Listen to me carefully, Hilda. It's not your fault. This is not your fault. You didn't do anything wrong. Joseph is a good man, you're right. But you didn't cause this."

"But what can I do?"

"I don't know, but you're not alone. I'll do whatever I can to help you, to help Joseph. We'll find better doctors. There's got to be better medication. We'll figure something out. Don't give up and don't blame yourself."

The security doors opened again and a doctor took the empty seat next to them. Even sitting, he towered over the petite sisters. "I know this has been hard on you, seeing your husband back here again, and now the suicide attempts. First of all, I want to tell you he's all right. We gave him a sedative and he's sleeping right now."

"What's wrong with him?" Hilda asked. "Why isn't he getting better?"

"His depression and paranoid schizophrenia must be treated. He needs to accept help."

"And if he doesn't?"

"His condition could worsen."

His final comment left Hilda feeling uneasy. This might only be the beginning of her hell.

Chapter Fifteen

November 1996: Jackie

Monday after the long Thanksgiving weekend, Jackie's co-workers discussed the drama of their family holiday get-togethers. Jackie remained quiet. She didn't want to admit to the partying she had done. On Saturday, she and Neil slept at a friend's house where they spent all night singing drunken karaoke.

On her way home, at the end of a long day at her new insurance sales job, Jackie pondered why the only employment she could find after graduating from college were low-paying, stressful, and unrewarding. She just wanted to come home and relax. Sleep, in fact, sounded great. She took some Valerian Root to relieve her anxiety.

She thought of Dad's cancer. Was it cured? Would it return? Helpless to fix his health problems, she could only worry. She thought of Dad's involuntary commitment to the mental hospital. Where was he now? Why was this happening to him?

Back at home in her sanctuary, her "sweet tooth" (which she inherited from Dad) got the better of her. She reached for her favorite ice cream, Ben & Jerry's Chocolate Chip Cookie Dough. With spoon in hand, she sank down onto the couch and indulged in creamy comfort, straight from the carton. She tried to melt her sorrows away, at least for one night. After scraping the last drops from the container, she closed her eyes, falling into a sugar-coma.

The phone rang. Contemplating whether or not to get off the couch to answer, she allowed it to ring again. Rather than move, she let the answering machine pick up instead.

"Jackie, it's Hilda. Please call me as soon as you get this message."

Jackie jumped to pick up the receiver. "Hilda?"

"Your dad's back in the Chino mental hospital."

"Wait, slow down. I thought he just got out and you went to Mexico." Jackie tried to throw off the sugar high she had been enjoying.

"He overdosed."

"Drug overdose? What are you talking about?" Jackie replayed the two minute phone call from Thanksgiving morning in her head. She didn't recall hearing about an overdose. Come to think of it, Hilda hadn't explained anything at all and even downplayed the seriousness of the situation. Jackie hadn't followed up with her.

"He was unconscious," Hilda said, "from taking too many medications. He tried to commit suicide again at the mental hospital yesterday with a bucket of water."

Jackie set the empty ice cream carton down. Was it her fatigue talking or had she heard correctly? "What do you mean? A bucket of water? I don't understand."

"Yes, he tried to drown himself in the trash can."

"What? He tried to commit suicide? Nobody tells me anything."

"I didn't want you to worry."

"Of course I would've worried. But you should've told me." Jackie felt guilty, but she couldn't explain why. She walked over to her cabinet and grabbed a pack of Reese's Peanut Butter Cups, her choice of confectionary comfort. She tore off the orange candy wrapper and gobbled up the two peanut butter cups.

"Can you drive up here tonight?" Hilda asked.

"No, I can't right now. I'm too tired to drive."

"What about tomorrow morning?"

She agreed.

After a fitful night's sleep, hardly worth the rest it was supposed to deliver, Jackie awoke feeling numb. She phoned work and pretended to be sick, rather than go into the details of her personal life with anyone at work. In all honesty, she did feel sick.

Jackie, Hilda, and Hilda's friend Esther, whom Jackie had also known for years, drove to the mental hospital. Hilda had been too upset to go visit him alone the day before, since she was scared of the husband she would meet.

The tight security—unusual for any hospital she had been to in the past—left Jackie with an eerie impression. Cameras were placed in blatant view. She figured security guards were watching their every move.

Once Jackie, Hilda, and Esther were cleared to enter into the hospital wing, the double doors buzzed open. These heavy metal doors were not like those Jackie had seen at any other hospital. They were thick with electronic locks...*secure*. They slammed shut.

The gray-speckled linoleum floor was perfectly waxed, the walls glossy white, and the overhead fluorescent lights glaringly bright. Everything was so...*sterile*. White doors alternated on each side of the wide empty hallway.

Esther gripped Hilda's arm and supported her as they walked. If Esther let go, Jackie thought, Hilda might just crumble to the ground.

At the nurses' station, nurses instructed them to wait in the TV room for Dad to be brought in. Padded chairs and simple wooden side tables adorned the small room. Even with the television on, Jackie couldn't stand the stillness. She strolled to the entryway.

To the right was the nurses' station, and further down were the two heavy metal doors, more appropriate for a prison than a hospital. To the left, the broad hallway continued until it ended in a larger version of the TV room, a grand living room populated with people, couches, tables, and chairs. Outside the black wrought iron barred windows, a few patients meandered around in a grassy, fenced courtyard. The chain link fence surrounding the courtyard was topped with curling rings of barbed wire, separating the inhabitants of the mental hospital from the real world. A creepy thought rushed into Jackie's mind: even if the patients wanted out, they would never be able to leave. Indeed, this was a prison.

Distracted by her surroundings, Jackie hadn't noticed the patients wandering back and forth in the hallway. These patients, wearing hospital issue gowns or robes, did not move in pairs or in groups. They drifted alone in no particular direction like real-life zombies. A few times they gave fleeting looks in Jackie's direction, but no sooner had their eyes rested on her face than their gazes slid past in whatever direction their bodies aimed.

Were they drugged?

One woman in particular, a thin woman in her early thirties with limp brown hair, slowly moved in Jackie's general direction. Drool dripped from her mouth, drizzled down her chin, and pooled onto the chest of her hospital gown, leaving a circular wet spot. Without wiping her chin or blinking, she roamed. Nobody else seemed to notice or care. Jackie observed the other patients and realized this one wasn't the only one drooling.

Sick to her stomach, Jackie slumped into a chair in the TV room. Not a single word could describe her horror. Dad was nothing like these zombies. Surely, there must be a mistake. Our doting, caring father, so full of life and love, had no business in this place.

A nurse escorted Dad in. At first glance, Jackie was relieved. There must have been a mistake indeed. Dad wasn't wearing a white sterile hospital gown. In fact, he was dressed like usual, in brown corduroys and a red polo shirt, neatly tucked in and held in by his leather belt. No drooling or aimless wandering. Jackie felt this was all a strange joke. In only minutes, he would go home with them and they would laugh about it all the way back to the house. This nightmare would end.

But that was not the case. He sat on a chair next to Jackie. His speech confined to single syllable responses, he didn't acknowledge anyone. Worse, his crystal blue eyes, so kind and bright, were dull and absent of life. His eyes were icy, his jaw tense, and his body language filled with an inexplicable anger, which broke Jackie's heart.

What had happened to him? What was causing all this pain and hostility?

Having taken several undergraduate psychology courses, Jackie tried numerous approaches. First, she coaxed with love and tender affection.

Stroking his thigh as a mother would to calm a frightened child, Jackie spoke softly. "It's okay, Dad. It'll be okay. I love you. You're safe now…with us."

His eyes remained fixated into space, his jaw locked, and his body rigid.

Jackie pleaded. "Dad, I want to take away all of your pain. How can I help you? What can I do for you?"

Hilda, clutching Esther's arm, remained quiet in the corner.

When kindness didn't work, Jackie became more forceful and irritated. "You need to stop this. You have a family. Amanda just had a baby. You have Keith and me and Hilda. This isn't fair. We missed Thanksgiving. We need you to be okay, to be at home. We need you."

Frustrated by his lack of response or acknowledgement, Jackie watched the television screen to keep from crying. An old western was playing. The four white walls were closing in. "Desperado" by the Eagles blared out of the tiny TV speakers. In the stillness of the room, the solemn lyrics told Dad to come to his senses and accept help while he still had time.

This was a song Jackie knew far too well. She had spent many a drunken late night with Neil and his friend Cathy singing to Eagles' songs. The lyrics to "Desperado," in particular, held special meaning to her. Now the words took on new meaning. It wasn't about her or her boyfriend. Those words were inexplicably being played out for Dad's ears. But he wasn't listening. He was too far gone to be able to hear them. Jackie's emotions, which she had tightly balled up and held down, bubbled up. Suffocating, she turned to Hilda and Esther.

"I think it's time we go," Esther said.

Nodding, Hilda and Esther rose. Jackie took Esther's other arm and the three, supporting one another, headed back in the direction they had come. White walls and the sterile setting blurred as tears welled in Jackie's eyes. The heavy metal doors slammed shut.

Chilly evening air stung their faces. Jackie and Hilda wept. Esther embraced both of them while sobs shook their petite frames. It seemed all they had left in this world was each other.

CHAPTER SIXTEEN

DECEMBER 1996: ACCUSATIONS

BY MID-DECEMBER, DAD had been released from his second involuntary mental hospitalization. Hilda suspected his discharge was more closely governed by insurance company limits, not due to substantial improvement in his health. When the day came, she heard the same speeches, received the same instructions and more prescriptions.

Dad seemed happy to be going home. Hilda had driven to the hospital every day for their hour-long visits, had washed his dirty clothes, and had taken care of the paperwork. How could he possibly be angry with her, his beloved?

At home, he hesitantly continued his medication regimen, but often complained of side effects, including fatigue, drowsiness, and loss of appetite.

Hilda accompanied him to his many doctor's appointments: counseling for couples, individual counseling, medical follow-ups, and medication monitoring. Counselors recommended keeping the stress level down for awhile, so Christmas was low-key. No spiked eggnog, no Christmas lights, no baked cookies. Hilda decorated a miniature table-top tree. Christmas music played in the kitchen while she worked around the house. The grooming salon put red ribbons on Shadow's and Star's ears.

On Christmas Eve, Keith, Jackie and Neil, and Justin and I came over for a brief celebration. We exchanged few gifts. Dad kept his time-honored tradition of giving each of us a box of chocolate-covered cherries.

Cordial cherries remind me of my happy childhood when Dad was Dad, the same dad who taught me how to play chess and checkers, who barbequed, or blackened, chicken, who took our family to the corner video rental store to rent a comedy for Jackie, Hilda, and me, and a horror movie for him and Keith, and who took us on weekend excursions and summer car trips.

It's sad to realize those times are gone but I have since learned to appreciate these memories. Not everyone had such a good time growing up.

Although he seemed stabilized, Dad still had a major issue: he and Hilda hadn't been intimate since before his surgery, four months earlier. His regular physician sent him to counseling sessions for men unable to function anymore. He tried Viagra. It didn't do a thing.

"Joseph, every medication you take needs time to work—give them a chance," Hilda pleaded with him. "Doctors are saying it's in your mind. You have to relax."

His doctor sent him to a fertility clinic where they gave him a shot. They said it would help him. It did, but only for one day.

"Well, at least the shot worked," Hilda sounded hopeful. "You can try that again."

"No, I'm not getting another shot," he said. "What if I'm in the middle of the highway and I have an erection?"

Hilda burst into laughter. He looked up at her and sheepishly cracked a smile.

"*Piggito*, you know I don't care about sex." She softly stroked his face. "I only care about you and your health. I love you so much."

"I love you, too."

On a Saturday morning in mid-January while Hilda was at the beauty salon earning extra money by giving the full slate of hair treatments to an old client of hers, Dad phoned my sister.

"Hi, Jackie," he said. "How's everything going?"

"Everything's fine. How are you doing?" Upon hearing Dad's voice, she took the cordless phone to the couch and sat, facing the short hallway leading into her bedroom. From there, she could see Neil sitting up in bed, stretching.

"Oh, I'm all right, dear. Maybe you can come over and visit sometime. Or maybe I can drive down to there to San Diego and see you. What about today?"

Neil massaged Jackie's shoulders. He brushed aside her wavy brown hair, kissed the base of her neck, and wrapped his arms around her slender waist.

"Dad, I kind of have plans today, but maybe tomorrow?" Jackie squirmed, dodging Neil's advances. She brushed his hand away. "Is something wrong?"

"Well, I don't know whether or not I should be telling you this."

"Tell me what, Dad? What's going on? Are you okay?"

"You, Keith, and Amanda are my children; you'll always be my children." He paused. "Hilda…she's a devil woman, she can't be trusted."

"What do you mean? What's wrong with Hilda?"

"She's like a demon woman. She presents herself one way, but she's not being true." He lowered his voice. "She's looking at other men."

"That's crazy, Dad. You must be mistaken. Hilda's not like that."

"When we go out, she looks at other men," he repeated, raising his voice. "You know I can't function sexually after the surgery. She can't handle that. You have no idea, Jackie. Hilda is a very passionate and sexual woman."

"No, no, Dad. Hilda's not that way," Jackie said. Neil brushed his fingertips along her exposed arms. Her green silk nightgown slipped off one shoulder. She knew what passion was and while she frequently indulged, Hilda was quite the opposite.

"You don't know her, Jackie!" he yelled into the receiver. He regained his calm. "Hilda put me in that mental hospital. I don't know what she's told you, but I know the truth. I'm completely fine. Ask me anything. I'm completely logical and sane. I'm telling you something's been going on. She can't handle the fact we can't make love. She's been cheating on me. I can prove it. It's really sad, you have no idea. I don't know where else to turn."

Because Dad had always been logical, his accusations against Hilda were out of character. His story didn't jibe with what Jackie had always known to be true about our stepmom. But since Hilda had skimped on details from the preceding months and Keith had been mum, Jackie had no idea that Dad had been suffering from paranoia. "Dad, I don't know what to say. It sure doesn't sound like the stepmom I know and love. I can tell you that."

"Don't you love your father too?" He sounded sad and frightened.

"Of course I do. You know that."

"You weren't there for my surgery . . . ." His voice trailed off.

Jackie felt the pang from the guilt trip he liked to lay. She justified her absence to herself and to him once again. "I didn't know how serious the procedure was, Dad. If I had known, if you and Hilda had explained to me what was going on, I would've been there. You guys made it sound like no big deal. I didn't think you were having a major surgery. You know I love you."

Disregarding his argument and her defense, he said, "I'm telling you Hilda has been cheating on me."

"With who?"

"Oh, there's been more than one. Remember her friend, Esther? She's been with Esther's husband, José. But he's not the only man. The psychologist, the psychiatrist—even the surgeon who screwed up my surgery. I would've thought she was more loyal than that. The worst part is that she acts one way around you and everyone else, so I don't blame you for not believing me. I understand."

"How do you know all this?"

"Look, I don't want to get into all of the details with you." His tone turned harsh. "Believe me. I know these things, Jackie. I'm not the idiot she thinks I am. She's obvious about checking out every half-way decent-looking guy anytime we go anywhere. Does she think I'm stupid? But I guess I am the fool. She had me locked up in that damn hospital."

Jackie was speechless.

He continued, "Honey, I love you. Don't tell Hilda anything I've said. If she knows I've told you who knows what would happen to me next."

"Okay, Dad." She was too confused to question him.

"All right. Maybe you can visit sometime or I can go down there to see you. Don't worry about me. I'll be fine. God will take care of me. I love you."

"I love you too, Dad." She set down the phone and leaned against Neil's chest. "I can't believe it. He thinks Hilda's been cheating on him." She closed her eyes.

CHAPTER SEVENTEEN

SPRING 1997: CARDS, TRICKS, & GAME OVER

JACKIE FELT LOST IN THE WORLD and tried herbal remedies and alternative forms of healing in her search for answers. A close friend introduced her to the study of Metaphysics, which resonated with her shifting belief system. Kim, an astrologer, read Jackie's birth chart, explaining the planetary alignments. How the planets lined up in the twelve different houses of her birth chart provided a glimpse into her personality, strengths, career attractions, love relationships, and future children. Kim forecast the year and sex of Jackie's first child—which later proved to be accurate.

"You like to travel. I can see you would be good as a lawyer. You're intelligent, analytical," Kim said while studying Jackie's chart.

In addition to planetary influences, Jackie wanted to know what information Tarot Cards had in store for her. Gertrude, an eccentric German pot-smoker, waved a bundle of smoking sage over the cards to cleanse the energy while Jackie took a seat at the table. In her colorful flowing dress, Gertrude, middle-aged and heavy-set with thick, flowing white hair, resembled an old hippie on a bad acid trip. Originally an artist in Germany, she maintained an artistic flair in her clothes, home decor, and lifestyle when she came to the United States in search of her long-lost son. Earthy in appearance, Gertrude's face reflected the full life she had led.

Satisfied the area was purified, Gertrude set down the sage and presented the stack of Tarot Cards. Jackie split the deck and chose cards. Gertrude flipped each one, revealing intriguing illustrations and symbols.

Gertrude pointed to the first card and rambled on in a strange flow of consciousness. "I see that there is a man in your life . . . your heart has heaviness from this man . . . he has a strong-hold on you." Jackie wondered at first if this referred to Neil. As Gertrude continued, this man's identity became crystal clear. "He is such an influence . . . a lot of pain and sorrow. You're so intertwined with him . . . . Yes, there is a male, you're very close to . . . a lot of your identity is tied to him, this person is heavy on your soul . . . this male energy is weighing you down where you cannot see beyond it . . . you're so sucked into this weight." Jackie raised an eyebrow. She felt every word to be true—this man was our dad.

The next card revealed aspects of her personality. Gertrude breathed in slowly and spoke softly. "Jackie, you are a nervous, anxious person when you're around a lot of noise and hustle and bustle. You would be more relaxed in a slower-paced environment . . . . I see a lot of trees . . . this would be better for your nervous system . . . you absorb a lot of other people's energies. You have a tendency to be pessimistic. You don't realize your own strengths. Jackie, you see the glass as half-empty instead of half-full. You don't give yourself enough credit. A lot of your anxiety and angst is because you don't realize the power you have."

A Queen card was next on the table. After a long pause, Gertrude explained, "This is a powerful card . . . you have the strength of a queen, but you don't own the strength you have. You play the victim and let circumstances dictate how you feel. Instead of changing your outlook…instead of seeing obstacles as something to overcome, they become hurdles that get in the way."

Throughout the remainder of her reading, Jackie received guidance on how to capitalize on her strengths to alter her future, not yet decided by destiny. Everything Jackie heard rang true.

After Dad's discharge from the mental hospital, Hilda took him to psychiatrists, psychologists, and even an acupuncturist to put an end to his erratic behavior. Jackie urged them to pay a visit to her astrologer.

Although Hilda believed in the possibility of the spiritual realm, Dad did not put too much credence in it, so both Hilda and Jackie were surprised when he agreed.

During the astrology session, they listened but didn't say much. As Dad drove home, Hilda waited until they entered the Interstate-15 freeway before speaking.

"What did you think of Jackie's astrologer, dear?"

"I don't know," he said. "It seemed vague. Like what she was saying could've applied to just about anyone."

"I thought so, too. I think the reading was a waste of our time and money."

"Yes, the main message was I was going to 'feel better soon.' Ha. Why not a specific time frame?"

Or the name of a medication that would work. Hilda looked over at him. "Well, it was nice to see Jackie, anyway."

The car rocked back and forth as it veered toward the dotted lines to their left and right.

Dad returned to work, again. Several months had passed since he disappeared, showed up at his office, and was involuntarily committed. His boss and coworkers minimized the awkwardness. Minh sat with him at lunch, like before. No one mentioned November 1st.

In the early mornings, Dad left the house with his tie straight, his shoes shined, and his button-up shirt tucked into his dress slacks, like before. He ate a quick breakfast with Hilda before catching the vanpool a few blocks away. Every evening he kissed Hilda on the cheek as soon as he walked through the front door. He changed clothing and exercised, as he used to do. Things seemed to be going well. Perhaps going back to work was a good thing.

Dad had been prescribed different medications, all with some kinds of unwanted side effects. When he took the psychiatric drugs, his visions and paranoia faded, becoming more manageable and under control. However, he complained of feeling drugged and "out of it." He couldn't sleep at night. His doctors prescribed sleeping pills, and he become entrenched in a vicious cycle of being forced awake and put to asleep by medications.

Dad questioned why doctors gave him medicine which made him feel so horribly. He complained to Hilda who urged him to continue taking the drugs. He complained to me. I agreed he had a distant look in his eyes, but at the time I didn't know anything about mental illness or drugs used to treat it, so my opinion was not an educated one. Dad became convinced the medication caused him misery. He stopped taking everything. None of us knew.

One day, Hilda received a phone call from Dad's boss.

"Hilda, this is Mike from Joseph's work."

Hilda froze, recalling the last time someone had called from his office. No news was good news, but unexpected news was usually bad. "Yes?"

"I wanted to speak with you regarding Joseph's performance here at work," Mike said. "I know it may not be my place to ask this, but we've known each other for awhile now, and considering what happened last November, has he been taking his meds?"

"I think so. Why do you ask?" She realized she hadn't refilled his prescriptions in awhile.

"Well, he is a good senior programmer and systems analyst. Hell, he's probably one of the best ones we have here. But, lately he hasn't been doing his job. I mean we can handle it if he's a bit slower than usual as he gets back into the swing of things. But it has nothing to do with his speed. His accuracy is far from desirable. He's simply not doing his job."

"Have you talked to him?" Hilda knew nothing about computers so she hoped Mike wasn't going to ask her anything she didn't understand.

"Funny you should ask." Mike wasn't laughing. "I pulled him into my office yesterday to speak with him regarding his performance. You know, we're all trying to be understanding. Well, he immediately got defensive and complained someone was sabotaging his computers and messing with his work."

"Is that true?"

"No, not at all. In fact, when I asked him to clarify, he accused Minh and Amit of being the culprits. Now, I'm sure you know Minh and Joseph have been friends for years now. Amit came over from India a few years ago, but he has never caused any problems and always got along well enough with Joseph."

"Is it possible though?" Hilda wanted to make sure this was indeed Dad's paranoia returning. "Joseph's such a smart man."

"Nothing is wrong with the people here. His coworkers aren't doing anything. Joseph is simply not performing at his best." He paused. "I'm calling you simply to give you a heads up on the situation here, so you know about this problem and his paranoid accusations. I'm urging you to check in with his doctors again. Let's see if we can straighten things out."

"Okay, I'll call the psychiatrist."

"Great. Well, hopefully Joseph will feel better soon. If you can think of anything I should know, call me."

What he wasn't verbalizing, but Hilda caught hint of in his tone, was Dad had to improve soon, if he wanted to keep his job.

Hilda dialed the psychiatrist's emergency line.

"Dr. Weisman," a deep voice echoed through the line.

"Doctor, it's Hilda, Joseph's wife."

"Yes, what can I do for you, Hilda? How's Joseph doing?"

She repeated the conversation she had had with his boss.

"So, I take it you don't believe he is taking his medication?" Dr. Weisman inquired. "Is there any way you can check?"

Even though Dad used to carry his pill bottles in his pocket everywhere he went, lately he had been leaving them on the kitchen counter, next to her vitamins. "Actually, yes I think so. Can you hold on a second?" She examined the cluster of bottles and read the date dispensed. One by one, she opened them and did a guesstimate as to how many pills remained. She trudged back to the phone. "No, he's not. The bottles are still full from the prescription we filled a month ago."

Dr. Weisman had apparently formulated an unorthodox plan. "Your husband's situation is serious and requires immediate intervention," he said. "Listen carefully. His condition will only worsen if he doesn't take his medication. You need to mash the pills for each dose in the morning. Mix them in with his cereal or whatever he eats."

"All right, I'll try it."

"Call me back if any issues arise. Let's keep our appointment in four weeks."

Hilda caught Dad by the arm when he stepped in the door that afternoon. After their kiss hello, she asked, "How's work going dear?"

Anger flashed across his face. "Not good. Someone's been putting things in my computer, trying to screw me. Look, I'm tired. I'm going to go lie down for a bit. Let me know when dinner's ready." He pulled away and marched down the hallway.

In the morning, Hilda leaned against the cold stove and sipped her maté. She had intended to follow the doctor's instructions, but changed her mind at the last minute. She couldn't do it. She had rehearsed it in her mind, but felt too guilty to carry through with the plan.

Dad finished his cream of wheat and set the bowl in the sink. He gathered his briefcase and kissed her good-bye.

She stopped him. "*Piggito*, are you taking your meds?"

"Yes." He turned and left for work.

Hilda remained there, sipping her tea. Her dear husband had stared directly into her eyes and lied. She resolved to hide his medication in his food the next morning.

It was easier than she thought. Hilda was up early anyway so she found it simple to mash up his pills and conceal the powder in his food while he was in the bathroom getting ready for work. It became so routine and effortless that she started mixing the powder into different breakfast foods: scrambled eggs, cream of wheat, cereal and milk, almost anything he enjoyed eating. Apparently the taste blended in well. She was careful to brush off the counter and wipe it down with a wet sponge before Dad entered the kitchen.

A week and a half passed in this manner. Dad began to complain about being tired. He cut back on his nightly exercise routine and took more naps. Still, the side effects were minor compared to what was at stake.

Star and Shadow jumped around Hilda's ankles, scavenging for scraps that might slip onto the floor. Dad's cream of wheat was ready. She stirred it again before turning towards her workspace. She closed the pill bottles and returned them to the corner. With the meat tenderizer and a dishtowel-covered plastic sandwich bag, she mashed the pills into a fine dust. Setting the instrument down, she hung the dishtowel back on the stove handle and slipped her fingers between the red and blue strips, separating the seal. It opened easily. With bag in hand, she spun around. Her eyes locked on Dad's icy stare.

"What are you doing?" he asked.

Hilda's eyes widened. "I'm preparing pills for the dogs, which the vet gave me." She opened the refrigerator and pulled out a slice of American cheese. As it was, Hilda often had to give the poodles pills from the veterinarian, requiring her to sneak it into their food. "You know how we always have to wrap up their medicine in a piece of cheese." She fumbled with the wrapper, never intending to really give the pills to the dogs.

"I hope it's not mine."

"No," she said softly. His stare burned a hole in her stomach.

He locked eyes with her for a moment. Finally, he reached around her for his orange pill bottles. "I don't need these pills anymore."

"*Piggito*, please," Hilda pleaded, "You need to take the medicine. You heard what the doctors said."

"Are you siding with them?" he challenged. "I don't trust those idiot doctors. They don't know what the hell they're doing. These pills make me feel horrible and it's no way to live. When I take them, I can't think straight, my mind's in a fog from these stupid pills."

"Dear, please. Don't you remember last year? Please, take your medication. We can talk to the doctor next week about changing the dose or something."

"Don't tell me what to do. I'm not going back to those idiots. They don't know what the hell they're talking about."

Hilda couldn't believe it. Was this the same man she married? He had never spoken to her like that before. She threw him a disapproving glance.

"Well?" he challenged, but she said nothing. "So, no more drugs for me." In one swoop, he scooped up the orange bottles of capsules lying on the counter and tossed them into the kitchen trash. He stormed out of the house.

She tiptoed to the trash can and waited. A minute of silence passed. She lifted the pill bottles out of the garbage. Because she sometimes cut and styled hair at home, Hilda owned a hydraulic chair, a contoured sink, a mirror station, and a wheeled three-drawer cabinet. She stored the pill bottles in one of her drawers. Seeing as Dad hadn't showed much interest in her work space before, she assumed he would not check in there.

Hilda phoned the psychiatrist.

"I'm worried for your safety," Dr. Weisman said. "Don't do that anymore. Make an appointment. This is urgent. I need to talk to him."

The appointments were of no use. Dad wouldn't listen to any doctors' instructions. Worse yet, he presented himself one way to the doctors and another way at home. He agreed with the doctors to placate their concerns and spoke normally. But he wasn't taking his medication. His behavior and driving became more erratic.

Hilda called his newest psychologist one afternoon.

The doctor responded, "I don't know what you're worried about. Nothing's wrong with your husband. He's an intelligent man."

Dad's ability to maneuver through psychologist questioning by calculating and delivering the expected answers would continue to cause strife for our family. After all, if he didn't think he was ill and he didn't like being hospitalized, why would he admit anything which doctors had used to justify hospitalizing him before?

Hilda wondered what to do next. Although she loved Dad and would do anything to help him, she feared angering him again. What options were left? If the doctors didn't believe her, who would? She could only hope Dad's condition would improve.

Chapter Eighteen

July 1997: Glimmer of Hope

With Dad's 54th birthday only a week away, Jackie, Keith, and I didn't know what to get him. We asked Hilda.

"I don't know," Hilda said. Worn down by the tumultuous past year, she thought of all of the framed family photographs that used to line the hallway, decorate the desks, and adorn the bookcases. Dad wouldn't explain why he stripped the walls bare. She told us kids little in an effort to shield us from some of the pain. Consequently, we had no idea what she had been going through.

Hilda suggested, "Why don't you three find some old pictures and put together a collage for your daddy? Perhaps we can remind him of better times and bring the old daddy back."

Dad used to bring his camera everywhere, make copies of our vacation photos, and offer them to us kids as souvenirs. Jackie and I had several photo albums to go through.

"There are so many of them." I opened an old album."What am I looking for?"

"Choose the photos that jump off the pages," Jackie said, "the ones that remind you of him or would remind him of us." She flipped through a leather-bound book. "Here we all are up in San Francisco. Look at your purple socks. I hated that jacket." She slid out the picture and placed it on the pile.

"Look, there you are in a white dress and a bridal veil. You look like you were only nine or so. Was that your first communion?"

"Yeah, your mom made me. I haven't been to church in like fifteen years. I hated Catholic school. We're not using that."

"Look at your sweet angelic smile."

Jackie moved her fingers along more photos. "Keith had the cutest toddler cheeks, I always wanted to pinch them."

"Look, Dad's holding Keith. They must have just brought Keith home from the hospital."

It didn't take us long to amass a myriad of memories and encase them all in an oak frame. In the process, we realized what a stark difference there was between the dad we grew up with and the one who was suffering from a severe mental illness.

The day of Dad's birthday party arrived.

With Justin, I pulled up to the curb in front of his house, the house I had known—even though only on weekends and holidays—for the past thirteen years. Hilda's skillful hand had coaxed the topiary bushes into their current animal forms. Multi-colored roses were in full bloom, bragging in ruffled layers about the care they had been shown.

Marisol, Marisol's daughter Elizabeth, son-in-law Oscar, and grandson were there. Her grandson, two months older and a head taller than Justin, wobbled over. He and Justin took off and occupied themselves in harmless mischief.

Jackie, Keith, and I went into the study to view the finished photo collage. Keith had wrapped the frame, using far too much tape, as was his custom. He seemed to gain some secret satisfaction from watching people struggle to scratch open their gifts.

"It's true what Hilda said about the pictures." Jackie guided us into the hallway, previously adorned with our baby pictures. White walls stood bare, only nail holes were visible.

"That's so sad," I said softly. "So, they're really all gone? Where are they?"

"He took them all down."

"Well, what can you do?" Keith said. "Nothing. No use in worrying about it."

"Hopefully," I said, "our present will trigger some happy memories for Dad. You never know. It could work."

The day passed in relative calm. Food was served and eaten, ice cream dished out and devoured, and stories swapped. Dad had been there physically, but not there mentally or emotionally. Everyone had noticed, but we collectively decided not to deal with him at the present. We were happy to visit with each other, to maintain a façade of normality.

When the time came to open gifts, we gathered around the coffee table. Jackie and I sat next to Dad while Keith maintained distance. Hilda encouraged Dad to open the large rectangular package.

Dad picked at the paper, eventually tearing open a corner. When he saw the framed photos, he showed no emotion.

"Dad," I said. "Here's when we drove up the coastline to Canada."

"Here, you're holding Keith when he was born." Jackie touched the glass plate.

"*Piggito*, remember when that picture was taken in San Francisco?"

Dad looked at the photos, but said nothing. He didn't seem capable of seeing or feeling the memories.

Hilda feigned a patient smile. "Joseph, aren't you going to thank your children? Look, at all the trouble they went through for you."

He smiled half-heartedly. "Thank you Amanda, thank you Jackie, thank you Keith." He reached over and gave us each a hug—not the warm embraces we fondly remembered, but more like the uncomfortable and emotionless hugs given after a reunion with a casual acquaintance. He stood up, rocked back and forth a moment almost as if considering whether he would open up the door of memories or not, and left the room.

"I'm sorry, kids." Hilda fought back tears.

Everyone, except Jackie and I, went back to the kitchen.

"Did you see his eyes?" Jackie asked. "I mean did you look into them? His clear blue eyes were empty, like he wasn't even here, like he was far away lost in thought, or just lost. I don't understand. Why doesn't he just snap out of it? He didn't even care about the pictures. He doesn't care about anything. I just don't understand how to get through to him."

"I don't know if we can," I said.

What I didn't realize then—none of us did—was that Dad was experiencing anosognosia, poor insight, and in his case, the inability to understand he had a serious mental illness. While he might have understood he had anxiety and depression, he was unaware that his paranoia was unfounded and his visions were delusions created by chemical imbalances in his brain. He didn't believe he was sick.

We believed Dad was either willfully denying he needed help or was being too stubborn to accept treatment. We felt he was pushing us away and we took it personally. Hurt turned to anger and frustration. If my family had understood anosognosia and the positive and negative symptoms of schizophrenia, our story could have turned out very differently.

Chapter Nineteen

November 1997: An Engaging Dinner

"Neil's parents invited us over for Thanksgiving dinner," Jackie said, "and they wanted me to extend the invitation to you and dad. Can you and Dad come? It's up near L.A."

Hilda remembered the previous Thanksgiving. Those fateful weeks Dad spent involuntarily confined in the mental hospital left no one with anything to be thankful for. The holiday held a bittersweet feeling.

"Yes," Hilda said, "that's wonderful. I would like that. I just hope Daddy will…well." She paused. She wanted to tell Jackie about his refusal to take medication and skipping his doctor appointments, but she felt it was no use to spoil Jackie's happiness. Hilda would continue to bear the pain alone. "We need the address and time we're expected. We'll drive up and meet you there."

On Thanksgiving, November 27, 1997, Dad and Hilda came as promised. Neil's extended family was there, including his sister and her family, his parents, some cousins, and aunts and uncles. With all of the guests, Dad's silence went unnoticed, and Hilda enjoyed the conversation of upbeat companions.

Dinnertime arrived. Long tables, of which two were put together for the occasion, had been dressed in fine linens, adorned with decorative china, crystal goblets, polished silverware, and folded cloth napkins. Neil's mom had placed party favor bags tied together with curled ribbons at each place setting.

She instructed the guests where to sit and everyone took their places. Neil was at one end of the table with Jackie by his side. Dad and Hilda sat next to them.

Neil's mom announced, "I'm trying something different this year. Everyone has a party favor, which we're all going to open at the same time."

At her signal, everyone untied ribbons. When Jackie gingerly pulled on the red ribbon, a small ring rolled out. With the dimly lit dining room, it at first seemed like a piece of costume jewelry, like the ones from the trinket dispensers. What a darling little favor, Jackie thought.

But no sooner had this thought crossed her mind than the room spun around her. Flashes went off in every direction from cameras previously hidden beneath the table. In a state of absolute confusion, Jackie looked at Neil who was kneeling. Dumbfounded, she experienced an out-of-body moment. Neil took her hand in his and held the ring up to her.

"Jackie, will you marry me?" Neil asked. "I know how you wanted to pick out your own ring, so I got you this to wear until you can choose the one you really want. I went back to Sea World last month hoping the pearl cart would be open and this ring would still be there."

A few months prior, Jackie and Neil went on a date to Sea World. They stopped at a pearl cart advertising "pick an oyster, find a pearl inside." A ring caught her attention. Delicate lines of gold swirled around a creamy iridescent pearl like a wave washing it clean. After peering at the price tag, she moved on and so did Neil. The moment passed. Within hours, she forgot all about her yearning for that simple, yet elegant ring. Neil had remembered.

The words tumbled from her lips. "Oh honey, of course, yes." Tears of joy streamed down her cheeks which must have been a bright shade of red. Her vision blurred from the continual camera flashes. She felt surrounded by paparazzi.

Coming out of shock, Jackie beamed at being able to share this moment, which she had dreamed of since she was a little girl, with her parents. Elated, she looked into Hilda's tear filled eyes with satisfaction. Jackie crooked her head at Dad, seeking his approval. But the ecstasy she experienced evaporated when she saw his stony glare.

"What's a wedding going to cost me," he grumbled with a scowl.

Hilda elbowed him sharply in the side. No one else heard. But Jackie had heard.

He did not just say that, she thought. Our dad would never have said anything like that. She tried her best to put on her happy face for the flashes still erupting around her.

Neil's mom boasted. "We were all in on it. Neil told me, and we set this up for you. The family was waiting for this moment, cameras in hand."

Conversation burst forth from all corners of the room and congratulations showered upon the newly engaged couple.

Yet what should have been one of the happiest moments of Jackie's life was tainted by Dad's shocking reaction. Jackie was crushed, although she tried not to show it. This was yet another reminder that her relationship with Dad would never be the same. He would never be the same.

CHAPTER TWENTY

DECEMBER 1997: THE FINAL ATTEMPT

NO MORE THAN A MONTH HAD PASSED since Jackie's proposal over Thanksgiving dinner; Christmas was around the corner.

Early evening, Hilda caught Dad sluggishly moving around in a drunken stupor. He stumbled against the wall. On the beige carpet lay empty orange pill bottles.

"Joseph! How many sleeping pills did you take?" Hilda demanded.

No response. Dad crumpled to the floor like a rag doll.

Her fingers shook as she dialed 9-1-1.

"9-1-1, is this an emergency?"

"Yes, it's an emergency!" Hilda screamed. She tried to calm down by focusing on her breathing. She needed to think clearly. She was afraid of resorting to her native language because of her panic. That would only complicate things further.

"What is the emergency?"

"My husband's unconscious. He's taken some pills—"

"Ma'am, is your husband breathing?"

Hilda hadn't thought to check. "I don't know." Wild thoughts raced through her head—maybe he was dead already.

"Okay ma'am, are you where you can check?"

"Uh, he's right over there," Hilda pointed at him, before realizing the woman couldn't see inside her house.

"Okay ma'am, I want you to check to see if he is breathing and if not, feel for a pulse. Come right back to the phone," the woman instructed. "Paramedics are on their way."

Hilda ran to her unresponsive husband. She couldn't tell if he was breathing, and was shaking too badly to be able to observe the subtle movement of his chest. She licked the back of her hand and held it underneath his nostrils. Cool air tickled her skin. Yes, he was breathing.

She rushed back to the phone, getting tangled in the long coiled cord. Twisting out of it, she held up the receiver. "Yes, he is breathing."

"Good. Ma'am, you said he took pills. What types and how many of them did he take?"

"Sleeping pills. I'm not sure how much, but I think he took several different medicines. I don't know how many."

"Okay, ma'am, I want you to stay on the line with me. Help is on the way."

Sirens blared. Lights flashed. Paramedics robotically moved around in unison. The room spun. Hilda didn't want to let go of her husband's cold hands.

"We need some room, ma'am," a paramedic said.

She stepped back. Paralyzed with fear, she stood by in horror of what her once-vibrant husband had become.

"No response." One of the paramedics radioed dispatch. "We're bringing him in."

Hilda, like a curious bystander, watched as they lifted and positioned his seemingly lifeless body. An arm dangled over the edge and was promptly placed at his side. The safety straps secured.

They wheeled him out. In a trance, Hilda floated behind. The past year replayed through her mind at lightning speed: the surgery, the mental hospitals, the overdose, the bucket of water, and now this is how it would all end. Outside, flashing red lights rotated and reflected off their garage door.

A paramedic turned to her, "We need to transport him to the hospital. You can ride with us, ma'am, or you can follow us in your own car."

She wanted to be next to her husband, holding his hand, but worried she didn't have anyone to pick her up at the hospital. Jackie, Keith, and I were all hours away. She grabbed her purse and car keys.

Before the ambulance doors closed, Hilda saw the paramedics start life-saving procedures.

She drove behind, her ears numb to the sirens, her eyes blind to the blue and red lights.

Minutes dragged into hours.

Hilda alternated between nervously pacing the waiting room and sitting still. At last, a man in blue scrubs opened the door and sat down beside her.

He placed a comforting hand on her shoulder. "We still don't know if he's going to make it. We're pumping his stomach. We're doing everything we can. I'm so sorry."

Hilda opened her mouth to speak, but couldn't. Her tears froze, her stomach dropped, and the oxygen around her dissipated, leaving her suffocating, unable to say a word.

"I think you'll be more comfortable in a more private room." He led her down the hallway to a small room. "I promise I will keep you posted."

Hilda knew it. He was gone. She blanked out.

Dawn illuminated the room. Hilda hadn't noticed the time lapse and didn't know whether she had spent the night awake or asleep.

A doctor opened the door and took a seat next to her. He rested his hand on her knee. "We almost lost him. I think he's going to pull through, but I can't say for sure yet. We're monitoring him closely. If all is well, we'll move him to the ICU soon." He shook his head. "Your husband had taken a lot of pills before you found him. If you had been any later…"

Hilda didn't know what to say. Nothing could be said.

She waited until he left her by herself before she cried. Until the past year, Hilda had hardly ever cried. She had cried when she broke her back as a small child. She had cried when she was later told the back injury would prevent her from having children of her own. She had cried when she immigrated to America from Argentina in her twenties and found her hopes deflated, and no work to be had. She had cried tears of happiness when she found the love of her dreams. And now that she was losing the man of her dreams, she cried tears of pain. The tears came hard. They were partly tears of relief for what was not to be, tears of fear for what almost had been, and tears of anger for what she had lost. Her husband would never be the same.

Hilda tried to stand, but her knees buckled. She slumped back down onto the hard plastic chair. Unable to move, she sat alone for what seemed an eternity. Time was irrelevant; the fragile future shattered.

CHAPTER TWENTY-ONE

DECEMBER 1997: FIGHTING DEATH

AT HER HOME IN SAN DIEGO, Jackie received the frantic call. She and Neil drove up to San Bernardino to pick up Hilda.

The drive to the hospital was silent. Yellowish parking lot lights flickered, a few buzzed like mosquitoes. The constant whoosh of the traffic blurred together, reminiscent of frothy ocean waves crashing on the shore and being pulled back out to sea.

The three walked toward the four-storied building. Lit in ominous red lights, the overhead sign read Hospital Emergency Room Entrance.

They walked toward the admissions desk. Jackie noted the patchwork of aged linoleum squares. Along the grey vinyl baseboards, which had separated at the seams, the linoleum curled. The pathway to the front desk was marked by deep-grooved gray skid marks worn down in some places to the concrete underneath.

An elderly man sat coughing in the corner with a quilted blanket wrapped loosely over his shoulders. A few seats down, a small child, brown hair matted with sweat, slept securely in his mother's arms. Across from them a stout-faced woman slouched, breathing heavily and wheezing faintly. No matter which direction Jackie turned, she saw more of the same.

She leaned against the wall for support. Faded white paint, now appearing a dull grey, was peeled away in the corners. She thought about the bright hygienic feel of the HMO hospitals to which we had been accustomed. She sat in a shabby chair, its stained padding as worn as the floor.

Hilda, after speaking with the receptionist, motioned to Jackie and Neil.

Glad to leave the dark, depressing waiting room, Jackie followed them into the elevator at the end of the hallway. The rickety doors shut and it struggled up. The elevator stopped, and the doors paused before opening. A sign on the wall directed them to the Intensive Care Unit.

In the ICU, they found themselves in an open area with no rooms. Curtains divided the room into sections. Mobile beds were locked into place along the walls with patients lying on them, some moaning softly, others in a deep slumber with tubes and machines all about.

The center of the great room appeared to be the work area where doctors and nurses attended to patients in greatest need.

"What's dad doing in this dump?" Jackie asked. "He's not low-life trash. He has money. He deserves better."

Hilda unenthusiastically said, "The staff is so nice, Jackie."

Jackie's eyes focused on a gurney in the center of the room. Curtains hanging from ceiling tracks created three floating walls around the bed. She followed Hilda and Neil. Tubes hooked up to IV drips on metal racks were on the right. On the left, machines monitoring vital signs beeped and displayed squiggly lines. Hovering over this patient, the attending physician glanced up and acknowledged Hilda.

The white blankets and sheets covering the mound of a body were probably the cleanest, whitest objects in the entire dilapidated building.

Jackie was afraid. She didn't want to see who the body belonged to. She didn't want to believe it. Tears welled in her eyes. Her eyes found their way to the top of the bed. She gasped for air. The room, the thin curtains, the fluorescent lighting, the dingy peeling paint, the nasty linoleum floors swirled around her. Her knees buckled. She fell to the floor sobbing. This wasn't possible. She gripped her eyes shut, trying to erase the image burned into her mind.

"What are you doing to him?" Jackie hyperventilated. "What's wrong with him?"

Hilda and the physician each took one of her arms and lifted her back up. Neil grabbed a chair and pushed it under her.

Now at eye level with Dad, Jackie gathered the strength to reopen her eyes. His body appeared alien-like with tubes going in and out of him. Machines pumped oxygen. IVs fed him. Just as she became capable of staring at the tired, helpless face before her, his eyes flashed open.

"He's regaining consciousness," the physician said. "But he might not understand you right away. He's heavily sedated."

This was unreal. Jackie pleaded, "Dad, you can't do this."

She thrust her hand in front of his eyes. Dim lights overhead set the diamonds sparkling against the gold of her engagement ring. She had picked it out only two weeks prior. It hadn't even been four weeks since Neil proposed to her on Thanksgiving. Dad had been there. Now he was here fighting for his life.

"Look at my ring, Dad. You have to be at my wedding. You can't do this to yourself. You can't do this to us. Don't do this to me." Her chest heaved. She yelled amidst the tears and sobs shaking her body, "You need to be alive to walk me down the aisle!"

With an apathetic look in his eyes, Dad gave the impression he had mentally checked out of this life. He looked like a corpse, devoid of life.

"He can't speak right now," the physician said. "I know this is difficult for you. It's not easy for anyone, but he's going to be okay."

"How do you know he will be okay?" Jackie screamed. "He's not okay. He's not. Look at him. He's never going to be okay."

Hilda embraced Jackie. Whose tears wet whose shoulders didn't matter. Nothing seemed to matter.

Four days later, doctors transferred Dad into the care of the Loma Linda mental healthcare professionals. Hilda and Marisol visited him. The first time they went together, they found him waking up out of a heavy sedation.

Dad saw Marisol and smiled. But when he saw Hilda, he widened his eyes as if the angel of death were standing there. He screamed at the top of his lungs, "Get her out! The devil's after me! She wants me dead! Get her out!"

That was the end of that visit. They returned several more times.

One day on the way home, Marisol said, "You know, Hilda, when you step out of the room to talk to the doctors, Joseph begs me not to let you lock him away forever. He says he trusts me and knows I'll do the right thing to get him out of there. I tell him you love him so much and you'd never do anything to hurt him."

"Just humor him," Hilda said. "Let him talk. Maybe he feels like someone's listening to him and believes him."

"Before he went to the hospital, he used to call me on the phone and say the same stuff. I do listen to him and don't judge him. I know he's not in his right mind."

"Marisol, I can't believe he tried to kill himself. I mean, the first time when I found him on the couch, I thought he had taken too many sleeping pills by accident. But there's no way this was by accident."

"What about the time he went to buy some milk late at night for his two bowls of cereal in the morning? You know, the time he took all the aspirin?"

"What do you mean?"

"Before the sleeping pills, you told me how he got sick to his stomach and threw up."

"Oh, he wasn't trying to overdose that time. He said he had a bad headache and took too many pills."

"And you believed him? Good thing mixing the aspirin with the milk made him sick."

"I don't know anymore," Hilda said. "I don't know what to believe."

Two weeks and several prescription changes later, Hilda took Dad home from his third involuntary hospitalization.

"Joseph," she said, "you need to take your medication this time."

"Yes, I know, dear." He reached over and planted a kiss on her cheek.

"You have to go to the psychologist and to the marriage counselor like the doctor said."

"Yes, I know, dear."

Regardless of the smile on his face, she feared he would never go back to normal.

CHAPTER TWENTY-TWO

JANUARY 1998: CROCODILE TEARS

JACKIE MOVED INTO NEIL'S HOME. They rang in the New Year together. They hoped for a better year and looked forward to their wedding scheduled for October. Dad generously offered to gift them $5000, but there were strings attached. He would part with $500 at a time and they would have to visit him to get each of the ten installments. Although Jackie and Neil enjoyed his company, the contrived arrangements felt like emotional blackmail and strained their relationship with him, creating a rift.

A few weeks later, tension erupted at the close of one of their visits.

After dining at his favorite local restaurant, Dad drove the four of them back to Neil and Jackie's small home.

The curved driveway was lined with lush green grass, the yard well-manicured. The backyard was large by Southern Californian standards. Hilda admired the fruit trees ripe with citrus towering overhead.

"I'd love to see whatever handiwork you've done to the place," Dad said. "You always seem to have new woodworking projects going on."

"Dad's never been the mechanical handyman type," Jackie whispered to Neil.

Neil led them inside. "I installed and polished the wooden floor. In the kitchen I refinished the cabinets, country style, with wood instead of worn out fiberboard."

"Wow," Dad said. "That must've been a lot of work."

121

"Surprisingly, not as much work as replacing the toilet in the second bathroom."

"You replaced the toilet by yourself?" His eyes widened.

Later, they relaxed in the living room and chatted. Neil sat between Jackie and Dad on the sofa, while Hilda settled into the loveseat nearby.

"Didn't you recently graduate college?" Dad asked Neil. "What did you study?"

"One of my double-majors was biology."

"Biology? That's great. You know, my father was a high school biology teacher. What drew you to that?"

"I've always been interested in unique plant species." Neil turned to Hilda. "You're into plants, too, aren't you?"

"Yes," Hilda said, "I garden and take care of all my roses."

"What other home improvements are you planning?" Dad asked.

The sun had set and dusk was almost gone. Although the day had been pleasant, the enveloping darkness brought a cool breeze in through the screen door.

Catching a chill, Jackie shuddered and nudged the front door shut. She wished Dad would hurry up and give her the promised $500 check. She felt she had done her daughterly duty entertaining them for the evening. Besides, she still wanted to have a few quiet moments alone with Neil before they turned in for the night. However, this was a delicate situation and she tiptoed around her intentions.

Feigning a wide yawn and dramatic arm stretch, Jackie said, "I'm tired. It's getting late."

Neil caught on and imitated her yawn. "Yeah, it's getting late; I've gotta get up early in the morning. I've got a house inspection scheduled first thing tomorrow." Neil, a health inspector for the county, performed various duties.

While most people would pick up on those subtle social cues, they flew right over Dad's head. "Oh yeah? What type of inspection?"

Knowing he could talk endlessly, Jackie didn't want the conversation to continue or he would follow up with a dozen more questions. Irritated—she was never good at hiding her emotions—she said, "Dad, it's been fun, but we really need to wrap up here. Neil said he wants to go to bed soon and I would like a few minutes with my fiancé before he falls asleep."

"Oh, so all you care about is the money, huh?" He leapt off the couch. "You don't even love me, do you?"

"Dad, that's ridiculous, you know that's not true."

"Were you there for me when I had my cancer surgery? No, you weren't, were you? What kind of thanks is that? You have a sorry way of showing your love for me. If I gave you a lump sum check for your wedding, I'd probably never hear from you again."

Jackie's heart stung from the accusation. She felt guilty in not attending to Dad before his surgery, yet thought he was faking this little scene to gain her sympathy. Having inherited his stubbornness, she refused to give him the satisfaction. She stared into his eyes, but his eyes were devoid of feeling, like a bare window in a dark house. "You're freakin' ridiculous. Don't play a guilt trip on me. It won't work. I don't have to prove anything. How pathetic is it that you feel the need to pay to see me?"

"How pathetic is it to not be at your only father's cancer surgery? You're an ungrateful daughter who should be more than thankful that I'm giving her anything. You don't know how to communicate love to your father after everything I've sacrificed for you."

Visions of him at the mental hospital and lying in the hospital bed after having his stomach pumped flashed before her eyes. Tears welled up and as much as she tried to hold them back, they burst out in floods.

"I cried the whole weekend about you and for not being there during your surgery. You have no idea."

Hilda leaned over to Jackie and stroked her face like a baby, trying to calm her.

Dad hardened his stance and rolled his eyes. "Oh, please. You can turn off those crocodile tears."

Jackie narrowed her drenched eyes, clenched her teeth, and flew off the couch. She came within millimeters of punching Dad in the face. She stared defiantly into his eyes. "I don't need your money."

Neil jumped in between them, creating a safe division between his fiancé and his future father-in-law. "Joseph, you have to leave now."

Glancing up for a brief moment, as Neil was a taller, stronger man than he, Dad studied Neil's eyes. "Fine, take your stupid money since that's all you both care about anyway." He reached into his pants pocket and tossed the folded check onto the floor.

Hilda grabbed his arm. "C'mon dear, let's go." She gave Jackie a hug and escorted Dad out the door.

CHAPTER TWENTY-THREE

SPRING 1998: ILLUSION OF PROGRESS

SHORTLY AFTER HIS RELEASE from his latest hospitalization, Dad began weekly individual appointments with his psychologist. One month later, he refused to go.

"Dear, you know you need to," Hilda pleaded, car keys in hand.

"No, I'm tired of it. It's not worth it."

"The doctors said you have to. It's only been a few weeks."

"I don't care. I don't even like him."

Hilda threw up her hands. "You can see another one."

The next day she made some calls and told him, "I've found a new counselor in Upland."

After his third visit with the new therapist, Dad walked back to the car and confronted Hilda. "You're in love with the doctor."

"What? That's in your mind. How can you possibly think that?"

"You're falling in love with him aren't you? You're seeing him behind my back." Dad glared at her from the driver's seat.

"That's not even possible. You know I only come here with you."

He opened his mouth, paused a moment, and asked, "Why do I have to see him? I don't have a problem."

She buried her face in her hands. Wisps of hope slipped away. At least tomorrow would be their next marriage counseling appointment.

Halfway through the drive to their appointment, Dad asked, "Why do we have to go and talk with him?"

Hilda said, "At least it's helping us. It's helping you."

"For what?"

"So we don't get divorced."

Towards the end of the appointment, when the doctor confirmed the next week's slot, Hilda said, "He doesn't want to see you anymore."

The doctor turned to Dad. "I expected this to happen considering your inattentiveness to suggestions and lack of response to your wife's complaints. You have to understand, Joseph, your wife has been very patient with you. One day she's going to get tired of the way you're treating her. Either go back to work or get out of the house. You can't just stay inside all day in a dark room, lying down. Take your dogs for a walk or something. Get outside."

Dad hung his head. He nodded and mechanically replied, "I'll try to be better. I know. I understand I have a problem. I know my wife is getting tired. I'm doing the best I can."

His answer placated the doctor and Hilda for the time being. In reality, the only physical problem he believed he was dealing with was his prostate.

Heeding the doctor's advice, Dad decided to return to work. His company graciously allowed him back.

Hilda was surprised by Marisol's visit and the abrupt news of her relocation back to Argentina. Marisol had been scant with details, saying she wanted to be closer to her parents and other siblings.

She hugged Dad and Hilda. "Thank you so much for agreeing to take over the car payments. I was so worried about what to do with the Ford Tempo before I move back to Argentina."

"No problem," Dad said. "We could use a second car."

Hilda shook her head. "I still don't understand why you want to move back there." Even though Marisol wasn't saying it aloud, Hilda knew it must have something to do with Marisol's ex-husband living there. She didn't believe Marisol would leave her daughter, son-in-law, and grandson in North America just to be back with the rest of her siblings and parents in South America.

By the time Marisol moved south, Dad had paid off the car. He donated it to the church. As much as Hilda protested, she was helpless to stop him.

One day in early August 1998, Hilda walked in the door from a busy day at the beauty salon. On her feet for hours, she flopped down on the couch, swung her feet up onto the coffee table, and closed her eyes for a bit.

Dad strolled down the hallway into the dark living room. All curtains were drawn shut, as they had been every day. He sat next to her and picked up her hand.

"Ducky," he said.

Hearing this term of endearment, Hilda kept her eyes shut and held on to the illusion of warmth and love.

He rubbed the back of her hand across his lips and face, turned it over, and kissed her palm. "I've decided to put the house up for sale."

She bolted upright and pulled back her hand. "Excuse me? What did you just say?"

"I listed the house with a real estate agent." His calm demeanor was in stark contrast to his shocking news.

"What? Why?" Hilda screamed. "Why did you do this? Why wouldn't you consult with me on this?"

"I took care of everything. Don't worry. It'll be good for us to have a clean start."

"Don't worry? We've lived here for fourteen years. You can't sell this place without asking me."

"Sure I can. The deed's in my name."

"You're out of your mind."

"There're too many bad memories here. I need to leave this place." He reached for her.

She backed up to avoid his touch. "Good for us? How do you know what's best for me? We have so many good memories here." She wiped tears from the corners of her eyes.

"It's already done. In fact we have a buyer." He smiled.

"What are you talking about?"

"Well, I only listed it for $107,000. I figured it'd sell quickly at that price." He shrugged, placed his hands behind his head, and reclined back on the couch as though he were proud of himself.

"You've got to be kidding me. Don't we owe that much? This house is worth a lot more than that." She frantically waved her arms. "This is absurd. I never would have thought you would resort to something as ridiculous as this. How could you do such a thing?"

"Dear, relax. We'll clear about a thousand dollars profit when all's said and done. That should be just about enough for a deposit on an apartment. In fact, while you were at work, I checked out a few. I submitted a renter's application to this wonderful complex in Hemet."

"Hemet?" Hilda's eyes widened. Could he possibly drop another bombshell on her? She slumped back on the couch and hid her face in her hands. "I can't believe this."

"The complex is really great. They allow dogs of course. And they have a clubhouse with a recreation room. It's got pool tables and ping-pong. Lots of trees and flowers, I thought you'd like that part. There's a heated pool—not that you need a heated pool in Hemet. Oh, and there's a Jacuzzi." He winked, scooted close to her, and raised his arm to put it around her shoulders.

Hilda stood up. "Joseph, you're insane. I'm going for a walk." She crossed the room. "Leave me alone." She grabbed the leather leashes attached to the nylon harnesses and took the dogs outside.

Dad couldn't believe Hilda would be so dead set against the move.

A week later, he packed and phoned us children asking us to come down and pick out what we'd like of his belongings. I was surprised to hear he was selling the house, but was too wrapped up in college and my baby to find out the details.

Jackie, Keith, and I gathered around him as he cleaned out the hall closet. He pulled out a few items he'd never shown us: a guitar, a pool stick cue, and two tennis rackets secured in wooden frames.

"Who wants what?" he asked. "Otherwise they all go to charity."

"I didn't know you played the guitar…or tennis," Jackie said.

"Or pool," I added.

Keith stepped forward. "I'll take the guitar."

"Okay, it's yours." He handed it to Keith.

"Well considering I don't play pool and Amanda does, I'll take the tennis rackets." Jackie picked them up.

"I used to play tennis with your moms fifteen years ago, but haven't used them since."

I gripped the cue stick. "I didn't even know you played. I love shooting pool, must have gotten that from you. We should play sometime."

There was a lot we didn't know about him. After Jackie and Keith walked off to speak with Hilda, Dad reached back into the closet. "Amanda, come here."

He pulled out his wooden Louisville Slugger. He rubbed his hands along the engraved label and the glossy smooth finish. "I want you to have this."

My hands drooped from the weight. "Are you sure?"

"Yes. My dad gave it to me, and since you always enjoyed playing ball with me, I want you to have it. Take good care of it."

"Oh, I will. Thank you, Dad. I love you." I wrapped my arms around him.

On August 14, 1998, the deed was transferred to the new owners. All the years, all the memories, all the pain…Dad attempted to leave it all behind.

CHAPTER TWENTY-FOUR

SEPTEMBER 1998: KEITH

DURING THE MIDDLE OF KEITH'S junior year, after a lengthy discussion with our mom and his principal, my brother checked out of his third high school. Albeit his previous two high school enrollments—freshman year in the High Desert at my high school and the start of his sophomore year at Jackie's in San Bernardino—were both cut short by Mom's foreclosure and Dad's illness, this third time was Keith's fault. He could hardly ever wake up in time. Although it sounded like a weak excuse, it was the truth. Having been moved through three different counties and high schools, Keith had to deal with Dad's cancer diagnosis and wild accusations, and was tired.

Our mom and the principal decided it best if he finished his third year of high school through independent study at the adult education center.

The summer of 1998 came and went, and brought many changes. With Mom's blessing, Keith returned to the desert—where he had lived for thirteen of his seventeen years of life—to move in with his best-friend Kotori.

Kotori's Native American family gave Keith the nickname "Bird," taught him to create dream-catchers, and promised to help him realize his dream of graduating high school with his childhood friends. Reinvigorated with happiness, my brother found no problem making it to school by 7:25 a.m. But a few weeks into the semester, he was called into the guidance office.

He fidgeted with the call slip, folding and unfolding it.

Mr. Carver called his name.

"Good morning, have a seat."

Keith sat on the edge of one of the plastic chairs.

Mr. Carter held an open file folder in his hands and reclined in his squeaky chair. "I've been reviewing your transcripts."

Keith focused on the fake wood grained desktop. "Yeah?"

"I've got some bad news," Mr. Carver said. "I know from speaking with your mom that you've had some unfortunate circumstances occur in your life recently."

What an understatement, Keith thought. Has your dad ever accused you of plotting to kill him? Have you ever witnessed your dad go crazy? Has your dad tried to commit suicide? Have you been shuffled from place to place without belonging anywhere?

Mr. Carver continued, "Different school districts in different counties have different graduation requirements. You went to school here, in Los Angeles County for your freshman year, San Bernardino County for part of your sophomore year, Orange County for the rest, and adult education for your junior year. That's a lot of moving. I see here you haven't done half bad academically. I'm sure you would've been on track for graduation had you been here for the past three years."

Keith had a sinking feeling in the pit of his stomach.

"Keith, you're several credits behind, in fact, over a semester behind. That means you won't be able to graduate in June."

The reason Keith had moved in with Kotori evaporated before his eyes. He had dealt with our dad's illness, worked, paid rent, bought a car, driven out here, and for what?

"Can't I make up the credits with independent study or something?" Keith asked.

"Well, yes, but not while being enrolled here as a regular student. We would need to enroll you in an independent study program. You can still earn a diploma, but not from here."

"That sucks." The reverberations of "not from here" rang in Keith's head.

Mr. Carver folded his arms across his chest. "If it means a lot to you to graduate from here, we can let you continue on next year as a fifth year student. We have a few students doing that now."

The blood rose in Keith's cheeks. "No way, I'd rather go on independent study and finish in June of 1999."

"Well, why don't you think it over?"

Keith headed to the parking lot. A warm breeze rustled through his brown hair and his bangs settled in front of his bluish-gray eyes. With the dry heat of the day fading into tolerable warmth, the animals began to move about in the distance. Waves of gentle winds swallowed up the sounds of scurrying rabbits in the brush beyond the school. The fields were strewn with dried thistle thorns from the parched tumbleweeds. A sudden gust lifted loose dirt out of the crevices in the cracked earth and funneled it into the sky, dragging small bits of debris with it. Just as in the Westerns, Keith watched as a few tumbleweeds, freed from their roots, rolled aimlessly down the paved road. He could relate.

As soon as Keith walked into Kotori's house, he phoned Mom. After numerous discussions, Kotori' mother decided to home-school Keith while her own son continued attending the high school. Lucky for Keith, she and her husband considered him a second son, because ever since Dad's illness, Keith no longer felt like he had a dad.

CHAPTER TWENTY-FIVE

OCTOBER 1998: THE WEDDING

IN THE DAYS LEADING UP TO HER WEDDING, Jackie stressed over the final preparations. She and Neil had invited almost 200 guests to their outdoor wedding and hotel reception. All of the final deposits had been paid, she had picked up her wedding dress and the custom designed bridesmaids' gowns for her four bridesmaids. Neil had ordered the tuxedoes for the four groomsmen. The DJ had their music selections, the hotel had the dinner and alcohol selections, the flowers were ordered, and both the photographer and videographer had their directions.

Jackie's mom, LilyAnn, phoned in a panic. "Jackie."

"Yeah, what's going on?"

"You aren't going to sit me next to your father, are you?"

"Well, yes. You two will be nice to each other right? I have you sitting next to Hilda and Dad at the parents' table, along with my brothers." Jackie referred to Keith and her two other brothers, her mom's sons from subsequent marriages.

"Please, Jackie. Don't you dare put me anywhere near your father, especially at the reception. I'm afraid that your dad is going to abandon Hilda for me," LilyAnn pleaded.

Jackie felt this concern was more than a bit exaggerated. They had been divorced for well over twenty years and besides, her mom seemed to get along fine with Hilda and usually tolerated Dad. "What are you talking about, Mom? This is kind of inconvenient for me. I've been busy all week with last minute arrangements. I've already finished the seating chart. What's the big deal?" Jackie thought her mom couldn't handle stress and was probably overwhelmed and emotional, because her only daughter was getting married.

"Jackie, your father's phoned me every day for the past couple of weeks. He's been saying crazy things, like he wants me to get back together with him. I don't need to deal with his crap right now. I have enough anxiety over my baby getting married. Why the hell's he calling me?" LilyAnn yelled.

"Are you kidding me? Dad's been calling you?"

"Yeah, he says we can get back together, but I can't have sex with any other men. He's telling me he's got some device to help him have sex because of the prostate cancer surgery. I keep telling him 'no' and he keeps calling. He's driving me insane! So, I told him, 'Don't you think you should help your daughter pay for her wedding?' since you told me he wasn't going to give you money."

"Seriously? Does Hilda know? She'd have a fit if she knew."

"How the hell should I know? I didn't want to bug her right now since your father has obviously been going a bit batty lately. But, I don't need him hitting on me either. I'm warning you not to put him next to me on Saturday."

Damn, Jackie thought. Why couldn't Dad allow something in her life to go right? His daughter's wedding. "Fine, Mom. I'll take care of it. I'll switch the seats, okay?"

LilyAnn's tone softened. "Great, honey. Thank you. Oh, I'm so excited for your wedding! I can't wait to see my baby walking down the aisle in her beautiful dress."

Jackie was now less than enthusiastic.

October 10, 1998. The day arrived. Jackie, her mom, her two brothers from her mom's later marriages, and Dad rode to the garden wedding location in the limo together. Located on a hilltop in Old Town, Heritage Park gave a wonderful view of downtown San Diego.

Jackie's stomach tingled, her palms were moist, and her knees shook. She was getting married to the man of her dreams. A year's worth of planning. Thousands of dollars spent. The honeymoon in Hawaii had been booked. The sun was shining, a beautiful day. Neil's best man had assured them he had the rings. Nothing could ruin this moment.

The limo inched along the private road leading up to the courtyard. From behind the tinted windows, she could see most of the guests had arrived. The violinist and harpist were playing music. The minister was talking to Neil. The purple and white flowers were impeccably arranged. Red and pink rose petals had been strewn across the white cloth center aisle. Her wedding would be as she had imagined it would be—perfect. Now all they had to do was sit and wait until the time came to get out. She turned her head and noticed Dad had been sitting next to her mom during the entire ride. LilyAnn looked annoyed and flustered.

Dad, dressed in his tuxedo with a buttonhole rose, turned to Jackie who prepared to hear his last few tender words of advice. She smiled at him. He tilted his head. His blue eyes behind his gold-framed glasses seemed to sparkle. All the disagreements she had with Dad faded, leaving only love.

"Jackie," he said. "Your mom won't answer me."

"Excuse me?"

"Is your mom dating anyone?" he asked. "Do you think LilyAnn still wants to be with me? What do you think?"

Jackie sat in shock, staring at Dad before she absorbed his words.

"Goddamn it. Why don't you just leave her alone? You have a wife." Jackie tried to hold back the tears, not wanting to streak her make-up.

LilyAnn scowled at her ex-husband, and wrapped her arm around Jackie.

Jackie pleaded, "Dad, can't you focus on me? This is *my* day. Can't you focus on *me*, just for today?" It took a lot of effort to fend off the pain of Dad's accusations challenging her love for him, his threatening outburst over money he promised to gift her for her wedding, and now, he was making passes at his former wife.

LilyAnn looked out the window. "They're ready. Keith's already seated Carol and Hilda. Neil and the minister are heading up to the altar." She pointed to a small clearing behind a historic Victorian house. "That's where the bridesmaids and groomsmen are lined up. Everything looks perfect."

LilyAnn opened the limo door and was helped out by her two sons. She turned back towards her ex-husband and narrowed her eyes. "Don't you dare screw this up for our daughter." She turned and walked across the grass.

Dad sat in silence next to Jackie. The violin and harpist played the beginning notes of the wedding march. Jackie pulled the veil over her face. Holding onto her heavy satin train, she approached the staging area.

Once there, Dad obediently held out his arm for her. Together they slowly came around the corner. When they neared the rows of white chairs, everyone turned their heads and stood up. Cameras flashed.

On the day Jackie had dreamt about her entire life, the day she had anticipated for the past year, she wasn't able to enjoy walking down the aisle because of Dad's behavior. She wanted him away from her. Her heels sank a bit in the grass forcing her to hang on tightly to his arm. The guests' faces blurred as she tried to focus on the music. They approached the altar and stopped.

"Who here gives away Jackie on this day, to be joined together in matrimony with Neil?" the minister asked.

Jackie turned expectantly to Dad and squeezed his arm.

"I do," he said.

After a long pause, the minister motioned with his eyes for Dad to step aside, like they had rehearsed the night before. He nodded and went to his chair. The ceremony began. Jackie and Neil joined hands and stared into each other's eyes. Rings were exchanged, vows repeated, and at last, the minister proclaimed, "By the powers vested in me, by the state of California, I now pronounce you man and wife. You may kiss the bride."

Neil lifted the veil. Jackie closed her eyes, her lips met with his, and she breathed in the emotional support she needed from the man she desired. The worries of Dad melted away.

The procession ensued. The photographer hissed out directions for the photos. Jackie forced herself to smile as she was sandwiched between Dad and Hilda, between Dad and LilyAnn, and between Dad and Neil. When she didn't have to stand next to Dad any longer, she relaxed. Thank God he's driving to the reception with Hilda and there's champagne in the limo, she reassured herself.

At the reception, after the wedding party was seated and toasts made, the DJ announced the father-daughter dance. Bette Midler's "The Rose" played while Jackie and Dad danced. She listened to the words about a long, lonely road.

In treating this special moment with the dignity it deserved, Dad displayed a serious countenance. Jackie also had a serious look on her face, which hid her fear that Dad was losing his mind. As she reflected on the words of the song in relation to Dad, she broke down and cried on his shoulder. Even knowing his daughter was crying, he did not react. The song played out, yet to her it seemed to fade out early. When a livelier crowd-pleasing song began, she was relieved to make her escape from the overwhelming emotions.

One bright moment happened when the DJ played a Greek folk-dance song which Jackie had asked him to play. Dad had taught us how to folk-dance, and we had danced together at the annual Greek festivals for many years. As in years past, Dad led. Jackie, Keith, and I joined him in a shoulder hold for the *hasaposerviko*. Hilda chose not to join the line. With a concentrated look in his eyes, Dad called out variations and we three followed his lead.

When the song ended, the moment passed.

Later that evening, LilyAnn's fears came to fruition. Even though they were seated at different tables Dad kept pestering her. "Would you like to dance?"

"No, Joseph. You have a wife." LilyAnn stared ahead at the dance floor.

"Come live with me. I'll take care of you. You can take care of the house."

"Y'know Joseph, this is our daughter's wedding day," she said. "You're spending more time on me than your daughter. Or your wife for that matter. Leave me alone."

Meanwhile, as though oblivious to her husband's inappropriate advances, Hilda drank glass after glass of wine. She danced with me and Jackie. She seemed too proud to let tears show on her face, and instead sat and vented to Neil's parents.

At the end of the evening, Jackie and Neil closed their hotel room door, yearning for a little privacy.

Dad bothered LilyAnn in the hotel lobby before walking over to a hotel telephone.

LilyAnn stopped him. "What are you doing?"

With his hands inches away from the phone, he said, "I was going to call Jackie to see how she's doing."

"Are you fucking kidding me, Joseph? What? You want to do to her what was done to us?" LilyAnn shook her head, referring to their wedding night back in April of 1967 in Chicago and their honeymoon at Chula Vista in the Wisconsin Dells. Since her family had paid for everything—my grandparents had refused to contribute a single cent—everyone knew where they were staying. Family continually called their hotel room and disturbed them. She would not allow him to do the same to their daughter.

His memory of that night long ago seemed to haunt him too. He sulked away.

Early the next morning, Dad phoned Jackie and Neil, apparently unaware of his violations of social decorum. "Good morning, Jackie. Would you and Neil like to go to breakfast with me?"

Jackie and Neil, tired from their long evening, had been sleeping in late and enjoying each other's company. She resounded with "No," and hung up the phone.

CHAPTER TWENTY-SIX

FALL 1998 – SPRING 1999: BREAKING POINT

AFTER THE SALE OF THEIR HOUSE, Dad and Hilda moved to a small apartment in Hemet in August 1998. He continued working in Pasadena. On a Friday evening in late autumn, he walked in the door from work and flopped onto the couch with a solemn look of despair on his face.

Hilda peeked around the corner. She had been preparing dinner.

"I was let go today," he said.

She raised her eyebrows but said nothing.

He continued, "They offered me an early retirement. They only want to hire younger workers so they can pay them less. Replace us old guys."

"Only you?" Hilda walked over and sat next to him. With his poor performance at work, she had figured this day would come. She reached for his hand. He didn't fight her this time.

"No, they laid-off ten of us—the ten of us had been there the longest, all good programmers. They offered us an early retirement package," he said. "I gave that company seventeen years of my life." He groaned.

To cheer him up, she suggested they rent a movie, something they'd done together for years. Dad chose *Patch Adams*, based on the true story of a man who spent time in a mental hospital and later became a doctor. The movie did seem to brighten Dad's mood.

For the next several weeks, Dad moped around the apartment. He spent his days and nights in the dark. He slept during the day. At night, he read the Bible and walked through the complex. His behavior, besides being erratic and irrational, also became downright scary for Hilda.

Early one morning in April while she slept, Dad came into their bedroom, grabbed her by the shoulders and jerked her back and forth.

Startled, Hilda awoke.

His eyes narrowed. The look upon his face pure evil.

She rubbed her eyes to make sure she wasn't dreaming

Like a shaken bottle ready to explode, he tightened his fists. "You. Devil."

She sat up and scooted away from him, off the bed.

"Devil!" He yelled. He opened his fists and stepped closer to the bed.

She screamed and jumped to the floor. "Joseph. Stop it."

He glared at her.

This was too much for her. Keeping her eyes on him, she threw on some clothes and ran outside. She bounded down the stairs and jogged through the apartment complex until she got to Francine's door. Francine, a female minister in her sixties, had befriended Hilda and Dad months earlier, when they first moved to Hemet.

Francine answered the door and pulled back. "Hilda. What's the matter? Here, come in, come in."

"Sorry for dropping by so early, but I don't know what to do or where to go."

"Honey, it's quite all right. I was already awake. Sit down and tell me what happened."

"Joseph's acting weird. He's yelling crazy things to me. I can't explain it."

"Why don't we get some fresh air? Come, walk with me down to the mailboxes."

Hilda confided in the minister while they walked under the trees together. She related what Dad had said. The minister already knew about his medical history.

Francine turned to Hilda. "You have to leave him."

"I can't do that."

"But you've told me how afraid you've been. I've seen his angry outbursts. I've heard his nonsensical words. I've witnessed his erratic behavior. I worry one night he's going to hurt you. He could kill you."

"I don't know what to do or where to go. I . . . I still love Joseph, but he needs help. He refuses to listen to the doctors."

"Why don't I come by later on and we can speak with Joseph together?"

That afternoon, the minister came as promised. The three of them sat on the couch. Dad acted as if nothing had happened.

"Joseph, I've come to talk to you," Francine said. "You have a problem and you don't want to accept you have a problem. I think you need to be on medication."

"I'm okay. The only thing wrong is that the devil is here in this house." He scowled at Hilda.

Francine tilted her head. "What are you talking about?"

"She's acting strange." He threw a distrustful look at Hilda. "I don't know what's wrong with her."

Uncomfortable under his stare, Hilda said, "Dear, stop it."

"You need to see a doctor," Francine said.

"No, I don't. I'm fine."

Francine shook her head and stood to leave.

"I'll walk you out," Hilda said softly. She and her two dogs followed Francine through the door.

They were downstairs and several yards away from the building before the minister whispered in confidence to Hilda. "You need to get away from here. He's going to do something to you. I can feel it. Go far away. Leave him today. Please."

"I don't know where to go. I told you my family's in Argentina."

"Fly down to Argentina. But whatever you do, get out of that apartment immediately. I don't trust him and am afraid of what will happen if you stay."

"He needs help."

"Well, while you're gone, it'll give him time to think about what he's doing. Maybe he'll realize he needs help."

Hilda nodded. She knew Francine was right. She did have to leave now. She didn't feel safe anymore. "I'll call my sister."

While Dad read the Bible, Hilda snuck on the phone. Whispering into the receiver, she related the day's events to Marisol.

"I've heard and seen enough of these stories to be afraid for you for a long time," Marisol said. "You better come down here and relax your mind. I agree with your minister."

Dad stood by and watched Hilda pack as many clothes as she could fit into a couple of pieces of luggage.

"Where are you going?" he asked.

"To Argentina," she said. "Want to go?"

"No, I'm staying here. I'm not going with you." He glared at her and left the room.

Within a few hours, as evening arrived, a cab came and Hilda was on her way to the airport. Dad didn't say goodbye.

After Hilda left the country, Dad paid a surprise visit to Marisol's daughter, my cousin Elizabeth. It took an hour to drive to his niece's house in Rialto. In the early morning, he parked his car at the curb across the street and waited until Elizabeth's husband left for work. When the taillights on Oscar's work truck disappeared down the street, Dad picked up his Bible and crossed the road.

Elizabeth, three months pregnant with her second child, answered the door. "Well, hello, *tío*. Didn't know you were coming over. What's going on?" Her two-and-a-half-year-old son peeked around her legs.

"Just wanted to say hi." Dad smiled.

"Okay. Well, you could have called." She held the door open for him. "Come on in. So, what's up?" Her mom and Hilda had kept her abreast of his mental state, so she knew not to expect the same smart and charming uncle whom she'd grown to love.

"Well, I haven't seen you in awhile." He took a seat on the couch. "How are you?"

Elizabeth sat down next to him. "Fine, if you don't count this morning sickness. It's been really bad this time around, not like last time. I can't even drive without having to pull over."

He rocked his head. "Oh. That's too bad. Have you seen any good movies lately?"

"That's a funny question. No, I guess not, unless you count kid movies."

"Have you seen *Patch Adams*?"

"No. What's it about?"

"It stars Robin Williams. He wants to help people, but the medical school is full of cold-hearted staff that don't care about the patients. So, he buys over a hundred acres of land in West Virginia to fix up an old house. That's where he creates a medical clinic where he can do God's work by helping patients using humor, without the old ways in medicine practice."

"Oh, that sounds interesting. So, you drove all the way over here to talk to me about a movie? How's Hilda?"

"You didn't know she's back in Argentina?"

"Yeah mom said something about that. Why did she go?"

He set a Bible on the coffee table. "What I really came to talk to you about is how you can get saved. Especially being with child now, you should convert before it's too late."

"Excuse me? What're you talking about?"

Over the next hour he preached to her and attempted to convince her that what he was saying was the true Word of God.

Dad's daily visits continued into a second week. He became more aggressive and insistent that Elizabeth convert to his personal beliefs. When he left, Elizabeth made a long-distance call to Argentina. Hilda answered.

"*Tia*, you're not going to believe this." Elizabeth updated Hilda. "I don't know what to do. I'm getting really uncomfortable when *tío* comes over. He's always talking about that stupid movie like he's obsessed with *Patch Adams*. Every day he reads from the Bible to me and interprets everything his way, no matter how much I argue with him. He raises his voice when I question him. He's scaring the crap of out me."

"Ai-yi-yi," Hilda said. "Do not open the door to him. You need to think about your baby and your son."

"I know. Oscar's getting mad, too. He doesn't want to leave for work when he sees Uncle's car there, especially cuz I'm home alone. It breaks my heart. I can't believe that's my Uncle Joseph. He's like a complete stranger now."

"I know, I know."

"What do I do if he flips out on me?"

"You better not let him in anymore," Hilda said. "No way. Look at me. I'm in Argentina because I'm a scared of him."

The next morning, Dad rang the doorbell and knocked on the door for awhile, before leaving. The visits stopped.

In early June of 1999, Dad gave all of his furniture away, either to charity or to us children. Keith needed a kitchen table and chairs, so he asked Jackie and Neil to drive their pick-up truck to Hemet.

While Neil drove, Jackie stared out the window. Vast expanses of dirt and dry weeds blurred together. The sky overhead had a depressing layer of brown-tinged smog. This was hell's land. A few trailers on blocks sparsely populated the horizon. There were rusty appliances, a broken down Chevy on wooden blocks, and an abused couch with the springs poking through the cushions on a front porch. This place reminded her of driving with Dad to pick up me and Keith in the desert.

The landscape changed a bit when they passed through a retirement town where homes and trailers backed onto golf courses. Small white rocks were used to decorate many front yards.

They pulled off the highway and came to rest under a tree in front of a small apartment complex. Since the abrupt sale of Dad's and Hilda's house in San Bernardino and their subsequent move to Hemet, Jackie had only visited them one other time. Relations had been strained since her wedding the previous October. With his current mental state, she found it difficult to be in Dad's presence, but felt obligated to come.

"You ready, doll?" Neil asked.

Jackie practiced the deep-breathing exercises she learned in yoga class. She had taken her anxiety medication this morning. "Yeah, I guess I'm as ready as I can be to deal with him. I feel so bad for Hilda. I wanna talk to her today and see how she's doing. I haven't heard from her in awhile and can't shake this bad feeling I have."

When they stood in front of the door, Neil squeezed her hand. She knocked and waited.

Within moments, she was standing face-to-face with Dad. He backed up a step, and motioned for them to enter.

Jackie was surprised to see everything so bare. Several pieces of furniture, a couple of bookcases, a desk, and a chair, were missing. No picture hung on any wall, no memento on any shelf, and no framed photo on any table.

Jackie took a tour of the small single bedroom apartment. Dad had James Taylor's somber song "Carolina in my Mind" playing on a portable CD player.

Amazed at how simply decorated the bedroom was, she stepped over the two poodles and ventured into the walk-in closet. Her eyes scanned the empty rungs and hooks. She turned to the dresser and opened up some drawers. Where were all of Hilda's clothes? Her jewelry? It wasn't just the photos that were absent from this apartment. She rushed out to the dining room where Dad was talking with Neil.

"Dad," she said. "Where's Hilda?"

"She's gone for about a month in Argentina, visiting her family."

That in and of itself wasn't unusual. Hilda flew down to Argentina every year to visit relatives. But this time, something was terribly different.

"Dad," Jackie persisted, "Where's all of her stuff? Where are her clothes? Her things?"

He swept his arm in front of her. "Oh, well, she took her clothes with her." He turned back to Neil and continued his conversation. "Come over here and I'll show you my new Jewish folk music." He reached to the countertop where a pile of CDs were neatly stacked and began shuffling through the stack. "This is some great stuff, and this klezmer band is really fantastic. This music takes me back to my childhood. Let me play you this one. No, wait. I know the one you will just love."

Jackie thought, nobody takes all of their belongings with them on a trip. Not *all* of their clothes and jewelry. Where were the photo albums and pictures?

Neil watched Jackie pace. "So, is this the kitchen table we're taking?" He pointed to the seventies-style octagonal checker-topped table with scrolled cast iron legs.

Dad stopped fumbling with the CDs "Yep, that's it. And these are the chairs." He rested his hand on the back of one of the six chairs which had been reupholstered brown from the original seventies red and black checkered vinyl.

After the last piece was placed in the bed of the pick-up like a Tetris puzzle, Neil unraveled a bundle of rope and secured the load.

"Wow, Neil," Dad said. "Where did you learn how to do the knot-tying?"

"Oh, I don't remember." Neil concentrated on pulling the rope taut and looping it around and through the legs of every individual piece and back to the other side of the truck. Jackie leaned against the side of the truck cabin while Dad stood a few feet away, in awe. After Neil tugged on the last knot confirming its hold, he jumped back to the ground.

After shaking hands goodbye with Neil, Dad turned to Jackie. His eyes lingered on her dark brown hair pulled back in a short ponytail. "I love you." He smiled.

Jackie, brooding about Hilda being M.I.A., feigned a smile as Dad hugged her goodbye and kissed her on the cheek.

"I love you too," she said.

Neil helped her up and got into the driver's seat. With the windows rolled down, Jackie waved to Dad and watched as he disappeared into the desert landscape. She would have hugged Dad longer if she had she known how many years would pass before she would lay eyes on him again.

CHAPTER TWENTY-SEVEN

APRIL – JUNE 1999: BORN AGAIN

EARLY IN JUNE 1999, Hilda phoned Dad as she had done every week since she left to Argentina. "Dear, how are you doing?"

"When you fly back, I'm not going to be here anymore," he said. "I'm looking for a small apartment."

"What's wrong with where you are?" She feared his response.

"This place is full of devils."

Hilda sighed. It seemed as if nothing had improved during her absence. If anything, he sounded even crazier. "Wait for me to come back."

"No," he said. "As soon as I find a place, I'm moving."

Not knowing what to expect back in California, Hilda, against her family's urging, flew home. It had been over a month since she had laid eyes on Dad. She felt rejuvenated and ready to face whatever awaited her. She was more determined than ever to get him help.

When her cab arrived in the parking lot, Hilda saw their bronze Mazda Protégé in the carport, which meant he was still there.

She unlocked the door to the apartment and stepped inside the darkness. Her poodles jumped at her feet. They wagged their tails while she scratched their ears.

She found Dad asleep in the bedroom. Hilda dragged her bag into the walk-in closet and flicked on the light switch. Her jaw dropped when she observed the empty rungs. Where were the rest of her clothes?

She turned to the dresser and threw open her drawers.

They were empty.

Her heart raced, and she directed her gaze to her jewelry boxes on the top of the dresser. With a sinking feeling, she swung open the small cherry wood doors with the brass handles.

Nothing. All her jewelry was gone.

Feeling as if the life had been sucked out of her, Hilda ran into the living room and tore open the draperies. The kitchen table and chairs were gone. The paintings were gone.

Frantic, she opened every table drawer and cabinet.

The photo albums. Where were the photo albums?

Hilda gasped as she came to the realization that a lifetime of memories had been destroyed. She knew they had over fifteen or twenty albums: pictures of their wedding, their honeymoon, us kids growing up, every vacation we had ever taken. And the horrible reality of it all set in—all the photos of *her* family were also missing, her father before he died, her sisters and brothers, nieces, and nephews, her trip to Spain, her birthplace of Bolivia—

Hilda had taken Dad to Argentina, Brazil, and Bolivia a few years earlier, when his mental state had only begun to decline. They went to Iguazu Falls, between Argentina and Brazil, where they spent a week in the jungle with a tour group. They went to the Carnival parade in Bolivia. Dad had joined in the parade and walked the entire parade route with her cousin who danced in costume. They all had so much fun.

Hilda couldn't remember what year they went. She knew it had to have been after Dad's surgery because she remembered taking him to the Bolivian Indians, dressed in traditional native garb, seeking a cure for whatever ailment he suffered from.

The Indians told them somebody practicing witchcraft had cast a spell upon Dad, that one of his wives did something to him. Dad said he didn't know which one. The witch doctor tried to cleanse my dad's body by giving him a strange concoction, which he drank. Other than the bitter taste, he didn't notice anything different. Dad partially believed their reasoning at the time, but seemed to have since forgotten it.

Distraught, Hilda took the dogs outside for some fresh air. She bumped into her next door neighbor taking out the trash. He seemed taken aback at the sight of her.

"You're home?" the old man asked.

"Yes, I was visiting family in Argentina." Hilda shook her head at the thought of everything that had disappeared. "Many of my things are gone, just gone."

"That's why I'm surprised to see you back," he said. "My wife and I thought you'd left or something. I mean, we saw Joseph throwing away many large black garbage bags, and boxes and boxes of things. We were shocked at how much stuff he'd thrown in the dumpsters." He paused for a moment as though trying to recollect the memory of it. "Yeah, that was back in May or something…weeks ago." He lowered his voice. "You know, my wife asked me to check and see what was in all the boxes. I peered in a few of the bags and saw your clothes, and in the boxes looked like photo albums."

With tears in her eyes, Hilda said, "Yes, everything is gone."

The old man set down the trash and placed a hand on her shoulder. "I'm so sorry, Honey. My wife and I almost thought about pulling some of the stuff back out. It's such a shame. What a waste." He added, "If we had known you would be coming back, we would have saved that stuff for you. I'm so sorry."

When she reentered the apartment, she found Dad waking up. She stormed into the bedroom and screamed, "Where's all of my stuff?"

He rubbed his eyes open and jumped a bit at the ghostly vision of his wife at the foot of his bed. "Oh. I didn't know you were home. Your stuff? Oh, I took all your jewelry to the Salvation Army and threw away your clothes."

"How could you? Why the hell would you do that?"

"Well, I didn't think you were coming back."

"I told you on the phone. You *knew* that I was. You never asked me if you could get rid of my things! How *dare* you?"

He showed no sign of remorse or acknowledgment of her hurt and anger.

Hilda stomped out of the apartment for some more fresh air to calm down.

During the time Hilda was gone with her family in Argentina, Dad had been focusing on faith to heal him. Hilda encouraged him to attend church and Bible study sessions with her which he had done on occasion.

On April 4, 1999, unbeknownst to Hilda who was in Argentina, Dad went to another church where he got baptized. He came home, feeling refreshed and reinvigorated. He didn't speak a word about his actions to her. Instead, he sat down on the couch and opened his Bible. On a notepad, he wrote, "What good is it to see children get old and die? That's hopeless. Maybe God calls on you and your children to give up your lives for eternal life in heaven, and every day gets sweeter. It's as the Bible says: the end of a thing is better than the beginning."

He set himself to the task of fervently studying his Bible. But the more he read, the more he became discontented. He stayed up until 1:00 a.m. to read the Bible. He would awaken at 5 a.m. and continue to read the Bible. Sometimes he didn't sleep at all and instead wandered the apartment complex, much like before, lost in thought. But this was more than mere soul searching. His Bible study was turning into an obsession.

After weeks of this, he came to the conclusion that "only a full body immersion under the water counts in the eyes of God" and so his baptism didn't count. He determined that the church which baptized him was a false religion. False, like the Catholic religion he had been baptized in with his second wife, my mom Carol, over twenty years before.

He sought out another Christian church and attended on a regular basis. But while other patrons merely listened to the words spoken during the service, he lived and breathed every word. At Bible study, while other members of the church group discussed religious matters with an open mind, Dad argued his points with passion. Some people tried to understand and accept his views, but whether or not they did was anyone's guess.

On Sunday May 2nd, while Hilda was still in Argentina, Dad became "born again." He was fully immersed under the water. As he triumphantly arose, the water washed down his face and dripped from his fingertips. He looked up at the myriad of colors shining through the stained glass windows that danced upon him. That day, he had confessed to Jesus and accepted God as his savior.

That night, the dreams began. Dad didn't speak a word of them to Hilda during their weekly phone calls. The next morning, he scribbled the following on a yellow sheet of paper in his legal-sized notepad: Night vision is a dream, have seen heaven, colors are heavenly, most beautiful, brilliant colors.

Chapter Twenty-eight

June 1999: Road Trip

While Hilda was in Argentina, Dad had made arrangements for them to move to Riverside. They took what little furniture they had left, and upon my stepmom's insistence, bought a new mattress.

At their new apartment, in the evenings when it had cooled off enough to be comfortable, they took walks with the dogs. Dad stopped to talk to anyone he passed. "Good evening, how are you doing?"

His latest victims took the greeting as innocent enough and returned with, "Good evening. Doing good and you?"

"I'm doing quite well ever since I discovered Jesus as my Lord and Savior. Do you read the Bible much?"

Even though they stepped backward and appeared uneasy, the couple was not outright rude. "Uh, no, not really," the man replied.

"Oh, that's too bad. Y'know what? I'm going to be a pastor," Dad declared.

"Oh that's great. Congratulations." The couple didn't feign any joy.

"Well, I've been saved and truly born again. I'll tell you how."

Hilda rocked back and forth, uncomfortable at the building tension. "Joseph," she interrupted, "I'm going in the house." She turned and stomped away. Shadow and Star pulled on their leashes, but were stuck in place.

The couple stared after Hilda, as she made a clean break. Dad, hardly paying attention to Hilda's departure, continued his evangelism. "I've been writing it all down. Y'know all the churches are wrong. They are false religions. I'll tell you the truth…"

Over breakfast in early July, Dad put down his Bible, turned to Hilda and said, "Let's take a vacation."

Hilda sipped her tea. "Where?" She wondered what unexpected surprise he had concocted. She set her cup on the coffee table and leaned back on the couch. Breakfast had been more difficult without the kitchen table he had given away.

"To Chicago." He shoveled a bite of jellied toast into his mouth, crunching on the crispy crust.

She threw him a distrustful glance. "We're not going to drive there, are we?"

"No. We can fly then rent a car in Chicago. It'll be a wonderful vacation." He smiled at her with crumbs at the corners of his mouth.

Hilda didn't mind a break from the summer heat and a temporary change of venue. She looked down at Shadow and Star, lying on the floor, patiently waiting for any food to drop. "What about the dogs?"

He flicked his hand into the air. "We can leave them at the kennels."

And so they did for the next couple of weeks.

Upon arriving at O'Hare Airport, Dad rented a sedan. After visiting his parents, aunts, and cousins, he and Hilda went to the Field Museum. They had only been in Chicago for a couple of days when, back at their hotel, he turned to Hilda and tersely instructed her, "Repack your bags. We're checking out of the hotel today."

"Why? I'm tired. Can't we rest for awhile?"

"No. We're going east. Trust me." He wheeled his bag out to the car.

She knew better than to start any arguments with him lately. Besides, she thought to herself, it could be a fun adventure.

Indiana, Ohio, Kentucky, Tennessee, North Carolina, Virginia, West Virginia. The states changed every other day. Hilda became nervous when she realized Dad hadn't taken his medications since they left California, even though he carried the pill bottles around in his pockets. "Dear, shouldn't you take your meds?" she asked.

"I am."

She stared out the window at the beautiful scenery. Trees and fields blurred by. She knew he was lying to her, but she couldn't do anything about it. She could only enjoy the view and try to ignore his speeding and occasional swerving mixed with irrational outbursts.

Everywhere they went, Dad stopped to check out apartments for rent and houses for sale. "How would you like to live here?" he kept asking Hilda.

And each time she replied, "That would be nice." She didn't take him seriously, but she wondered where and when their sojourn would finally end. It reminded her of her childhood, and how her father sporadically moved his family across countries in South America. After working on the building of an air force landing strip in Bolivia, he came home with monkeys as pets. There was also the time he bought a boat and dragged the family to Brazil for a business venture. When that failed, he loaded everyone on a bus that stopped at the river's edge in the wilds of the Amazon. After the bus left them there, Hilda had been frightened waiting in the darkening jungle with a group of people, hoping a boat would come for them. When the snakes, cats of prey, and half-naked natives approached them, she grabbed onto her dad's coattails and never thought she'd make it out alive. But she did, and they retired from traveling when they got to Argentina, where she grew up. After a childhood like hers, growing up in a male dominated culture, no wonder she had the patience to deal with my dad's spur of the moment adventures.

As they drove through Clay County, West Virginia, he pointed out the window. "Oh, Hilda, look at this town." They had driven through several small towns with old homes and main streets. They all began to appear the same. Towards early afternoon, at the end of a country road, Dad slowed down in front of a two-story country house for sale. He peered at it through the windshield. "Look at this home." He parked at the curb and skipped like a child on Christmas morning around the property. "Look. Beautiful, by the river."

She got out and took a few steps towards where he pointed. She squinted through the sunshine. A winding river was less than a quarter mile from the back porch. "Yes, dear. It's beautiful." She turned back to the car.

He ran up to her and grabbed her arm. "Let's buy it." He took out a pen and paper and copied down the real estate agent's contact information from the for sale sign.

"I don't think we can afford this."

"Sure, we can. Let's check with the realtor, see how much." He pushed his gold-framed glasses back up on his nose.

"Joseph, wait a minute. Let's go back to the hotel." She got into the passenger seat.

He capped his pen, neatly folded the paper up and slipped it into his wallet. "Okay, but I want to call the agent when we get back." He started the car. His eyes lingered on the house, surrounded by pine, oak, and maple trees. While he drove off, he kept repeating, "I love it, I love it, I love it."

"Joseph, think about it," she warned and tried to drown out his annoying mantra by focusing on the trees whizzing by her window.

Back at the hotel, he immediately phoned the real estate agent. He hung up and turned to my stepmom whose eyes were fixated on the television screen.

"Hilda, the real estate agent is going to meet us down at the house in about an hour."

"That's nice, dear."

"Well, let's head out."

She turned off the TV and followed him out to the car.

The real estate agent led them up the stairs. "And up here is the master bedroom and bathroom, as well as a second bedroom. So along with the bedroom and bathroom downstairs, this place has three full bedrooms and two full bathrooms. It's quite a desirable floor plan actually. I'm sure you would agree the downstairs, along with the spacious living room, comfortable den, airy kitchen, and carpeted dining room would be more than adequate for the two of you. Plus you've got the basement for storage as well." He paused letting his potential clients have a look around. When they had finished inspecting the upstairs, he led them back downstairs.

"How's the neighborhood?" Dad asked.

"Oh, it's a safe community. Lovely folks live 'round here. Me and my wife been residents of a nearby town for years now. Great thing about this particular house is its location, right by the water." He walked them out to the back porch. "What with the nicely done front porch and this here back porch leading right up to the Kanawha River. Well, you can't get more peaceful and quiet than this here place. Quite a desirable location, really." He motioned back towards the front. "And you're not really too far from several Interstate highways…convenient location. But, you'd be far enough away not to get any noise though," he added.

Dad and Hilda stood together under a canopy of trees and stared across the river. Water burbled serenely in the background.

"Well folks, the agent said. "I apologize, but I've got an appointment I've got to get back to the office for." He handed them his business card. "Just give me a ring if there's anything else I can do for you. And if you want to see other properties in the area, I'd love to help you out."

"Thank you." Dad grinned from ear to ear as he shook the man's hand. "I'm sure you'll be hearing from us soon."

"Sounds good, Joseph. You and the missus take care now." He waved and was gone.

Dad turned to Hilda. Green, tree-covered rolling hills surrounded them. Monarch butterflies fluttered by. "How would you like to live here?"

"It's beautiful," she said, "but why here? Why in the middle of West Virginia?"

"It's a peaceful place to live."

Two golden winged warblers flapped their wings and hopped about the trees. Along the river, a handful of ducks floated by, dipped their heads underwater and preened their feathers.

"But, dear," she said, "we don't know anyone here."

"That's the point. We'd be far away from all those problems in California, away from the traffic, away from the family, away from everything." He took a deep breath and closed his eyes. "It's perfect weather here. Feel the breeze?"

"Yes, but, dear—"

"Shhh. Listen." A couple of birds sang merrily, and a few woodpeckers occasionally knocked their beaks into the nearby oak trees.

"Yes, it's lovely here," she said. "But, can we please go back to the hotel and at least think this through?"

"Okie-dokie." Half-way back, he continued his childish refrain, "I love it, I love it, I love it."

Once in the hotel, he incessantly prodded her. "Can't we move here?" He scooted next to her and leaned his head on her shoulder. "Please?"

Hilda pulled away and studied his face. "Are you sure?"

He jumped up. "Yes. Yes. Yes."

"I'm tired, Joseph. It's getting late."

"Okay, in the morning, I'm calling the agent back."

"Fine, whatever." She ignored him for the time being.

The next day, Hilda found herself sitting on a plush armchair passively listening to negotiations between Dad and the real estate agent.

"Okay, so it's settled." Dad nudged Hilda. "I need the checkbook, dear." Hilda absently reached into her purse, pulled it out, and handed it to him. "So, I'll give you the ten percent deposit. We'll be back here in about a month to finish up the transaction."

"Sure, no problem, Joseph." The agent held out a pen and the contract to Hilda for her signature, which she obliged in giving. He exchanged their check for a copy of the paperwork. "Well, congratulations to the both of you. I know you'll be happy here. You'll find that we're all like family." The agent held out his hand.

Dad stood and shook his hand vigorously. "It's been a pleasure. We're sure looking forward to starting anew out here." He smiled, took Hilda's arm and headed out to the car.

She kept quiet. Her thoughts jumped between denial and hope that perhaps the move would be good for his mind.

They drove back to Illinois and flew home a few days later. He wouldn't stop talking about the house in West Virginia. Hilda tried to believe this time things would be different. But, she couldn't shake the uneasiness.

CHAPTER TWENTY-NINE

JULY - AUGUST 1999: GROWING DISTANCE

IN JULY OF 1999, DAD AND HILDA announced their plans to move to West Virginia. The news was not well-received, as Hilda expected it wouldn't be. Marisol argued the move was a bad idea. Hilda felt they had gone too far to turn back. Dad decided to get rid of everything and to bring nothing but themselves and their dogs to start their lives anew. Before advertising in the Penny Saver, he offered the rest of their furniture to us. With Jackie living with Neil in their furniture-packed house, and me having already decorated my new apartment, Keith was the only one still in need of anything. He had recently graduated from high school and was renting. Keith accepted this peace offering, albeit without serious intentions of patching the broken ties between himself and Dad.

"Thanks for renting the U-Haul and driving me out here, Mom," Keith said.

"No problem, sweetie." Our mom, a strong, heavyset woman with pale skin, had brown eyes, and short brown hair with natural red highlights that lightened up her face.

During the drive to Riverside, Keith considered Dad's insanity, and how he'd accused Keith of trying to murder him. He thought about his last visit with Dad, when they went to lunch. Except for religious undertones, the visit had been uneventful.

Mom parked the truck. Opening the car doors, she and Keith were hit by the scorching heat, reminiscent of where we lived in the desert.

They walked upstairs where they were greeted by both Dad and Hilda. To Keith's dismay, the building didn't have air conditioning. *That should be a crime in this damn heat,* he thought.

"So what am I taking?" Keith looked around.

Dad led them throughout the apartment. "You're going to get all of this." He gestured to two couches, a brand new bed, two wooden end tables where he used to keep his maps for our family trips, a glass and brass side table, and a floor lamp.

Keith and Dad carried the furniture out. They went up and down the stairs more than a dozen times, loading the U-Haul while Hilda and Mom discussed the upcoming move to West Virginia.

After they hoisted the mattress into the truck, Dad paused to catch his breath. "It's so beautiful in West Virginia. The house is next to a river and it uses actual well water. It's a really big two-story. Y'know Keith, there's nothing like the outdoors and fresh air."

"That's great, Dad. I hope it all works out."

"See, that's where you're wrong. You don't need to *hope*. You just need to have *faith*. You see, I've been *saved*. God has shown me things, revealed through visions, things you and Hilda just wouldn't understand. You need to have *faith* in Jesus, your Lord and Savior. After you are baptized with a full-body immersion—all religions are false religions though—and, if you listen, maybe He will come to you, too. Not all will be chosen." He smiled and patted Keith on the head as he had when Keith was a small child. "I'm going to be a pastor, you know."

"Okay, Dad. That's great, whatever you say."

Dad headed back to the apartment while Keith lagged behind.

While Dad and Keith loaded the truck, Hilda leaned over and confided to my mom. "Carol, I hope the change in scenery will help him. I don't really want to move back there."

"I'm surprised at how well you seem to be taking all of this," Mom said. "What's the house like?"

Hilda had a sad look in her eyes. "Oh, the house is fine. It's a large two-story house, near the river and the woods. I mean the area is nice and quiet, but I don't want to move so far away from everyone."

After clearing out the apartment, Dad and Hilda loaded the luggage containing their clothes—what little clothes she had left—into the trunk and put the dogs inside the car. They headed north on Interstate 15. By nightfall, they had crossed into Nevada.

Driving nearly ten hours a day between the two of them, they made good time heading East on Interstate 70. They sent a few postcards back to us as they drove through Utah, Colorado, Kansas, and Missouri. After a brief detour north in Illinois to visit with his family in Chicago, they continued on their way through Indiana and Ohio. They changed direction and headed south on Interstate 77 into West Virginia, their new home state.

When the real estate transaction was finalized, they bought a minimal amount of furniture and moved in at the beginning of August.

Dad set the keys down and kissed Hilda on the cheek. "See, Ducky, this is our *new* home. Isn't this exciting?"

She grunted. "Yeah, very exciting." The dogs jumped about the room. Their claws skidded across the wooden floors. Hilda stared at their little paws. She too, would have to get used to this new territory. Unfortunately, she was already homesick.

CHAPTER THIRTY

SEPTEMBER 29, 1999: THE NIGHTMARE

DAD SAT DOWN AND opened his Bible. Hilda shook her head. There they were in Clay County, West Virginia, an area smack dab in the middle of the state near the city of Charleston, and nothing had changed. The dogs scratched their claws on the front door.

"Oh, you two want to go out?" They ran circles around her feet, nearly tripping her. "Want to go for a walk?"

The two black poodles jumped up and down, their tongues hanging out. Star, always the friskier of the pair, barked.

"Okay, okay, hold on you two." She opened the unlocked door. The dogs scurried past her and disappeared in the tall grass among the trees. The sun had already set, but left enough light enough to see. She stood on the covered front porch of their new home and surveyed her surroundings. Not another house in immediate view. Theirs was the last structure on this street, before the river. The elderly couple living in the next house down seemed nice enough and offered to have them over for some pie and coffee sometime, after they had settled in.

"Star. Shadow," Hilda called into the twilight. A bark resounded from a little way off. "Oh where have you two run off to?"

When she stepped down the stairs, the wooden planks creaked. She walked through the tangled blades of wild grass which brushed against her knees. During the spring, purple, white, and yellow wildflowers dotted the countryside, but the blooming season had passed. A light breeze was

165

blowing along the river and every couple of steps or so a cool spot in the air passed by her. She stepped under the great oaks and Maplewood trees. Their crooked limbs had grown outward in skewed directions. The trees' long arms seemed to embrace, casting dark shadows on the fields below.

"Shadow. Star." She whistled. The dogs trotted through the undulating grass and sat at her feet, wagging their tails. "At least I have you two. Nothing else here is familiar. If it weren't for my little doggies, I would be so lonely." Their ears pricked up. She squatted and rubbed their heads. They leaned their front paws on her knees and reached their drooling tongues to lick her face. She turned to the side to avoid them and stood up. Not far off, water sloshed about.

"C'mon, let's go check out the river. It's not too dark yet." She patted her thigh. The dogs followed. The tall grass dropped off along the riverbank, marked with sand and stones. She thought about balancing on the rocks to make her way down to the riverbed, but stared up into the sky. The wispy clouds were now a dark gray along a midnight blue backdrop, darkening by the second. "Okay, maybe tomorrow," she conceded and turned back towards the two-story craftsman house with the steep peaked roof. The realtor had claimed it was Victorian style, but having been built in the early twentieth century that was highly unlikely. It looked more like a common country home. But it didn't matter; the house was homey with the worn wooden floors. The eaves and siding had been given a fresh coat of paint before the sale. She walked up the creaky steps, holding on to the railing of the spindle banister supports on the way up.

She slipped her shoes off in the foyer. Shadow and Star bounded behind her as she walked up the flight of stairs.

In the last year and a half, Hilda had become accustomed to going to bed alone. Dad stayed up and read the Bible until 2 a.m. He woke up at 5 a.m. to continue reading the Bible. She stopped nagging him to come to bed months ago. Instead, she hoped he would find spiritual guidance to restore him to his former self. But sleeping alone in the new house only worsened her homesickness. At least she had the dogs.

After getting ready for bed, Hilda went downstairs to kiss Dad goodnight. He was hunched over on an armchair underneath the floor lamp. A yellow legal-size notepad balanced on his lap. He held a pencil in place between his teeth while he flipped through the gilded Bible pages. Light illuminated the shiny brass base of the lamp. She stared at a distorted reflection of him on the brass pole and gave him a hug and kiss. "Good night, dear. I love you."

He pried his eyes from the Bible long enough to glance at her. "Okay, love you, too. Good night." He frantically scribbled notes on his pad of paper.

The dogs were already fast asleep at the foot of the mattress. Careful not to disturb them, Hilda pulled the chain on the bedside lamp to click off the light. She slid underneath the comforter and sheets and closed her eyes. Sleep came quickly.

"Wake up, the devil is here." Dad shook Hilda from her sleep. She mumbled and rolled over, away from him. He reached over and shook her again, and shouted, "Wake up, Hilda! I'm telling you the devil is here."

She sat up and rubbed her eyes. The harsh ceiling light made her squint. She stared at her him. "What time is it?"

In one swift movement, Dad shoved both of the sleeping poodles off the bed and onto the floor. Their little paws slipped on the wood as they attempted to regain their balance.

"What's going on?" She looked over at Dad. His fists were clenched and his body shook in anger. Hilda's heart pounded. She clutched her blanket, unsure of what his next move would be.

"These two dogs are devils." He kicked Star's side propelling her into Shadow who attempted to run away. He loomed over them as they cowered in the corner, tails between their trembling legs.

"Joseph!" She shrieked and gasped for air. "Stop. Leave the dogs alone." Tears streamed down her cheeks.

He glared at her. "You know them, they are devils." Without mercy, he swung open the bedroom door, pulled back his right leg and swung it straight at both helpless creatures. They whimpered and yelped in pain. She hoped they might run away, but they approached him. Their faithful qualities remained.

"Please, Joseph." She sobbed. Her body trembled.

He followed through with his left leg, sending the dogs tumbling down the staircase. Whining in the darkness, they landed with a thud.

Hilda felt each blow they were dealt and feared Dad's next move. She jumped from the bed. Sick to her stomach, she backed against the wall, raising her hands to her face in defense of whatever was coming her way. Her chest heaved. Her muscles tightened. She held her breath and peeked between her fingers. He exited the bedroom and descended the stairs. She prayed, please God, let the dogs be okay. Run and hide Star and Shadow. My poor little babies. Oh God, don't let him kill them. What's he going to do to me? She felt too paralyzed to move.

Her prayers were answered. She could tell by Joseph cursing at the dogs. "You devils. Stay away from me." She looked at the clock. It was after one in the morning. She tiptoed out to the rail above the stairs and leaned over the side. Dad had settled back into his arm chair and picked up his Bible. She hoped he would fall asleep downstairs like last night. Too afraid to go down there, she had no other option but to get back into bed until morning. She flitted between unconsciousness and consciousness, waking up at every nightmare, only to toss and turn back to sleep.

As soon as dawn broke, Hilda got up and threw on some clothes. She wasn't hungry; she had too much on her mind. Dad went upstairs and walked by her as if nothing had happened, as if last night was her nightmare alone.

"Morning." He opened his dresser drawer and pulled out an undershirt and pair of briefs. "I'm taking a shower." He shut the bathroom door.

When she heard the shower turn on, she grabbed her purse and flew down the stairs, car keys in hand. She called, "Shadow? Star? Where are you my babies?" They came out of hiding at the sound of her voice. Star had a slight limp. Hilda picked them up, one at a time, and felt their injuries. Fortunately, they both had survived relatively unscathed. Just in case, she put them in the car with her. Afraid of the noise alerting Dad to her whereabouts, she quickly turned the ignition. Once on the road, she allowed the car to crawl past the house before gunning it to the highway.

Hilda drove to the nearest hospital and ran inside, grabbing the first doctor she could find.

"Excuse me, doctor," she said, "please, I need your help."

The doctor stopped. "What can I do for you?"

Hilda relayed the previous night's escapade.

The doctor listened before saying, "I'm sorry, but we can't help you."

She put her hands together and begged, "Please, I need help."

"Did he kill someone? Try to kill you?"

She looked down at the tiled floor. "No."

"We can't help you. Try the mental hospital. Good luck. " The doctor gave her directions, feigned a smile and disappeared down the corridor.

Increasingly worried about what awaited her back at the house, Hilda drove to the nearby Shawnee Hills Psychiatric Hospital seeking help.

She got the same reply, "There's nothing we can do unless he tries to kill himself, tries to kill you, or somebody else."

"He has to *kill* somebody to get help?" Hilda shouted at the clerk in frustration.

"Pretty much," was the cold reply.

Shivers ran up and down her spine. "But it's an emergency."

"Has your husband threatened to harm himself or someone else?"

She grumbled. "No, but he's been in a mental hospital twice before, in California."

"I'm sorry, but there's nothing we can do here without a court order," the woman replied. "The law prevents the hospital from helping patients who don't want help."

Hilda's mind raced. "Court order? How do I get one of those?"

"You have to go down to the police station and talk to them."

"Okay, okay. Where's the police station?" She felt in a rush against time. Even with Dad shaving, she figured he was probably dressed already. She could picture him sitting at the kitchen table, eating his Mini Wheats while reading the Bible and taking notes.

Hilda needed to say whatever she could to get him help. She was too afraid to spend another night in the house at the end of the empty road along the river, alone with him, at least until a doctor could examine him. Then she could once again feel safe.

She sat in the police station lobby as instructed, and waited for someone to come out to speak with her. She stared at her watch, at the wall clock, and back at her watch, observing the seconds tick away.

A uniformed officer strode up to her. "Good morning ma'am, my name's Officer Davis. How can I help you?" A slight Southern twang was detectable in his husky voice.

For the third time in the last thirty minutes, Hilda related her story. This time she added, "Something is not right with my husband. I'm scared of him. I'm worried for my safety and my dogs. I don't know if he's going to hurt me when I go back there today." She looked up at him in earnest, with tears in her eyes.

Officer Davis took notes on a small notepad as she talked. He maintained a stern countenance. When she had finished, he looked down at his notes and paused for a moment. "Okay ma'am, don't worry." He said the words she had been waiting all morning to hear. "We can help you. I'll send an officer down to pick him up from your house and we'll take him to see the court's psychologist for an evaluation."

She had been holding her breath and now released it. Her muscles tensed again and her neck hair bristled. "How can we do that? He doesn't *want* to see a doctor."

"The judge can take care of that."

"Excuse me, sir. Do I have to go with you?" Hilda cringed.

"No, in fact it's probably best if you don't in case there's trouble."

Hilda's eyes widened. She hadn't thought about Dad resisting transportation. Wild arrest scenes from cop movies flashed through her mind.

Officer Davis must have seen the terror in her eyes. "Don't worry, ma'am, you're doing the right thing. We'll get him back here safely. You can just wait at the courthouse."

"Thank you, thank you very much," Hilda said. She went back to the car to let Shadow and Star out on the grass for a bit. She didn't know how long this was going to take.

Dad searched the house for the demon dogs, messengers from hell. "Praise God. Praise to Lord Jesus Christ, our savior," he said. "The demons have been expelled from this house." I shouldn't have doubted God, he thought, or God will rebuke me. He knew ever since accepting God as his savior and being truly born again, he would be tested.

He pulled the cereal and a bowl out of the cupboard and sat down for breakfast. Of course, he brought his King James Version of the Holy Bible—the only version which held the *true* testament of Christ—and his yellow notepad to the table as well. He didn't seem to pay much attention to the absence of my stepmom. He looked down at his notes:

✓ Destroy all photos

No pictures (KJV Holy Bible, Exodus 20: 4, Deuteronomy 5: 8). Just words.

Also, (KJV Holy Bible, Isaiah 66: all, but especially Isaiah 66:4, 2 Thessalonians 2: all, but especially 2 Thessalonians 2: 10-11)

He flipped through a set of twelve 8 1/2 by 11 sheets of plain white paper he had tucked in the back of his notepad. Twelve—like the twelve Disciples of Christ—twelve sequenced pages of truth and the secret to life everlasting. This is what he believed God had called on him to do, witnessing for His son, Lord Jesus. God had spoken through him.

He took a spoonful of cereal and skimmed through these twelve sheets of paper.

*TO LIVE FOREVER = ETERNAL LIFE, YOU MUST BE "BORN AGAIN" = "SAVED".

REPENT OF YOUR SINS.

*BE BAPTIZED EXACTLY ONE TIME COMPLETELY UNDER THE WATER IN THE NAME OF THE FATHER, AND OF THE SON, AND OF THE HOLY GHOST (NOT THE "HOLY SPIRIT") WHEN YOU ARE OLD ENOUGH TO UNDERSTAND ALL THIS.

*THE KJV HOLY BIBLE: KING JAMES VERSION = KJV = AUTHORIZED VERSION IS THE ONLY ENGLISH-LANGUAGE HOLY BIBLE INSPIRED OF GOD, AND CORRECTLY

TRANSLATED FROM THE ORIAMANDAL. DESTROY ALL OTHER VERSIONS.

*FEAR GOD. BUT DO NOT FEAR MAN! KEEP HIS COMMANDMENTS. LOVE GOD (FATHER) AND LORD JESUS (SON).

*FAITH WITHOUT WORKS IS NOT ENOUGH. IF YOU HAVE NO GOOD WORKS = GOOD ACTS = GOOD DEEDS, THEN YOUR FAITH IS FALSE, AND WAS NEVER WRITTEN IN YOUR HEART.

*DO NOT GIVE PRAISE, GLORY, HONOR, OR THANKS TO ANY MAN, AND DO NOT ACCEPT ANY FROM OTHER MEN. THIS INCLUDES THE CLAPPING OF HANDS. DO NOT STAND UP OR SIT DOWN FOR ANY PERSON OR FOR THEIR COMMAND OR REQUEST, AND DO NOT ASK IT.

*PREACH THE GOSPEL TO EVERYONE. HAVE PATIENCE. ENDURE TO THE END.

*DON'T JUDGE. DON'T CONDEMN. DON'T RETURN EVIL FOR EVIL. HAVE COMPASSION. SHOW MERCY. FORGIVE OTHERS. EASE YOUR BROTHER'S BURDENS. BE LONGSUFFERING. BE KIND. GIVE FROM YOUR ABUNDANCE TO THE POOR AND NEEDY.

*THE dEVIL IS WITHOUT HOPE, SO HE WANTS YOU TO BELIEVE THAT THERE IS NO HOPE FOR YOU. HE IS AN EVIL SPIRIT.

He nodded, took another spoonful of cereal. After thinking for a moment, he picked up his pen, uncapped it, and added a final paragraph:

IF YOU <u>READ</u> (OR <u>HEAR</u> FROM ANOTHER) <u>ALL</u> THAT IS WRITTEN IN ALL THESE TWELVE PAGES, <u>BELIEVE</u> IT WITH ALL YOUR HEART, AND <u>DO</u> IT, YOU WILL GAIN EVERLASTING LIFE IN PARADISE, AND WILL <u>KNOW</u> THAT GOD <u>IS</u> YOUR HEAVENLY FATHER, AND THAT YOU <u>ARE</u> A CHILD OF GOD!

Dad *knew* God had spoken through him and his message was now complete. He tucked his twelve page message into the back of his yellow notepad, sat back down at the table and opened up the Bible to where he left off earlier.

Someone rapped loudly on the front door.

Dad opened it, but was confused to see two policemen standing on his doorstep. "Can I help you, officer?"

"Officer Davis. Are you Joseph?"

Dad nodded. He thought, the devil has come to test my faith now.

"We need you to come with us." The uniformed man motioned with his hand for Dad to step out of the house.

"My wife's not here."

"We're not here to see your wife. You need to come with us to see a doctor."

"May I bring my Bible?"

Officer Davis smiled. "Of course you can, sir."

Dad knew more suffering lay ahead. He sensed the evil, but was unafraid. He had no man to fear.

Dad entered the courthouse. He gripped his Bible with both hands as the officers accompanied him inside. My stepmom was sitting in the lobby. The officer instructed him to wait there until the psychologist called for him.

Dad leaned towards Hilda and whispered, "I don't know why you did this."

She crossed her arms across her chest. "Why did you kick the dogs? I'm scared of you because the things you did in the house. It's not normal."

He whispered, "Nothing's wrong with me." He bent over trying to look her in the face.

She turned away.

A man in a dress shirt and slacks appeared and called out, "Joseph?"

Dad, still holding onto his Bible, stood up and so did Hilda. The doctor acknowledged her. "This is a closed door session. You'll have to wait here ma'am."

Hilda nodded and slumped into the chair. This was like déjà vu. She half expected to see a gurney with her screaming husband strapped to it being wheeled in front of her. She waited. But nothing happened. About twenty minutes passed by before the doctor reappeared without Dad. *I knew it,* she thought. *They took him to the mental hospital.*

"Hilda, is it?" he asked. "Right this way, I'd like to speak with you for a moment."

She bit her lip and followed him down to the end of a hallway, where they entered a room. She figured they needed her to sign paperwork again and hoped this mental hospital would have better care than the other ones.

The man led her into another room and shut the door.

"Have a seat." He motioned to a buttoned leather couch. "We let your husband go."

"Excuse me?" Blood rose to her cheeks.

"Your husband is a normal, intelligent man. Nothing's wrong with him."

"Are you kidding me?" She raised her voice. "What about the dogs? He's not normal. You have no idea what he's put me through. He's crazy."

"To me, he looked normal," the doctor said. "I did give him a prescription."

"He won't take medication." She ground her teeth and took a deep breath. "He thinks God is going to heal him."

"Being religious is not a crime."

"It's not religious. He's insane. I'm telling you he's crazy. He reads the Bible all night. He doesn't even sleep."

"Did he hurt you? Did he try to kill someone? Did he try to kill himself?"

"No, but he kicked my dogs down the stairs."

"Nothing we can do." The man shrugged.

"Doesn't that make him crazy? What good are you if you won't help him? He's sick."

"Ma'am." He leaned forward in his chair. "Have you ever thought about talking to someone? Have you considered going to counseling? I can refer you to someone down your way. He's a good guy, been in practice for—"

"You think *I'm* crazy?" She laughed maniacally. "Oh, that's just great. Ha. Waste my time. I'm going to leave now."

"I urge you to at least take the counselor's card." The man opened his top drawer and pulled out a business card. He held it out to her.

"I will not." Hilda stood up. "Have a good day." She stormed out of the office.

Back in the lobby, she found Dad scowling.

"Let's go home," he said.

She hesitated before leading the way back to the car, trying not to imagine what would happen to her when they got home.

Dad insisted on driving. Along the way back, he braked in the middle of the deserted country road. She peered ahead in the distance to search for the cause. Nothing there. His hands gripped the steering wheel, his muscles rigid, his jaw tense.

Her stomach fluttered. "Dear, let's go home."

He narrowed his eyes and jerked the car into gear. A few minutes later, with his eyes transfixed into the distance, he parked the car in the center of the street, as if contemplating his next action.

"What are you doing? Please dear, let's keep driving." She nudged him. After an uncomfortable silence, he let off the brakes and hit the gas pedal. She wanted to get out of the car as soon as possible. She didn't feel safe stranded in there with him.

Their house came into view. Already after sundown, a thin cloud layer had hidden the crescent moon and stars. The gravel crunched under the tires as they pulled into the driveway. The headlights illuminated the fields around the house.

Dad turned the ignition off and sat with the keys in his lap. The headlights dimmed and turned off. Shadow and Star jumped up into the front seat, eager to get outside. Their claws scratched at Hilda's pants, scraping her skin underneath.

She looked towards the house. In the daylight the high peaks and ornately decorated eaves gave the house a regal feel to it. At night, with only the yellowish front and side porch lights on, the patterns cast eerie shadows along the ominous peaks.

Her heart thumped. She was like a lame duck under the car's bright interior. She grabbed her purse and got out. Dad got out as well and the car went dark.

He decided to take a walk and she didn't try to stop him. The dogs disappeared, too.

A cool breeze swept along her face. Something rustled in the grass beside the house. She turned in that direction and heard it again. She approached the house. As her right foot stepped down on the first wooden step, the dogs jumped out from the grass. She swallowed hard.

With the dogs at her side, she went inside and flipped on the lights. She walked through the rooms, turning on the lights as she went until the house was lit up like a Christmas tree.

Hilda was alarmed. What would he do next? What if he tried to commit suicide again? What if he tried to hurt the dogs again or worse—what if he tried to hurt her? Unable to sleep, she headed onto the back porch for some fresh air. Shadow and Star curled up at her feet. The chilly autumn wind blew through her hair and she shivered. She leaned forward to rest her tired head on her hands.

In the blink of her eye, there he was. Dad, like a ghostly apparition, stood in the tall grass staring up at her. Hilda felt a punch to the gut. She blinked to make sure she wasn't hallucinating. Her heart raced, but she maintained a poker face.

Dad floated through the field and approached her. With a crazed look in his eyes, he yelled out at her, but not to her, "Devil! Devil! Get away from me devil! God help me!"

She had had enough of this already and said, "I *hate* God." She went into the house, leaving him outside mumbling to himself. The poodles followed her upstairs. Once safely inside the bedroom, she locked the door and lay in bed, clutching her pillow. The dogs snuggled alongside her legs.

Hilda felt alone and helpless. She cried herself to sleep.

PART THREE

CATACLYSM

CHAPTER THIRTY-ONE

SEPTEMBER 30, 1999: HOMELESS

SHADOW AND STAR BARKED, awakening Hilda. Rubbing her puffy eyes, she saw the dogs dance in circles at the bedroom door, signaling their need to go outside to relieve themselves.

"All right. All right, my little doggies. Just wait a minute, let me put my clothes on first." The poodles sat down and wagged their tails.

Everything flashed through her mind: the dogs being kicked down the stairs, the police station, and the anger in her husband's eyes.

Hilda hesitated before unlocking the bedroom door, afraid of what awaited her on the other side. She listened for a moment. Shadow barked again. "Okay, let's go." She turned the handle and swung open the door. The dogs raced downstairs ahead of her. She followed closely behind. No sign of Dad. She stepped outside onto the back porch. The dogs disappeared into the tall grass. A riverboat floated by in the green murky river along the house. She walked down to the water's edge and stood there. A couple of birds wafted in the breeze.

Her stomach growled. She hadn't eaten anything yesterday.

After feeding the dogs, she fried an egg, jellied a couple of pieces of toast, and brought her plate and tea to the table.

When she raised her fork, Dad walked into the kitchen. Her stomach fluttered. She nibbled her food. He came towards her.

"I'm going to see my parents in Chicago," he said.

"Why? We just came back from there a month ago."

"I want to go to a Greek festival."

Hilda knew, at least in California, the Greek Festival season typically lasted from about May until September. She doubted he would find any Greek festivals in Chicago. "But, we just moved in, we need to take care of the house and the dogs."

"It's fine." He stood at the opposite end of the table.

She ate some more of her eggs and toast before she responded. "I'm not going. You can go by yourself."

"Are you sure?"

Her blood pressure rose. "Joseph, you wanted to be relaxed, you wanted to get out of California. I listened to you against my better judgment. I left everything and everyone behind and came here for you. Now why are you doing this?"

"I want to see my parents. Are you sure you don't want to come?"

"I'm sure."

He headed upstairs to pack his bags.

Within minutes, he came back down. "Are you sure you don't want to go?" He held two large pieces of luggage, one in each hand.

She couldn't believe he was actually leaving. "I'm sure."

"Okay then." He gave her a hug good-bye.

She sat there, unresponsive to his touch.

He loaded his bags into the car, their *only* car, and back out of the driveway.

He was gone.

By the next day, the silence in the house was comforting. She was glad he was gone but at the same time, she missed him. Hilda never suspected in her bruised and battered heart that he was really leaving. But that day would be the last time she would ever feel her beloved husband's arms around her. How could she have possibly known?

Reality set in. Dad was gone and so was the car. Hilda was stranded, with two dogs, at the end of the road near a river in West Virginia. She walked to the neighbors' house.

The retired couple next door welcomed Hilda into their home for cake and coffee, over which Hilda related her tale to these two complete strangers. Fortunately, they became friends and offered to drive her to town whenever she needed.

Weeks passed. By late November, Hilda still hadn't heard any news regarding Dad. She had just arrived home from another trip to her attorney's office when the telephone rang.

"Oh, Hilda." the nasally voice said. "Thank God you're home." It was my grandma.

"Marion?" Hilda asked. "Have you heard from your son?"

"Yes, yes he's been in Chicago for awhile now."

"What?" Hilda shook her head. "Why didn't you call me? Why didn't you tell me…all those times I've called you?"

"He didn't want me to," Grandma said. "Listen, you need to fly out here immediately. Joseph's in the hospital."

"Why? What happened to him?" Hilda's heart sank. A million crazy thoughts played through her mind. Was he in an accident? Was he going to die?

"Hilda, you have to come."

"Yes, but I need to know what happened to him."

Grandma became agitated. "Oh, he's really sick and needs you. Will you come?"

Hilda realized my grandma was not going to make any revelations at this time. "Yes, I'll fly out there as soon as possible. Which hospital is he in?" Hilda grabbed a pad of paper, and a pen.

"I . . . I don't know. His father knows. He's with him right now. I . . . I don't know."

"Never mind. I'll try to be out there tomorrow. I'll call you as soon as I get in."

"Ok, good. Thank you. I didn't know what else to do. I . . . I had to call you. I know he needs you here though. Call me when you get to your hotel."

Hurt that Grandma hadn't offered to let her stay with them, Hilda went ahead and arranged for a flight and hotel. She landed at O'Hare Airport late at night. Snow glistened in the moonlight. Bundled in her scarf and coat, she couldn't escape the sting of winter whipping across her face and numbing her ears. She hailed a cab.

As she took the elevator up to her room, Hilda was troubled my grandparents didn't offer to pick her up from the airport. That's not the way family is supposed to act towards each other.

My grandma always seemed a little neurotic. When my dad, their only child, was born, my grandpa chose to be by his sick mother's side rather than stay at the hospital with his wife. Grandma never forgave him and fell into a dark depression. From that point on, Grandma became a recluse and rarely left her condo.

Hilda phoned my grandparents.

Grandma answered, as always. She never allowed my grandpa to speak on the phone, another one of her idiosyncrasies.

"Marion? It's Hilda. I'm here in Chicago. Where's Joseph? Which hospital?"

"Oh, I don't know. Here, talk to John."

A strange occurrence indeed.

"Hello, Hilda," Grandpa said. He dictated the hospital address.

"What happened to him? Is Joseph okay?"

"Yes, he's going to be okay. He had his nose broken by a couple of drug dealers though. He took quite a beating. They stole all his money and took the car. The cops haven't gotten any leads. They doubt they can recover any of it or even catch the perpetrators."

"Oh, my God. How could that happen to him? He's such a kind, gentle man."

"Well, he's been around shady people lately….preaching his beliefs to the wrong sorts of people, y' know? His mother and I don't like those dirty women—" He stopped mid-sentence.

Hilda's eyes widened. "What women? What are you talking about?"

"Oh, it's no use. Marion and I are convinced you were right all along. Joseph is ill and needs help, but his mother and I are getting old. It's hard for us. He's our only child. We didn't want to believe it. We've worked our whole life, given him everything we could. I taught science all those years while Marion stayed home with him. It's so heartbreaking for us. Hilda, I'm so sorry for you. I know you two are still married. I'll have you know Marion and I refused to let him bring any of those prostitutes, or girlfriends as he's been calling them, here, into our house, absolutely refused, never saw such trash. He's been talking, saying crazy things, been talking a lot about God. He's just about driven Marion crazy with all that talk about religion, you know with us being atheists now and everything. We're tired of hearing it. Something's just not right about him. We love him though."

"I know," Hilda said. "So do I." She knew her husband had been sexually dysfunctional since the surgery, so she chose to ignore the mention of other women, the prostitutes, for now. She ran her fingers through her short black hair, just like Joseph used to do for her. "What was he doing around drug dealers? He doesn't do drugs."

"Preaching to them I assume, like he does with the prostitutes. He tries to save everyone on the street with his preaching. It's gotten so it's hard to take him anywhere."

"I need to go see him."

"But, they don't allow visitors this late. You'll have to go in the morning. I'll probably be heading over there as well. Perhaps I'll see you there."

"Yeah, maybe." Hilda, irritated at not receiving the offer of a ride to the hospital with her father-in-law, wanted to get off the phone.

She had hoped to see Dad right away. She still had no solid information regarding his condition. If it weren't for exhaustion, she wouldn't have gotten any sleep.

The wake-up call rang at 7 a.m. as ordered. A cab was waiting for her. The ride downtown was silent, other than the honking of impatient drivers, and the construction sounds of jackhammers and other earthmoving equipment in the nearby streets. Unfortunately, the drive took longer than expected because the Kennedy Expressway wasn't living up to the "express" name during morning rush-hour.

When she arrived at the hospital, she rushed over to the admittance desk.

"I'm here to see my husband." Hilda wondered how Dad would react to seeing her, and imagined what he would look like with his injuries.

The receptionist took her information. She spent a couple minutes on the phone before turning her attention back to Hilda. "Ma'am, I double-checked with the nurses upstairs. I'm sorry, but your husband was released this morning."

"What are you talking about? How's that possible? I just flew in last night."

"Ma'am, I don't know, but you can speak with our social worker. I think he handled things this morning."

Hilda stared at the woman. "Okay, where's the social worker?"

"Please, have a seat, ma'am, I'll have him paged."

"I'll stand." Hilda moved to the side. Her nerves were frazzled. Where was Dad? Why was he released? Hilda paced back and forth alongside the wall.

A man in business attire with a name tag clipped to his shirt pocket entered the waiting room and walked up to her. "Hello, I'm the social worker handling this case. Hilda, is it?"

"Yes. Where's my husband? What happened to him?"

"Well, he suffered a nose fracture and was in pretty bad shape when the medics brought him in. But the doctors patched him up, and he was released this morning."

"Where did he go?"

"I'm not entirely sure. His father picked him up."

"Excuse me? Did you say his father? I can't believe this. I flew in last night from West Virginia—where my husband left me last month and since then I hadn't heard from him. His parents called me to say that he was in the hospital and his mom told me to fly here. I talked to his dad last night. I don't understand what's happening."

"Come have a seat over here for a moment." He led her to some empty chairs in the corner. "The reason Joseph was on my caseload is because he's homeless."

"Homeless? What are you talking about? Joseph has a home. We just bought a house in West Virginia, but he went crazy and left me there, by myself. I didn't know where he was."

"I hear what you're saying, but he came into the hospital homeless. Unfortunately, I don't have too much information to share with you. The best advice I can give you is to check the local shelter. There's one not far from here." He wrote down an address.

Homeless. How could Dad's life have come to this?

CHAPTER THIRTY-TWO

LATE NOVEMBER 1999: LOST

THE WINDY CITY LIVED up to its name. Short on cash, Hilda braved the snow and wind for many city blocks until she reached the homeless shelter. Even with gloved hands tucked into her pockets, she couldn't feel her fingers.

With snow caked on her shoulders and back and her red nose, Hilda fit in with other inhabitants of the building. Unwrapping her scarf and removing her gloves, she approached the front counter.

"Excuse me, sir."

A black man with white stubbly beard looked up. "Yes, can I help you?"

"I hope so. I'm looking for my husband."

"Well, now's not the best time to find him. This here shelter is open for meals and for evenings. We don't allow folks to hang out around here all day. Sleep and meals only."

"Please, sir, my husband Joseph was just released from the hospital early this morning. I need to find him."

The man raised his eyebrows. "Did you say your husband, Joseph? Is he in his fifties or so, white guy with glasses, brown hair, and blue eyes?"

"Yes. That's him." Her heart pounded. She had tracked him down. He was going to be okay. She would be able to bring him home, where she would find a good doctor to help him.

"Well, hold on now, ma'am. He was here, but he got his things and left hours ago."

Her knees almost buckled. "He's gone? You said he came to get his things? Was he staying here? Did he leave with his father?"

"Well, if I remember correctly, I think your husband's been staying here almost a month, at least a couple of weeks." He thought for a moment. "This morning, he came with an older man, probably his dad, you say. But his old man left, so Joseph hung around here for a bit, gathering his stuff and whatnot. He checked out with me. Didn't say where he was going. Don't think his dad knows he left."

"Oh, no. Is there anything else you remember? Anything else you can tell me?"

The man stroked his stubbly beard. "Well, he sure looked messed up. All bruised up and bandages across his nose, looked like he had his nose broken or something. Oh, and his glasses were missing. Well, I guess it's a bit odd his old man dropped him off since I think Joseph was one of the few ones here with a car."

She shook her head. This wasn't happening. "Some drug dealers broke his nose and stole his car. I don't know what to do."

"I'm sorry to hear that. Having been a past resident of this shelter, I know first-hand how dangerous the streets are. Your husband seemed like a nice guy, pretty smart, too, always preaching about God and the Holy Bible. Probably at the wrong place at the wrong time."

"But what can I do? Where can I find him?"

"If I were you, I'd check in with the local police station."

After thanking him for directions, she bundled up and headed outside.

The afternoon sun was fading behind the brick buildings. She braved the snow; the police station shouldn't be much further. As she walked by, some people on the streets mumbled to themselves. Others lay on the ground around the building corners huddled under piles of rags. Snow drifts silhouetted their bodies. Hilda shivered, and sped up her pace.

"I'm sorry, ma'am," The officer said. "Ain't nothing we can do."

"Can't I file a missing persons report or something? Can't you find him?"

The officer motioned to his side, towards the wall covered with photos and descriptions of individuals, some labeled Wanted, others Missing.

"Do you know how many homeless people there are?" he said. "We can't keep track of them all, unless they commit a crime. If he does, we'll find him. If you call us, we'll tell you if we've booked anyone matching his description." He handed Hilda a business card.

Wait to find out if he's arrested? She had to find him. Instead of returning to the hotel, she wandered the city streets, looking into the face of every homeless man to see if any of them could possibly be Dad.

Night fell and snow flew in flurries. Under the moonlight, the snow appeared muddy gray. No cars were parked on the streets in this part of town. Several buildings had windows shot out or boarded up. Some homeless men and women nestled in for the night under overpasses. She felt their eyes on her.

Hilda was lost. With aching legs, numb toes, and wind-chapped face, she continued. The thought of Dad sleeping alone on the freezing city streets kept her going.

Please God, protect me. Protect him. I pray to you, Lord, watch over us both.

She passed under bridges, through dark tunnels, and came to a covered walkway leading up to a train station. She had no idea how often the trains ran at this hour, if they did. The gloomy entryway, lit by a dim yellow light, reeked of urine. If her fingers had been of any use, she would've used them to hold her nose from the putrid stench.

Rowdy laughter echoed from the top of the train station. She shuddered. A group of drunken people yelled back and forth at each other. She figured they were waiting for the train or were going to sleep at the station under the heated lamps. She stepped onto the platform. They all hushed and stared at her like she was a cat in a dog park. Their argument continued with them screaming at each another.

Forget it, she thought. Something told her not to stay, she wasn't safe. She turned around and slipped back into the darkness. Pulling her coat sleeve back, she looked at her watch. It was after midnight. No sign of him.

Hidden under her scarf, her ears throbbed. Her nose was stinging. Snow came down harder. She sped up her pace. More street people eyed her strangely. One yelled at her, shaking his fists. Another followed her across the street and incoherently called after her.

I have to get out of here, she thought. Her heart raced and burned into her chest. She didn't know which way to turn. A couple of vagrants closed the gap between her and them. Her stomach and throat tightened.

A Yellow Cab pulled up to a red light. She flailed her arms and hopped in. The hot air in the cab felt suffocating, but she was relieved to be out of the cold.

"I need to go to my hotel at O'Hare Airport," she said.

"Way out to O'Hare? Are you sure? Not Midway?"

She nodded.

"All right, no problem." The cabbie turned on the fare clock.

Hilda watched the dark streets blur together outside her window: the drugged persons on the corners harassing the drunken bar hoppers, the lumps of rags in front of the doors to the shops, the unruly youth roaming the streets. Hilda closed her eyes and focused her thoughts on the heat blowing in through the vents. She was going home empty-handed.

The plane's wheels retracted after take-off. Jet engines roared.

She leaned her head against the seat. She promised herself if Dad returned one day to West Virginia, she would do anything to help him. She reflected on what else she could have done. She had brought him to doctors and treatments. Psychologists, psychiatrists, acupuncturists, a psychic—nothing helped.

He was a wonderful person, husband, and daddy. She did the best she could, but worried she hadn't been strong enough for him. Maybe it was her fault.

I don't know why Hilda didn't tell me, Jackie, or Keith how dire Dad's situation had become. We had no idea.

Maybe Hilda understood there was nothing any of us could do at that point, but to watch in horror as Dad lost control of his mind. She tried to spare us the pain.

CHAPTER THIRTY-THREE

DECEMBER 1999: VISIONS OF A PROPHET

YEARS LATER, DURING PHONE CALLS with me, Dad related details about his auditory and visual hallucinations. He was very specific about certain dates, such as the day he left Hilda and the day he left the country. While much of what he told me didn't make sense, I kept an open mind and imagined what he had experienced, whether true or not. Although bizarre, his stories enthralled me. I took notes during phone calls, which I used to update Hilda and my siblings about Dad's mental and physical health.

Nearly a decade passed before I shared Dad's stories with doctors, several of whom said many patients who suffer from paranoid schizophrenia do not trust anyone enough to divulge information of their delusions. Considering this, I felt it important for others to be aware of how altered brain chemistry changes a person's views of life and reality.

The first vision came to Dad as he and Hilda drove into Chicago on Milwaukee Avenue, near a forest reserve at 11 a.m. It was a beautiful spring day, likely spring of 1999, with not a cloud in the sky. The trees in the reserve were still bare from winter; buds had not yet appeared. Dad's vision split. As if he were looking out through a pair of binoculars, two round pictures appeared in front of his eyes. In one circle he saw trees covered with green leaves, in the other circle appeared trees with snow tufted on the branches. He came out of the vision and found himself still driving along the curvy road.

Eight hours later, at 7 p.m., Dad and Hilda got in the car to go to dinner. They drove in the opposite direction. Out of nowhere, wet, sticky, heavy snow fell like in the vision he had earlier that day with the snow tufted on the boughs. It was a message from God. He didn't tell Hilda.

Soon after, Dad had another vision, this one of a cemetery crowded with tombstones. Two months after this occurrence, while he and Hilda were driving along an embankment in West Virginia, the vision came true. Weather-worn tombstones littered the old cemetery surrounded by grassy fields, exactly the same as the one from his vision. Another message from God. Again, he didn't tell Hilda.

And now he knew why he hadn't told her. The devil had possessed her. "Remember Lot's wife," he said. "Never look back."

And he didn't. After all, God had commanded him to leave on September 30, 1999. Almost having second thoughts as he left the state of West Virginia, Dad reminded himself, "She tried to lock me up and put me away. Satan entered into her."

As he continued his journey, loneliness crept up on him.

He repeated, "Those not *with* me are *against* me."

By late 1999, winter had brought Chicago's trademark bone-chilling winds. Dad longed for spring with buds on trees, which would unravel, revealing colorful blooms amidst boughs of green. Instead, all around him gray twigs and branches resembled unfolded arms of white. Frost had taken hold of the grass. The undulating icy water of Lake Michigan joined the breeze in a tango not far from shore.

Storm clouds scattered across the sky. The Chicago River idled under the bridges. Along the skyline, glass buildings glistened in the sun and beckoned visitors to the Miracle Mile. Sellers offered shoppers exquisite clothing and fine foods, but none of that interested Dad. Business people in cashmere and wool coats shuffled on and off the El-train and in and out of cabs carrying umbrellas and briefcases.

Tourists braved the cold and hustled about with cameras, maps, and scarves. They hurried from the Sears Tower to the Hancock Tower, from the Field Museum to the Museum of Science and Industry, from The Chicago Art Institute to the Shedd Aquarium, and from the Planetarium to Buckingham Fountain.

Although he enjoyed museums, Dad could only visit the more affordable Flower Conservatory. Considering the weather conditions, he appreciated the Conservatory's warmth and beauty. It gave him a chance to defrost and relax.

After he left Hilda, Dad had returned to his hometown, or as he lovingly referred to it, the "Farmer's little New York City."

He paused at the steps leading up to the stoic stone structure. He didn't know what led him to this church in the suburbs of Chicago. He gripped a manila envelope in one hand and opened the heavy wooden door with the other. Sunday service was already in progress. The welcoming heat smacked him in the face.

A pastor, as round as he was tall, in a robe tied loosely with a rope around the waist, heartily belched out, "Praise to you Lord, Jesus Christ. A-men."

The God-fearing masses joined the choir in singing God's praise.

Dad slipped into the back pew. Morning light shone through the multi-colored stained glass windows. The colors' reflection danced on the walls. His heart felt lighter and he raised his arms in praise.

A group of middle-aged people in the front of the church caught his attention. These regular folks in their street clothes weren't seated in any of the pews. They were grouped in a circle singing in front of the pastor. Dad focused in on their cloudy faces as they sung God's praises in perfect harmony. He blinked. In the next moment, the fifteen individuals clasped hands, ran down the aisle, and floated out the door together. They disappeared.

Dad stared at the worshippers around him; nobody else had seemed to notice them. They were angels. God had sent him here to this church in Chicago today to see them. Unbelievable.

The church choir's song came to an end and the minister began his sermon.

Dad exited the church. He turned his head in all directions, searching for the angels. They had vanished.

He stared up into the heavens and raised his arms. "Praise to you, Lord."

Cold evening winds rushed at him from the East, but Dad didn't care. He had a lot on his mind. The dreams of God, Jesus, heaven, the visions of angels—what did it all mean? Coincidences weren't coincidences—they were signs he had been chosen to be a prophet, by God himself.

Lost in thought, he walked to Navy Pier. He warmed up indoors before returning to the chilly city streets. He stepped off the sidewalk but stopped when he spotted the glossy black Lincoln limousine approaching the curb.

The chauffeur pulled the limo to a sudden stop in front of him. The rear side window lowered. Two people sat inside. Dad's eyes widened. His heart pounded. One of the occupants, a man with steely cold eyes, gave off an aura of the devil himself. The man directed his icy stare at Dad and peered into Dad's soul, violating him.

Dad couldn't move. He watched in horror as the man opened his mouth and revealed a ghastly tongue which unraveled out almost an entire foot. It slithered out the window at him. Reaching for Dad, the tongue turned into a forked tongue like a snake's.

"Dear Jesus, my Lord and Savior, save me from this evil abomination." Dad prayed. The tongue recoiled back into the devil's mouth and the limo rolled down the street. It disappeared around a corner. That *was* the devil. The demon was again trying to get in his way, but he was not deterred.

The further he went, the less Dad felt the stinging winds. He reflected on seeing the devil in the limousine. He wondered what else he would have to face.

After drug dealers had brutally attacked my dad and broken his nose, my grandparents tried unsuccessfully to keep him off the streets. His tragic hospitalization, vivid hallucinations, and irrational behavior were not considered sufficient evidence to justify a need for involuntary treatment.

Since my dad was an adult, there was nothing anyone could legally do to protect him from himself and his dangerous transient lifestyle. Hilda and my grandparents had to stand by helplessly and wait for the next calamity to strike. Even though Dad no longer had the mental capacity to provide his own food, clothing, and shelter, he was not, according to the law, considered gravely disabled. His mental state spun further out of control.

One evening, while wandering the streets of Chicago, Dad reached his hands into the air, waved a manila envelope containing his religious writing, and proclaimed, "Thanks be to you, God. Praise to Jesus Christ, my Lord and Savior. Since I am now divorced in God's eyes, I pray to You, Lord, for a new wife. I pray for a wife who will preach with me and help me to spread Your word."

Up ahead were a few liquor stores and bars. Loitering around the corner of a building stood two "ladies of the night" as Dad commonly referred to them. This part of town was notorious for prostitutes, drug dealers, drug addicts, and other rejected members of society. It was where God had tested him. Even though his car and wallet had been stolen and his nose broken, Dad's spirit did not falter.

He approached two gaunt ebony-skinned women on the corner. He pulled off a glove, opened up the manila envelope, and slipped out two sheets of paper. After handing them to the prostitutes, Dad evangelized.

"God sent me here," he said. "He has a message for you. God calls on you to give up your life, and then you will receive eternal life in heaven. Every day gets sweeter, as the Bible says: end of a thing is better than the beginning. Many are called, few are chosen. Walk after the spirit, not the flesh. I didn't know one verse before all of this. I just knew I *hated* this life. God gave me peace and joy, took away the anxiety, the depression, the fear. I found God. Or rather God smacked me in the head and found me. The whole thing is about getting into heaven. You have to want that *more* than anything else. Don't wait until it's too late."

"Honey, I can't be thinking about heaven," one woman said. "You hear me? Like Jesus gonna want me?"

"I have *seen* Jesus in my dreams seven times already," he said. "He looks like a man; it shouldn't surprise you. His voice sounds just like mine. That's why He calls me His little lamb. It's not that He looks like me; He made us to look like Him, like a person. Jesus' mother believed in Him but his brothers and sisters did not believe. God sent me here. You are not going to remember this life. We're all sinners. I sin. But I repent and God forgives me. Don't look back. When you're in heaven, you won't care. I have *seen* heaven. The colors are most beautiful, brilliant colors, like another dimension. It's not a dream, it's an existence."

The women had spoken with him before. They allowed him to continue talking.

Dad held his hands to his eyes. "Remember my glasses? I don't need them anymore, because God has healed me. God will heal me because I *believe* He will. Through God, *all* things are possible. This whole life is temporary. The flesh will fall apart." He threw his hands up. "I have work to do. Take it or leave it. Just know this: whatever sins you have committed, *God* forgives you. *He* will heal you. God sent me here because God loves you."

"Oh sweet Jesus," one woman said. "I believe you."

"You *are* a prophet." The other woman cried.

She had called him a prophet. He knew it. God had chosen him to do His good work. His heart soared, he held his hands on her shoulder, and bowed his head. "I heal you in the name of God." He stepped back and faced her. "You have been healed."

She wiped her eyes; mascara had streaked dark lines down her face. "Thank you."

"Don't thank me, thank Jesus. Read and believe and you will be saved. I have to go now. I'll return if God wills it."

Dad's chest swelled with pride. He had done another ministry. While walking away, he replayed the prostitute's words. She had called him a prophet. So it was true, God was working through him. He would be protected until the time came to give up his own life for God. That's what all prophets have to do eventually.

Snow started to fall. He strode down the cold wintry streets, alone.

By the end of the month, with my grandpa's help, Dad obtained a new ID card and passport. His previous employer's 401(k) servicing company accepted his request for funds. He had saved over a quarter of a million dollars in his retirement fund. The company withheld a 10% penalty for early withdrawal and nearly 40% for taxes. In the end, Dad drained his retirement savings, a hefty six-figure sum and proof of his life-long financial discipline.

On December 31, 1999, Dad, with only a single backpack for luggage, left the United States of America. God had called on him to go.

He stood at O'Hare Airport and scanned the international departures on the electronic screen. *Where is God sending me? How will I know?*

Trust in God.

He walked up to the ticket counter. "Good morning, Miss. I'd like a one-way ticket on the next international flight out."

"Where will you be heading?"

"Wherever the next flight out leads me."

She shook her head.

"How long have you been working here?" he asked.

"Twenty years, but no one has ever said that to me before." She paused. "Okay, sir, how will you be paying?"

"Cash." Dad opened his wallet.

The woman gave him a strange look and clicked away at the keyboard. "All right. The next flight out will be to Amman, Jordan."

After completing the transaction, and with his ticket in hand, Dad pulled a slip of paper out of his manila envelope. "This is for you. This is the word of God." He grinned.

The woman snickered, glanced down at the sheet, and tossed it into the trash below. She looked up at the long line in front of her. "May I help whoever's next?"

Over the airport speakers, they announced his flight was now boarding. He handed his passport and ticket to the gate agent.

"Enjoy your flight." The agent handed him back his documents.

Dad took a deep breath and settled into his seat. God was calling all the shots now. He would go to wherever God commanded him to go. He rested his eyes. Now, leaving all his troubles behind him, he could relax. When he arrived in Jordan, it would be the year 2000. A new year, a new millennium, a new beginning. Praise be to God.

Chapter Thirty-four

Spring 2000: Fata Morgana

Neil flipped the switch on the table saw and guided the block of wood through its hungry blades. Shavings curled off and fell onto the cement floor. The squeal reached a high pitch before dying back down to a hum. He paused to wipe the sweat from his brow and rub the itch on his nose caused by the raw scent of freshly cut wood. Using the built in ruler and protractor, Neil rotated the block forty-five degrees and pushed it through the blades again. Vrrreeeeeeeerrrrr. He picked up the wood and blew off the dust. After shifting his goggles onto his forehead, he held his work up to eye-level for inspection. With a nod and a grin, he set it down on the table.

Neil pulled up his stool and took a break. He grabbed a glass of water, took a few sips, and leaned against the table. He surveyed the sunlight shining on the front yard and noticed the grass needed cutting. Jackie was shopping this morning and wouldn't be back for at least another hour. A few birds landed on the telephone wires across the street. A light breeze made its way into the open garage and lifted up sawdust swirling it around before leaving it in a spot a few feet away. He loved San Diego with its mild weather; today being a fine example. He took another gulp of his ice water and crunched on a frozen fragment that found its way past his lips.

A taxi cab stopped at the curb in front of the house. The back door opened. After the door slammed shut, the cabbie drove off. Neil squinted in the bright midday sun, trying to identify the man walking up his driveway. The older gentleman, dressed in tan khakis, brown belt, and blue polo shirt, tucked neatly in, paused for a moment and peered in the garage. Neil removed his gloves and brushed his hands off on his jeans. He stood up to meet the stranger halfway.

With his eyes adjusted to the sunlight, Neil stared at the apparition in front of him. His eyes widened in surprise. It couldn't be him. Nobody's seen him in nearly three months. He's been long gone. Where are his glasses? Where is his hair? I've never seen him dressed so hip.

"Hi, Neil." As if nothing had been amiss, Dad added, "How are you doing?"

"Uh, fine, Joseph." He offered his hand. "Sorry about the dirt, I've been doing some woodworking in the garage."

"Can I see? I think it's fascinating how you're able to create so many things."

Neil nodded and led him into the garage. He tried to carefully pose one question at a time. "Where have you been?"

"I've been around. Here and there, you know, wherever God sends me."

His excuse gave Neil pause. "We've all been worried about you. I mean, I know Jackie can't stop talking about you. She's been concerned about her missing dad. She'll be happy to see you safe and sound."

"Is she here?" Dad maintained an unusually calm composure.

"No, she went shopping. She won't be back for a little while yet." Neil picked up the rectangular wooden placard. A curve jutted out on the top where he had pierced a hole. He pointed to the hole. "That's so it can be hung up on the wall."

"What are you making it for?"

"Oh, just a little something Jackie wanted me to make for Amanda. We're going to paint it white and add a little message on the front here. She was thinking something like 'sisters are friends forever.'"

"That's nice."

"Do you want to come in? Can I get you something to drink? Or are you hungry?"

"No, thank you. I'm going to be heading out now." Dad motioned to the yellow cab waiting at the curb.

Neil hadn't noticed the car had returned. "Well, that was fast. You're leaving already? You just got here."

"Yeah,. I gotta get going. Nice seeing you. Tell Jackie I said 'Hi.'" He held out his hand.

Bewildered, Neil shook it again. He knew he needed to ask so many questions, but Dad wouldn't give him the time. "Okay. Can you come by later to see her? I know we're all wondering where you've been and what happened. Hilda, she's been searching for you. She's all alone in West Virginia, where you—"

With his hand on the door handle, Dad turned to Neil and cut him off, "Well, I'll be going now. Nice seeing you, Neil. Take care of Jackie." He got in the back seat and shut the door. A moment later the engine revved and the car was gone.

Neil stood there, speechless, and still in shock. Dad came unannounced, out of nowhere, and was gone as soon as he came. Neil tried to think how he would explain this to Jackie, Keith, Hilda, and me.

CHAPTER THIRTY-FIVE

NOVEMBER 21-22, 2000: FROSTBITE

HILDA'S FINGERS SHOOK WHILE she dialed the long distance phone number to Argentina.

Marisol answered. "*Hola.*"

"Oh, Marisol." Hilda wiped the tears from her eyes. "The police, they found Joseph frozen on a park bench in Chicago."

"What? Is he alive?"

"Yes, they got him to the hospital. He had frostbite on his feet and legs. He could've lost his legs or worse if he'd been out there much longer."

"Oh my God, didn't that happen to him in New York City, too? Why doesn't he sleep in a shelter?"

"I guess sometimes they're full. I just don't understand why he would sleep on a freezing cold bench while it's snowing. He has a house. I wish he'd come home." While she had made friends out in West Virginia, she hated living alone. Not a day went by when she wasn't praying to God to bring her husband back home.

"Ai-yi-yi, Hilda. It's so sad. I'm so sorry. Are you going to see him?"

"I called the hospital. He's already checked out."

"But where did he go to?"

"I don't know. They used the Cook County Hospital's address and phone number for him, because he's homeless."

"I'm so sorry. That's so sad."

"Yes, it is. It's terrible." Hilda didn't know how or why she waited for him to return, but she kept the flicker of hope alive. She saved every correspondence he sent her.

By then, contact between Dad and the rest of the family ceased. He stopped sending postcards to Hilda, stopped calling me, stopped talking to his parents, and disappeared. For the next two years, Hilda remained in constant contact with the US State Department. She frequently phoned them to check if any Americans had been found dead overseas.

Two years passed without word from him. We figured Dad wasn't coming back. When she looked into the legalities of her situation, Hilda discovered a person must be missing for seven years before being declared dead.

We began the grieving process and waited.

Chapter Thirty-Six
Two Years Later, after Dad's Disappearance

July 2002: Prayers

ONE EVENING AFTER PUTTING Justin to sleep, I lay down on the couch with my boyfriend Tom to watch TV. For two years, I had been dating Tom, whose almond shaped eyes accentuated his kind smile. I'd met him years ago when I was in high school.

A young pig-tailed girl on a commercial spilled some milk. Tears welled in her eyes. Her television mom wiped away her tears, brought out some brand name paper towel, and soaked up the spilt milk in one swipe. They shared a smile while the paper towel company logo flashed across the screen.

Without provocation, I felt I had been punched in the gut. Gasping for air, I began to shake. I sobbed. I couldn't explain it. Tom wrapped his arms around me.

"What's wrong?" he asked, giving me a strange look. "What happened?"

Embarrassed at my reaction, and with tears flowing down my cheeks, I laughed while still crying. "Oh my God, I don't know what the hell's wrong with me. I don't know why I'm crying. Look at me. This is ridiculous. Over a stupid commercial. You got to be freaking kidding me."

Tom hugged me. "It's okay, sweetie. The mom cleaned up the milk and the girl's not in trouble."

I continued to shake, sob, and laugh—all-together delirious. "It can't be that. Wait a minute." Today's date flashed across my mind. "Oh my God, today is Dad's 59th birthday." I stopped laughing. It had been over three years, since I had last seen Dad. I hadn't heard his voice in well over two years, when he offered to baptize me and Justin in my apartment pool.

I told Tom to let me be alone. I ran into my room and threw myself on my bed.

Dad more than likely was dead.

We all knew it. I didn't want to believe it, but I felt it must be so. It had been three years since he had abandoned his wife, abandoned us, his children, and abandoned his life

I rolled onto my back. I hadn't closed the curtains. The evening light projected shadows of tree branches and leaves on the ceiling. I focused on counting the branches which swayed back and forth, and calmed down a bit. But no sooner would I gain control, than I would lose it again.

"Please, God," I prayed aloud, "I just want my daddy back. I'll give you anything, if only for a day, I could have him back. God, I've worked so hard in life.

"I bought a brand new car four years ago with my own money and I graduated from college a year and a half ago on my own. I bought this condo last year on my own. My *old* Dad would have been proud of me. But Dad will never know."

The shaking sobs started up again, as I pleaded more desperately than before, "God, just one day. I need to tell him I love him. I never got to say goodbye. I need to see him. God, please give me back my Dad." Like a lost child, I lay there in fear and agony.

Two weeks later, Tom was playing with Justin while I cleaned up the dinner dishes. The phone rang and I answered.

"Hello?" I hoped it wasn't an annoying telemarketer. I'd been meaning to sign up for the new "do-not-call" list. The caller ID came up as unavailable.

"Hi, Amanda?" The man sounded a bit agitated.

"Yes, this is she. Who's calling?"

"It's me, Dad," he said.

The impossible had happened: God had answered my prayers. "Oh, my God. Dad?" My eyes widened and I fell back onto a dining room chair.

Tom looked at me and crooked his head. He mouthed the words, "Is that *really* your Dad?"

I nodded, still in disbelief.

"Are you okay?" Tom asked

I nodded again, tears in my eyes.

Tom picked up Justin's coloring book and crayons. He whispered to Justin, "C'mon, let's leave Mommy alone so she can talk on the phone." They went into Justin's bedroom.

Was this a dream?

"God told me to call you," Dad said.

"Thank God you're alive. But, why now? Why haven't you called me for so long? Wait, how did you even get this phone number? My number's unlisted."

"I called your old apartment phone number and a recording gave me this new number. Did you move or just change your phone number?"

I couldn't believe my good fortune. I had paid for an extension on the call forwarding service from my previous apartment's number to my new phone number at the condo. I wasn't even sure why I had chosen to do so at the time.

"I moved last year," I said. "I bought my own condo. Oh, and I graduated from college a year and a half ago. Justin is almost six, he's so big now." The words flew from my mouth in a flurry. I was afraid Dad would disappear again at any second and I wanted to tell him everything. "Dad, I love you and miss you so much. I was praying to God last week for him to let me talk to you again . . . and now . . . you're on the phone . . . I can't believe it."

"Have faith. I don't question His motives, but He sent angels into my dreams telling me to call you. He provided me with the money to buy this phone card. I have seen visions and heard amazing things. I am a true prophet of God."

I ignored this unbelievable claim. "Dad, where are you? What have you been doing? Why did you leave? Why didn't you say good-bye?" I wiped my eyes with a napkin.

"I'm on the streets. I'm doing as God has commanded me to do. Don't be sad. I'm not afraid."

"Why did you abandon Hilda in West Virginia?"

"I've already told you this before. She is not my wife."

"You're still married."

"We're divorced through God."

"That doesn't count. You're still legally—"

"God's law is the only true law. I don't need to recognize man's law."

"But—"

"Amanda! I left her in September of 1999 because the devil had gotten into her. We are divorced by God." Dad raised his voice. "I will not listen to any more talk of that devil woman. I called to speak with you."

I didn't want him to hang up, so I dropped the matter, for now. "Dad, where have you been?"

His tone softened. "I've been all over the world. I've been to over thirty countries."

"I know, you told me about all of the countries the last time you called. Why did you leave?"

"I go where God commands me. In the past, God told me 'Go to Turkey, take a cab,' so I did. I have been through a lot. I've been arrested in Israel."

"Arrested?" I gasped. "For what?"

"Well, let me tell you something. Y'know the Israelis don't treat the Palestinians very well at all. They're treated like second class citizens. My cab driver? He was Palestinian...got pulled over by the police. The policeman was giving him a hard time...the cab driver, he did nothing wrong. So, I said something to the policeman about it...well, God spoke through me..." He snickered. "One good thing about Jews is they can't agree on anything. So after I was arrested, when they had a panel of psychologists discussing my case, they each had a different opinion and couldn't agree, so they had to let me go."

"Wow Dad. That must've been scary."

"I knew God was with me. I've been all over the world. I've seen things you wouldn't believe. I could tell you things that are really scary. Demons have grabbed me at night . . . I couldn't move . . . claws dug into my flesh . . . my body was paralyzed. I said 'Jesus!' I woke up with a scream. A couple of seconds later, I hear a scream down the hall. I put my hand on the hotel door and made the spirit leave."

I was speechless. How do you reply when your dad says something like that? "That's horrid," I heard myself say.

"My life is like a James Bond movie. I once jumped off a ten-foot high wall with my backpack on and landed on my feet."

"Why were you on a wall?"

"I was being chased by wild dogs and helicopters sent by the devil."

I didn't know whether to laugh or cry at hearing Dad's stories. "What happened? Why were you being chased? Where was this?"

Without acknowledging my questions, he continued telling stories. "On a park bench, I woke up at 2 a.m. and saw an evil spirit walking down . . . a soulless creature wandering around . . . this was in Savannah, Georgia while I was sleeping on a bench…it was horrifying…black, smoky looking . . . see Daddy knows…God shows me things…I'm a prophet." He took a breath and kept going, while I took notes. "God came to me and showed me two tablets; the commandments were actually written on both sides. He held a tablet of my life which showed me God is chronological and knows what is going to happen in the future. All the experiences were written in Hebrew, so I didn't understand. One day, God will provide me with a new wife. She and I will lose our lives in Jerusalem. The Gentiles will overrun Jerusalem one day. No prophets are killed outside of Jerusalem."

"What are you talking about? How do you know you're a prophet?"

"According to the Bible, God spoke through them—prophets—from time to time. I have had visions. In Ft Lauderdale—I had seen this seven times in my dreams before it really happened. Well, there I was in Ft. Lauderdale, and I went into a Haitian church. Men were seated on one side, women on the other. I saw my guardian angel glowing white, next to a Haitian boy. Nobody else saw him, but I did. Before that, back in Chicago suburbs in 1999…coming out of a church . . . pews in the back . . . fifteen angels…they looked like regular people, middle-aged in regular clothes…singing in harmony, cloudy faces, they ran out of the door together, nobody else saw them . . . .On September 9, 2001, in an Atlanta rescue mission sleeping on a thin mat . . . I woke up. I had a vision of a big explosion, bodies flying. Two days later, the twin towers came down . . . .God shows me things, Amanda."

I interrupted his strange flow of consciousness. Even though incredulous, I was fascinated. "Do you still have these visions?"

"Used to have them more a long time ago." Dad went back into his wild train of thoughts. He told me about the prostitutes in Chicago and the dual round visions of the landscape which started it all.

This wasn't making any sense. "What do you mean, Dad? Do you still have visions?"

"God proves to you when you are younger. When your faith is stronger…when you are older, not so much."

"Have you met any other prophets?" I humored him.

"I have talked to other prophets . . . all living in the streets in America…three out of four were black."

"How did you know they were prophets?"

"I just know…Holy Ghost, you know that you know. You will see things, and hear things, and you know."

"In Chicago?"

"No, in different places . . . . One prophet told me that every time he goes out, he can see people whose arms are snakes. He knew they are evil. See, God showed him the evil people. He was a prophet, too. I've been all over the world. I could tell you stories. Since October 26, 2000, I've been all over America, in most of the fifty states, living on the streets…Boston, Miami, Nashville, Charleston, Memphis, Atlanta, Savannah, D.C., New York City, Manhattan, Oklahoma City, Las Vegas, Columbus, Ohio, Tampa, Orlando, Ft. Lauderdale, Jacksonville, Florida, Los Angeles, been all over . . . homeless . . . I walk three miles a day; I look ten years younger than I am."

I couldn't listen to any more of my dad's nonsense. "Dad, you don't need to be homeless. You have a family who love you. You have a wife and a house in West Virginia; you have your three kids here in California."

"We'll see. I'll pray to God."

"You can stay here with me, if you want."

He was quiet on the other end for a moment. The first moment of silence since this insane wild ride of a phone call began. "My phone card's running out. I got to go."

"But, Dad," I protested, "when will I hear from you again? When will you call me again?"

"When God commands me . . . sends me a sign to. . . I must go now...Listen, Amanda, I hope you still have that Bible I mailed to you in 1999. I'm going to mail you a sheet of my writing. I want you and Justin to be saved. Share it with Keith and Jackie if you want. You need to read it and do it. Believe and profess with your heart. It's all there. What's your address?"

I gave him my new address. "You can always e-mail me if you want." I gave him my e-mail address, as well. "But, Dad, if you're homeless, where do you keep your notes?" I had so many questions I still wanted to ask him.

"In my head," he said. "Sometimes, I've had to write things down on toilet paper. But then, I flush it. That way, no one can get to it. Don't trust anyone...had my wallet stolen . . . I keep all the important information in my head...oh! The call's ending in fifteen seconds. I love you . . . praise be to God."

Click. The line went dead. He was gone, yet again. I sat there trying to process all the information Dad had just conveyed. My head was spinning.

CHAPTER THIRTY-SEVEN

OCTOBER 2002: THINK FAST

SINCE MAKING CONTACT WITH Dad in July, things on the home front became pretty messy. In August, Tom and I broke up. Money grew tighter without Tom's contribution. Much to my chagrin, I had to charge the credit card for food and necessities. Mortgage payments and bills ate up my savings, so I found a better paying job to try to remedy the situation.

After coming home from work on Friday, September 6, 2002, I got my first e-mail from Dad. Actually, he sent seven e-mails within a span of thirteen minutes. Because he was using an alias, the emails had landed in my junk e-mail file. The first of his numerous online identities was the mother of the cartoon character, Dennis the Menace: Alice Mitchell. In his letters, Dad preached to me, commanding me to research various sections of the Bible and to act on his instructions to be "saved."

I was relieved he was alive. Not wanting to have his delusional religious beliefs thrust upon me, I skimmed through the e-mails. In a brief reply, I told him I loved him.

The next day, I spent time with Justin, celebrating my first week on the new job. Mindful of my low bank account balance, I charged groceries on the credit card, again.

After dinner, Justin wanted to take a bath, an hour-long ritual of playing with boats and toys. I was relieved to have a little bit of quiet time to myself before bedtime.

I opened my e-mail. I figured I must be getting spammed because my "junk folder" was jam-packed, even though I had cleared it the day before.

It wasn't spam. And it wasn't from Alice Mitchell. Dad had sent twenty-seven e-mails that day, from two of his newest aliases: Rosita Gonzales and Hector Delgado. Twenty-seven! I glanced at Justin through the open bathroom doorway. He was making sputtering noises and floating his boats on the little lake.

Turning back to my computer, I scrolled through the subject lines until I came to the first one which read: "emergency – help – please read this before all others – read it carefully – thanks!" I read it twice:

Hi, Amanda! Hi, Justin! You see, I have a new electronic address.

So I noticed. I see the paranoia is acting up again.

I am on the streets

Well, you have a house and a wife in West Virginia.

and without money.

I know the feeling.

I will surely die – cannot even buy water.

Is he exaggerating? I thought water was still free.

Please send me money! God will reward you, in the name of Jesus for doing so! I need you to send me money from a Western Union office. I need one hundred dollars. If you can send more, say, three, four, or even five hundred dollars that would be wonderful. God, in the name of Jesus, will reward you more so for whatever you can give. At this moment, even fifty dollars will save me.

Because I have no ID, here is what you must do: send it to Kent Franklin Clark. These initials KFC mean to me that the King Forever is Christ. Do NOT use my real name.

Tell them to "Waive ID" because I have no ID. Tell them to send it to the state of New York. Do not provide a city. If you can do all this before noon, that would be great! Then, send a message to this e-mail address. Again, the more you can send, the more God will bless you and Justin with!!!

And, NEVER tell anyone about this or the name I will be using with you. Do not even tell Justin. Do not even tell yourself aloud. Keep the matter private between you and me and God and Lord Jesus and all the heavenly host.

I thank God through Christ Jesus for blessing me with such a daughter as you are!
Hoping to hear from you soon!

I didn't know what to think. I scrolled through the other twenty-six e-mails, skimming the subject lines. All of the e-mails contained Bible verses about the subject lines. Some of the titles jumped out at me, in succession: "Relationships to your children," "Giving," "Relationships to your parent," "Dad is still hanging in there – where are you, my daughter in Christ?" "Do not reveal a secret to another." "Humility," "Hypocrisy," "One more thing about the emergency," "True disciples of Christ," "Afflictions, sickness, and healing," "Mourning, and heaven," "Endure to the end," "Money," "Prayer," "Patience." As the time date stamps grew later, a couple of the subject lines took on a different tone altogether. One said: "God may withhold blessings until you submit to Him, following the Holy Ghost."

I stared at the screen. A mixture of emotions stirred up: irritation at the number of e-mails, anger at the directives, sorrow for Dad's apparently dire situation, and frustration at my inability to do anything about his disease. I answered him:

I love you and I miss you. You do not have to live on the street. You can get all the food and water you need. You are an intelligent person that God has blessed with many skills. I do not have any money to send you, Dad. I pray you will voluntarily seek some help or get a job like you used to have so that you won't have to be homeless and without food and water. You are welcome to come visit me and Justin here in California.

Justin wants me to tell you, "I love you, Grandpa."

I love you, Dad. You have always been a wonderful, loving, caring supportive father whom I always admired, and respected. Please come back to your family. God would want you to take control of your life again and not lose the precious time we have left to spend together as a family.

I hit send, and sat hitting the screen refresh every couple seconds. Ten minutes later, his response came through. The subject line read: "My last reply." I opened the e-mail which read: "These are the words of God." A few Bible verses followed, ending with "Get saved…you have not achieved eternal life. Don't take it from Justin."

I turned off the computer, shut my eyes, and slumped onto my bed.

During the first week of October, I got a strange call from Dad in the morning while I was getting ready for work.

"I'm glad to hear from you, Dad, but, I can't talk now." I pulled on my pantyhose. "I'm running late for work. I still gotta take Justin to school. Can we talk later today?"

He sounded a bit flustered. "Well, I *really* need to talk to you. How would you like it if I came to stay with you for awhile?"

With only one heel on, I hobbled over to the bed and sat down. "Yeah, sure, Dad. That would be wonderful. Y'know, I said you could stay here. I mean I gotta work and Justin's got school, but yeah, you're welcome to stay with us." I debated going in late and sending Justin off with some excuse for being tardy.

"Oh, well, I know you have to go to work now. Um, I think I can get a ticket from this organization out here, but they need to talk with you. Y'know, they just wanna verify someone would be there to get me. It won't take long at all."

I didn't know what he was talking about. "Uh, sure. Want to call me back when I get home tonight?"

"No, that won't work. It'll be too late here. I need your work phone number so the man here can speak with you."

Remembering the twenty-seven e-mails he had sent me in a single day, I worried Dad had lost all sense of reasonable boundaries. I didn't want to jeopardize my new job. I had only been there a month.

"It won't take long," he insisted.

"Okay, fine." I gave him the phone number quickly, before I had time to change my mind. We said our good-byes, and I rushed Justin out the door.

At work, my coworker Isabelle said, "Hey, Amanda. Your dad is on line two." Having been friends for a year and a half, Isabelle knew the whole story, including this morning's development.

I picked up the line.

"Hi," Dad said. "Here's a man who would like to speak with you."

"Good afternoon, Amanda," a man with a slight southern drawl greeted me. "I'm with Traveler's Assistance in Atlanta, Georgia. We can provide your dad with a one-way ticket on a Greyhound bus, if you agree that you will be there to receive him. I believe Anaheim is the closest station for you."

"Oh, that's great. Yes, it is. Yes, of course he's going to stay with me," I said. This was unreal.

"So, just to confirm…Amanda, you are Joseph's daughter?"

"Yes."

"Okay, great. We'll go ahead and get him a one-way ticket to California," he said. "Have a good day."

He hung up.

That's when I realized I didn't get any of the details, the date and time. And I had no call back number, either. My excitement turned to panic.

During my lunch break, I called Greyhound and attempted to explain my conundrum. "So, you see, I need some help. When would my dad arrive in Anaheim, assuming he leaves Atlanta, Georgia today?"

The woman said, "I'm sorry, honey. It appears no buses are leaving out of Atlanta right now. There's a hurricane watch."

"Seriously? When are they going to let them leave?"

"I don't know. It depends on the hurricane." The woman laughed.

"Okay, let's say, hypothetically speaking of course, my dad left on the nearest bus around Atlanta that is departing. When would he arrive here?"

"Ma'am, where would he be leaving from? And that also depends on when he can get to the next bus station."

"Okay, I don't know. Just whichever bus leaves the soonest . . . a station which he can get to by a cab or something . . . a bus departing for California."

"I can't really answer that."

I was probably being a pain with my unreasonable requests. "I'm sorry. It's just that my dad is homeless and a traveler's group is sending him on the next bus out here so that he can stay with me."

She paused to take in this new information. Understanding the circumstances helped. The telephone representative tried to give me a guesstimate. "All right, hold on a sec…this might take me a few minutes…"

"No problem," I waited patiently, crossed my fingers, and prayed to God for some intervention here.

I heard her typing away at the keyboard. She paused and resumed typing. She returned to the line. "All right, now ma'am, you understand this is highly circumstantial and I could be way off here?"

"Yes, yes, I know."

"Well, if he leaves from the nearest Greyhound station that isn't under a hurricane watch, I think that would put him into your local station at about 7 a.m. on Sunday morning."

I thanked her for her extra help and went back to work. My break was over, but I couldn't concentrate for the rest of the day.

Saturday night came. I hadn't received another call from Dad. I remembered back in 2000 when he offered to baptize me and Justin in the apartment pool. He didn't show. I decided he wasn't coming, but set my alarm clock for 7 a.m. anyway.

On Sunday, October 6th, I awoke to the buzzing of my alarm. Still tired, I hit snooze and rolled back into bed. A few minutes later, the phone rang.

"Amanda?" Dad asked. "Where are you?"

I bolted out of bed. "I was just walking out the door," I said. "I'll see you in a little bit."

"Okay, I'm waiting for you."

I threw on some clothes, pulled Justin out of bed, grabbed a bag of dry cereal, and flew out the door. Dad was really here, in California!

I pulled into the Greyhound parking lot. With Justin still in his car seat in the back, I stepped out and scanned the area. I didn't know what to expect since Dad had been homeless for almost three years now. I looked for a ragged, dirty, haggardly thin man, with gold framed glasses. Nothing. I walked up to a middle-aged man exiting the building.

"Excuse me, sir. I know this is going to sound a bit strange, but I'm looking for a homeless man. Have you seen any guy in his fifties, with glasses, brown hair, probably appears a bit dirty? He was on that bus." I pointed.

The man gave me a strange glance like I was speaking in a foreign tongue. "No, sorry, I didn't see anyone like that. Good luck." He strode off.

Now what? I didn't see anyone else to ask. Just as I headed back towards my car, I spotted a gentleman, in the far end of the parking lot, walking in my direction. I squinted at him as he slowly approached. No, he couldn't be Dad. That man was bald, didn't have glasses, had a bit of a belly, and didn't at all appear homeless. He wore a blue short-sleeved polo shirt tucked into a pair of dark jeans that were cuffed at the bottom, polished black leather shoes and a black leather belt. The only item the man carried with him was a small blue backpack, casually slung over one shoulder. He was now a few car lengths away. He came towards me.

I had no idea who this stranger was or why he was walking in my direction, until I looked into his unmistakably pale, blue eyes, which were now framed by sun-kissed wrinkles instead of gold-rimmed glasses. "Dad?" I hesitantly asked.

He smiled. I embraced him. Dad was alive. God had brought him back to me.

He got into the front seat of my Accord. "Remember, you cosigned this car for me, over four years ago?" I still needed him to sign off on the pink slip.

He wobbled his head side-to-side as if contemplating something else. When he opened his mouth to speak, I saw no resemblance of Dad, as he used to be. He didn't acknowledge anything I said, and simply evangelized to me the entire way home. I let his words slip through my ears. I was overjoyed at being able to hear his voice again. Silently, I thanked God the entire way. Dad was coming home.

Wide-eyed at meeting his grandpa, Justin stood next to my bed. We watched as Dad carefully and deliberately unpacked his backpack. He meticulously took out several items, each secured in separate plastic grocery bags. Dad untied the first bag, revealing a handful of individually wrapped wet wipes, the kind a restaurant hands out to you after a meal of messy ribs. "These come in handy….and here are my socks. It's important to always have clean socks when you're walking miles a day." His eyes had a vacant quality about them as he spoke.

I stared as he laid out two pairs of socks on my bed. "How do you wash them?" I asked.

"Well, that's a silly question. With water, of course."

"But, where do you get the water to stay clean?"

"Oh, different places. Sinks, fountains." Dad brought out a clean pair of white briefs which appeared to be in good shape. "I wash my underwear every day, too." He laid a large manila envelope on the bed. He opened up a bag that had a toothbrush and tube of toothpaste in it. He also had a razor. Next he untied another plastic bag which contained brown and white paper napkins from various restaurants. After this, he proceeded to tie, untie, and re-tie all the bags again. Dad placed each item back into his backpack as if his mind were in a fog.

"Is that it?" I asked. "That's all you have?"

He paused before unbuckling his belt. "I have this. And, do you know these fine Italian leather shoes cost over one hundred dollars?" He lifted up a foot to show them off.

"Wow, they look really nice, but how did you pay for them? I thought you didn't have money." Although he skimped on school clothes, Dad always made sure his children had the finest shoes on our feet.

As had been the case earlier today, he disregarded my question and spoke whatever came to his mind. "Shoes are of the utmost importance. I've been in the hospital with frostbite on my toes before. I've been all over the world. God has taken me to many places."

"Where do you sleep?"

"Benches, shelters…look, that doesn't matter. God has provided for me."

I thought for an appropriate response. Instead, I turned to my desk and grabbed my camera. "Dad, I want to get a couple of pictures of you and Justin."

I stood Justin next to him and snapped a few photos before Dad could think to object. I was still afraid he could disappear at any moment. The photos would prove to me this day was real.

Chapter Thirty-eight

October 2002: Confessions

My friend and coworker Isabelle had given me one of her father's old jackets, a few button-up shirts and a couple pairs of pants, all of which her father had intended to donate. Although I had never been good with a needle and thread, I sewed up a loose button on one of the slacks.

I took Dad to the Salvation Army to buy whatever I could afford to get him. We searched through the racks together.

"No, absolutely not, Dad. I can't have you preaching around my office. I don't want to lose my job." I replied in response to his request to go to work with me in the morning.

"Well, people shouldn't punish you, or God will punish them."

"Dad, we need my paycheck to eat. Now, I have three mouths to feed." On second thought, I added, "And please, don't preach in my condo complex." I didn't need him angering any of my neighbors.

"This is my job, Amanda. I am a true prophet of God. Are you against—"

"I know, Dad." I tried to placate him. A few shoppers gave us sideways glances. I didn't feel like drawing any more attention at the moment. "Is there anywhere else where you can do your work? The park?" I lived along a busy street in a busy city surrounded by other busy cities, whose borders blurred together. There were many shopping malls and parks nearby. "Maybe we can get you a bus pass or something?" I found it easier to go along with his beliefs than to try to argue against them. That would be a losing battle.

"I'll see. Just tell me what time you'll be home from work, and I'll come back after that." Dad conceded. "Do you have any money I could use for lunch?"

"No, but we can pack our lunches together. I hope you like peanut butter and jelly." I laughed. I didn't particularly like them myself.

Dad shrugged. I saw half a grin creep up along the corners of his mouth. However, by the vacant stare in his eyes, I could tell Dad was still far away

When I made the dinner invitation, Keith answered with irritation. "Why would I want to do that?"

I gripped the phone. "But, you haven't seen him since 1999. That was over three years ago."

"I've talked to him since then." Through his tone of voice, I could hear him thinking, 'here we go again.'

"Oh, really? When? Don't you feel sorry for him?"

"I talked to him a couple of times after he and Hilda moved to West Virginia. They were short calls…nothing memorable. Dad also called me a couple of times while he was in Jordan and some other countries. Do you know what he told me? He said he was trying to get twelve wives and was living in some four or five-star hotel. So, no, I don't feel sorry for him. He brought this on himself. If he hadn't thrown away a quarter of a million dollars—his life savings and everything he had for retirement—he wouldn't *be* homeless."

I cringed. "If you'd came over, maybe the two of us could help Dad snap out of his delusions. Perhaps we could remind him of better times."

"You can talk to him if you like. I don't have to. He's not the same person. We don't have a relationship anymore. Period. He tried to convince me to go out there with him to Jordan or Turkey or some other country. Want to know what else he said to me?" Keith, usually a man of few words, was sure letting me have it this time. "One time, he said God told him I was above him….that I was Jesus' equal while Dad was just a disciple. He was mad about that. He's insane, Amanda. He tried to convince me to go preach with him. He said, 'I'll buy you a ticket and you can come tomorrow.' He told me he would pay for me to go and live with him in a hotel. Of course, I fucking told him no, I wasn't interested. But, damn. He wouldn't get off the phone until I said, 'I'll think about it.' That was the only way to end the conversation. At least, I've never hung up on him before…Can't say I didn't think about it though."

"Yeah, I know. Mom said Dad called from Turkey and tried to convince her to fly out there and become another one of his wives again."

"See? He's fucking nuts! He said the Bible told him he needed twelve wives and that he wasn't married to Hilda. He told me that God said that that wasn't a real marriage. That really sucks what he did to her. Although we haven't talked much lately, she's told me she went to the FBI and they wouldn't do anything for her because he wasn't really missing…a missing person, I mean. She couldn't do anything with the house because Dad wasn't around."

"Yeah, I know. They said he had to be missing for seven years before you can declare someone dead—even though he did abandon her. But, Keith, he is mentally ill. I'm sure he didn't do this stuff on purpose. You know the *old* Dad wouldn't have done anything like that."

"Exactly. The *old* Dad wouldn't have. This is not Dad. I don't think of him as the same person. He goes into crazy mode. Besides, I've got my own shit to deal with. The *old* dad wouldn't have called me telling me he'd been arrested in some country because he was preaching and got himself into trouble. You know he was in jail for a couple of days? That's crazy, and you know it, Amanda. The *old* dad wouldn't have put me through this shit. You have no fucking idea. I was only fifteen when I went to live with him."

"He's still your dad." I didn't know what other angle I could possibly take to convince my brother. "Maybe, you can just come by for dinner….see how things go. I'm sure there are a lot of things you would like to say to him which you never had the chance to say."

Keith hesitated. "I don't know if it's a good idea."

"Please. If it doesn't work out, you don't have to see him or talk to him again. Who knows? Maybe he'll remember the *old* times and actually accept some help."

"All right. But, don't get your hopes up. I don't think anything good will come of this."

Friday, the night of the dinner arrived. Since I was on a budget, spaghetti and salad had become staples in my house. Dad sat on one side of the table, next to Justin. Keith sat next to Dad, and I sat across from Dad.

"God has taken me many places, Keith," Dad said. "Did you get the packet I sent you? If you read it, believe it, and do it, then and only then, you can be truly saved. Daddy knows these things, because I am a true prophet of God."

Keith leaned over to me. "Do you have a beer?"

I nodded.

Under his breath, Keith added, "I think I'm gonna need one tonight."

"In Egypt, I gave away $1000 on the street. I handed out $100 bills in Cairo. Gotta watch out for street kids, though….they're barefoot, dirty, pathetic….y'know there was this girl…eight years old, holding her baby brother, probably about eight months old, his nose was dripping….the parents train these kids to beg for money."

I caught bits and pieces. Tension rose like a thick layer of fog and hung over our heads.

"In Romania, the gypsies live down in the sewer hole…there's prostitution…they go to the bathroom in the street. The Romanians were standing around with pick-axes watching the gypsies . . . one had a baseball bat, he was threatening me . . . but, in the upscale areas . . . there was this guy, a gypsy in his 60's, the Romanians—they wear crosses and are Christian—well, they cracked this guy's head open with a pick-ax . . . I saw it with my own eyes as God is my witness. You know in Europe, the police laugh…they're cruel."

I glanced over at Justin to see his reaction. Almost done eating, he seemed more interested in playing with tomato sauce and noodles than in the disturbing conversation at hand.

"So whenever a gypsy gets on a bus, everyone else makes the sign of the cross. This big woman got on the bus. She tried to say she was the police. She came up to me and told me to show her my ID. I refused, I know their tricks . . . want to steal my ID and money . . . well, she tried to grab me…she commanded me to get off the bus. I turned to her and said, 'fuck you!' She spit in my face and left the bus."

I choked on my salad. "Dad, you shouldn't use that language around Justin."

Justin had been falling asleep on his hand. He pried his eyes open to see what commotion he had missed.

Dad gave a sheepish grin. "Sor-ry. Daddy forgot."

This was a strange new habit of his—to refer to himself in the third person.

"Never mind. It's okay." I looked over at Keith. He had finished his first beer and was opening a second. I could feel trouble brewing. "Justin needs to go to bed now, anyway. It's late and he's done eating."

Justin looked up at me, his face streaked with spaghetti sauce.

While I walked Justin down the hallway, I could still hear Dad say, "West Bank. You know with Iran and Iraq…the whole problem with Kuwait, well they refused to raise the price of oil above $9. Well, Iraq needed to raise the price, so they burned Kuwait's oil. The King of Jordan said he won't help Kuwait…not go against another brother…Hezbollah is not about religion or land…Ishmael's sons are terrorists…Ishmael from the Bible…born to go to hell."

After putting Justin to sleep, I hurried back to the dining room to see what I had missed. Keith looked annoyed, and Dad was back on the topic of religion.

His thoughts were jumbled and spilled out like a mess upon the table. "I enjoin you to do the sheet while there is still time…I can sense evil people…Long time to get off the sleeping pills, almost did me in…Hilda, I know she was fooling around on me…I know things… I have been praying since 1999 for a wife. I have to be patient…don't try to prevent…don't try to make it happen. Let God take care of it."

I grabbed Keith's beer and took a gulp.

Keith opened his mouth and spoke for what seemed like the first time this evening. "So, Dad…I've been here for over an hour. Are you going to ask me how I'm doing? Do you even care?"

I took another swig from Keith's beer.

Dad stared at Keith for a moment. "Well, if you do that sheet of paper and get saved, I will know how you'll be doing. Stop being so stubborn."

Keith narrowed his eyes which seemed to light with fire. "Oh, really? That's fucked up. What about all the shit you did to me when I was living with you? Are you going to apologize for that? Yeah, I didn't think so."

I thought about trying to quell the situation, but realized my efforts would be futile.

Keith raised his voice. "There's a lot you don't know about me. While you're off living in your delusional world, you're fucking missing out on your family's lives."

Dad thought for a moment. He stood up and paced across the dining and living rooms. "Keith, Daddy knows things. You don't know what you're talking about. Daddy knows…God tells me things…I am a prophet."

Keith stood up. "You are not a prophet! You're fucking delusional! That's right, I said it, you're crazy!"

Keith followed Dad who was now pacing across my hallway.

I winced as screams erupted between Keith and Dad. I felt for sure the police would show up any minute. I was surprised Justin, behind his closed door, was sleeping through this. I grabbed the phone and dialed Jackie's number.

"Jackie? It's Amanda," I whispered. I curled up at the end of my couch to watch the fireworks display. Jackie could hear the yelling in the background. "I tried to stop them. When Keith gets angry, he yells a bunch of shit and doesn't remember what he says after the fact." I filled her in on the preceding conversation and gave her a detailed play-by-play of the action. I repeated every obscenity and word I heard. "I swear, Jackie, it's like a Jerry Springer show in here right now. I'm sure my neighbors are going to call the cops on us."

While still pacing in the hallway, Dad raised his arms over his head, and clasped them behind the back of his head. He rubbed his shaved head, but gave Keith no response.

Keith followed him, screaming and trying to get a reaction. He stopped and stared Dad in the face.

"Look at me!" Keith yelled. "You know what? I'm gay. That's right, you heard me. Your only son is gay. How does that feel?"

My jaw dropped as Keith threw that information at Dad. I didn't expect that admission.

Keith stood in front of me. He looked down at me. "I told you this wasn't a good idea. I need to go home."

Down the hallway, Dad, lost in thought, stroked his shaved head, and continued to wear down a trail in the carpet.

Keith never did get a reaction out of him.

CHAPTER THIRTY-NINE

OCTOBER 2002: DANGER

"I TOLD YOU NOT to preach to my neighbors." I set the grocery bags on the kitchen counter.

"This is my job. I will not deny God," Dad said.

I rolled my eyes. He believed he was a prophet. I did not.

Changing the topic, I said, "So, did you straighten out all of your tax problems with the IRS and the Illinois, California, and West Virginia tax boards?"

"God has taken care of it for me. I gave a good testimony over the phone to a woman with the IRS." Dad grinned.

I placed a pot of water on the stove to boil. "So, is everything settled?"

"They tried to double charge me for the taxes, their mistake, not mine. I took care of everything, all the penalties and taxes before I left the United States on December 31, 1999."

It amazed me how capable Dad was at handling things rationally sometimes. At other times, he was completely irrational like when it came to blowing his life savings, stranding my stepmom in West Virginia, his hallucinations, and his paranoid delusions.

Surprisingly, most people who spoke with Dad had no inclination he was off his rocker. Most assumed he was simply a religious zealot. But with all of his dirty and racial jokes, his eruptive anger, and his inability to keep himself from being homeless, I highly doubted he could *really* be some rare prophet-of-God.

I waved a paper in front of him. "Well, your birth certificate is probably in this envelope." I handed Dad the letter from Jackie. "So, when do you want to go down to the social security office and the DMV to get your new ID?" With his wallets constantly getting stolen on the streets, Dad was continually replacing his identification. While in Chicago, his dad helped him to obtain new identification cards; now, it had become his kids' job to do so.

Dad opened the envelope. "We can go as soon as possible. I can get a bus pass. My work around here is almost done. With a bus pass, I can go to new places to give out my writing." He raised his eyebrows. "Are you sure I can't go to your job with you? You're really doing a disservice to your coworkers in not allowing me to go." As unreal as his argument was, it felt like a "Dad" lecture.

"Absolutely not." I refused to tell Dad where I worked for fear he would come and disturb me. I could just see it now: Isabelle and my manager facetiously referring to me as the prophet's daughter.

"What's for dinner?" Dad asked.

"Spaghetti and salad." This seemed to be the regular menu item around here: cheap and tasty. "Don't you like spaghetti?"

"Yes," he replied absently.

Noodles drained in the colander. Steaming red sauce sat in a ceramic serving bowl nearby. Justin sat in his booster seat at the end of the dining room table, next to his grandpa; both were hungry. I had to use the restroom before serving up the plates.

I was washing my hands when I heard Justin's screams and subsequent bawling. I darted down the hallway.

His cheeks damp with tears, Justin stuck out his lower lip. His cries died down to sniffles upon seeing me.

"What happened?"

Dad's face twisted into a scowl. He pointed accusingly at Justin. His voice shook in anger. "It's all *his* fault."

Justin whimpered. "Mo-mmy, I didn't do it."

"Do what?" I squatted beside my sad little angel. "What happened, sweetie?"

"He spilled water across the table." Dad lunged off his chair at wide-eyed Justin.

"Seriously, *water?* Dad. Leave my son alone. You're being ridiculous." With a couple of swipes, paper towels soaked up the evidence.

Dad sulked back into his chair.

Justin sniffled. I felt terrible for him. After I placed a plate in front of him, I served Dad. Holding his plate in my hands, I poured spaghetti sauce on top of the noodles.

"Mommy, I didn't do it," Justin whined. "Grandpa spilled the water. I didn't do it. I was just sitting here."

Before I could say anything, Dad jumped up. His voice rose to a fever pitch. "It's *his* fault. He talked and *made* me spill the water. Kids need to learn to keep their damn mouths shut." He raised the back of his hand at Justin, who slinked back in fear.

I was shocked. Dad never hit any of us as children. "Don't you *dare* speak to my son that way. I will tell him what he can and can't say. That is not your place or you can just leave."

"He needs to respect me and keep his mouth shut. If you aren't going to teach him how to behave…." Dad got dangerously close to Justin whose little eyes stared up at me helplessly.

Without a second thought, I flung my Dad's plate of spaghetti into the sink. It slammed against the white porcelain. Miraculously, it didn't break, but red sauce splattered across the white countertop. I turned and glared at Dad. Grinding my teeth, I growled. "That's it."

"Oh? Just like your mother, huh?"

A bitter memory flashed to mind: Mom threatening to throw a pot of boiling spaghetti at Dad while I, at the age of four, stood by in his defense.

I couldn't believe his provocation. "How dare you?" Adrenaline pumped through my veins. "Get away from me. Now."

Dad must've have seen hell reflecting in my eyes as he took a step backward.

"Go to Justin's room, now," I yelled. "We need to talk."

Dad moped down the hallway.

Like a mommy bird, I swooped down and wrapped my arms around Justin. "Honey, look at me." I placed a finger under his chin. "I'm not mad at you. You didn't do anything wrong. I love you very much. Do you understand?"

Justin's lower lip quivered. "But, Grandpa said—"

"Never mind what Grandpa said. I want you to know something. You know how sometimes you get a cold and get sick?" I tried to break it down for my five-year-old. "Well, Grandpa's sick in the head. He doesn't mean to say or do the things he does. He says those crazy things because he's sick in the head."

Justin perked up a bit.

I brushed his hair behind his ear. "He shouldn't have said anything to you. This wasn't your fault, Honey. Can you finish eating while I go talk to Grandpa?"

"Okay, Mommy." He gave me a kiss.

After calming Justin, I went to deal with the instigator. Mentally preparing to deal with a screaming lunatic, I wondered whether it would be safe to allow him to remain in my house, especially since he was sharing a bunk bed in Justin's room. I quietly shut the door behind me.

"Dad, you can't yell at Justin."

With his head bowed down, Dad paced back and forth.

"He's my son, not yours. I don't ever want to hear you scream at him like that. Do you understand? You will never yell at him again."

To my surprise, he nodded. "Daddy's sor-ry. You're right. You're his mom."

There went his third person references again. But at least, he calmed down and the friendly face I'd loved my entire life reappeared. For that reason, I blindly trusted him. I believed—much like Hilda—that my dad was still there, the old dad. I couldn't yet accept that mental illness had completely claimed his mind.

Bedtime drew near. Justin raised his arms, so I could slip his pajama top on.

Dad entered the bedroom.

Justin innocently stared up at his grandpa and asked, "Are you sick in the head, Grandpa?"

My eyes widened. I was mortified.

Dad tilted his head. "What did you say?"

I squeezed Justin's shoulders, hoping he would take the hint. "Nothing, Dad. Are you ready for bed?"

I endured another long week at work and another stressful evening at home arguing with Dad. He had a way of slinking under my skin. Sometimes I could handle his forceful preaching, but not tonight. Tonight was the last straw.

"Stop it," I said. "You're not a prophet of God. You're delusional."

"Amanda, you're stubborn, you know that?" he rebuked. "You don't know what daddy knows. I see people, when they are hell-bound, while they are still alive. I've seen my dad hell-bound—standing there—still in the sky. I saw fire in the vision, burning under his feet—all because he was angry and didn't want to hear about God. I've seen it in my mom, Jackie, Neil, and Hilda. Keith has reduced himself to a speck of dust. They won't see and believe the truth. You know what? Justin had a dream; he told me, 'There's a fire under Mommy's bed.' You know what that means? Those are the angels of fire. God is revealing how close you are to being lost."

"What are you talking about? Fire under my bed?" I was horrified because I knew those words would never have come from Justin's mouth without help from my dad. "What have you been saying to Justin?"

"You need to accept that sheet of paper. I'm telling you, before it's too late."

"Don't you dare preach to Justin, do you understand me? I'm tired of this shit." I stared into his eyes.

Dad's face made me sad. I felt like a little girl again. Here was my dad, the one who pushed me higher on the swings, the one who patiently taught me to play chess, the one who gave me a kiss and hug goodnight each night. And now here was my dad, completely out of his mind. I couldn't grapple with this new reality.

"Dad, this is ridiculous," I said. "While you've been off in your own little imaginary world, you have no idea what I've been through. You don't know how hard things have been for me. Where were you when I needed you? Somewhere across the world, pretending to be a prophet? Get real."

Mourning the loss of Dad, I was too hurt to do anything but yell at him, even though on some level I knew the mental illness wasn't his fault.

The argument escalated as we exchanged hurtful words. His were masked under the guise of prophecy; mine were blunt. It felt good to get everything off my chest that for fear of hurting his feelings, I had kept inside. On the other hand, my heart ached. I felt so sorry for him. I wasn't yet ready to say goodbye to my daddy. I wanted to hang onto him before he slipped through my fingers like sand, but he was becoming an increasingly unpredictable storm.

I didn't want to accept it. Dad was disappearing.

CHAPTER FORTY

NOVEMBER 2002: MANIPULATION

SINCE DAD SEEMED TO have gotten over the shock of his only son's sexual orientation, I invited Keith's partner Abe to dinner.

Keith prepped Abe ahead of time about Dad's past and recent mental health status; he felt he was prepared for whatever form of crazy Dad would present. During dinner, Justin, Keith, and I were quiet, unusual since we were never short on words.

Dad rambled on about churches and faith. "So, Abe, what religion are you?"

Abe glanced at Keith for a moment and swallowed his food. "Well, I was raised as an Adventist."

Keith clenched his fist around his fork.

"Has Keith shown you my writings?" Abe shook his head. Dad took that as the green light to advance his personal beliefs.

Keith tapped his foot against the floor.

After dinner, I unfolded the blue sleeper sofa in the living room for Keith and Abe. Late at night, we all got ready for bed.

Keith turned to Abe, "So, what did you think?"

Abe paused, choosing his words carefully. "Well, your dad seemed nice. He rambled on about religion too much. Other than that, he seemed normal. I didn't get the crazy vibe."

"He isn't normal," Keith said. "He's just good at fooling others."

"Yeah," I said. "People have to really know Dad to realize he's not just some religious zealot, but that he's out of his mind."

I was exhausted. I think the anticipation and worry over how well Dad would receive Abe was more stressful than the actual evening. I tucked Justin in before I went to my room and fell into a deep sleep. Drifting in and out of consciousness, I heard whispers blending into my dreams. I strained to hear the voices and was able to distinguish Dad's muffled words. I opened my eyes. The room was dark. Nothing stirred.

I heard the whispering again. I quietly sat up in bed. A crack of light came from underneath the bathroom door; my condo only had a single bathroom, accessible from either my bedroom or the hallway. I tip-toed over and held my ear to the door.

Dad was whispering.

"Yes, I need you to send the money as soon as possible, so I can get out of here."

Incredulous, I listened on.

"Amanda's taking my money. She's only after my money."

My body warmed as anger took hold of me. Did Dad really say that horrible lie to someone on the phone? The same dad I had graciously taken into my home and provided with meals, clothes, and a bed to sleep on? It's true he had contributed a small amount towards the food and rent, since he started receiving pension checks, but it didn't come close to what I had paid for his care. I used some of the money to buy his bus pass and to take him out. I never stole money from him, nor did I ever intend to do so. I thought for a moment, trying to untangle sleep from my nightmarish reality: Dad had been manipulating me.

I inched over to my desk, fumbling in the dark for the phone. I glanced over at the clock, but since my contact lenses, which I slept in, were blurry, I could only estimate the time, either four or five o'clock in the morning. Gently, I lifted the receiver and listened.

"Joseph, I don't know. Your father and I are tired of this."

I recognized my grandma's voice. Even though Dad was her only child and I was only her grandchild, I felt intensely protective toward her. I didn't want Dad to swindle money from my vulnerable grandparents. They were retired and not completely in good health.

Dad whispered, "It's true. She took my money. I need you to send the check today. When I get it, I can leave. I can't trust Amanda. She's stealing."

Something inside me snapped. Over the previous six years, I had held nothing but love for Dad, sorrow over the mental illness that had taken hold of him, and hope that one day he would return to normal. I had been the only family member, besides his parents, able to maintain contact with him. My patience was strong even when it pained me. And though I was struggling financially and potentially putting my son in danger, I had taken Dad off the streets to live with me. And for what? What did I have to show for all it? Dad was as paranoid and delusional as ever, with no end in sight to this madness.

I had mistakenly believed Dad could conquer the mental illness on his own. I had been wrong. In this moment of realization, I was overcome with hopelessness and despair. I lost control. Pent-up pain of hearing about Dad on the verge of death by suicide, of knowing he had been committed to mental hospitals, of watching him abandon Hilda, Jackie, Keith, and me—exploded and turned to anger. Anger at Dad. At the world. At God. I was losing my faith.

My sense of reason and sensibility evaporated. I jumped into the phone conversation head first, without care for what profanities would escape. Hysterical, I yelled, "That's *bullshit!* Don't tell Grandma fucking *lies* about me. I never stole any of your damn money."

My grandma stuttered. "Uh…uh…Joseph, don't, don't call me anymore." She hung up.

Dad flung open the bathroom door and stormed out in a fit of rage.

I rushed into the hallway, flicked on the light, and confronted him. "What the *hell* are you doing?" I demanded. "Why are you lying to Grandma about me?"

"You shouldn't have gotten on *my* phone call. I know what you're up to."

My chest heaved. "I think it's time for you to go."

As if he had a multiple personality, Dad's tone softened. He kindly asked, "You wouldn't kick out your dad, would you? At least let your father take a shower first."

"No." I wasn't buying any of his manipulative bullshit anymore. I stood there, blocking him from going back into the bathroom. "You need to leave my house, now."

Dad took a different approach. He whined, "Would you really throw your dad out onto the streets? In the cold?"

"Yes, I would. Since you were secretly planning on leaving anyway, you might as well get out now." I stared at him. "I can't believe you. I tried to help you out...and this is the thanks I get? Get . . . out."

In a split second, his demeanor changed. Like a savage beast, he lunged at me. He tried to grab hold of my arms to push me out of the way.

I backed up.

He stepped forward and raised his hand.

I was shocked. This was not the dad I knew and loved.

I held my ground. "Don't you hit me. Don't you *dare* try to hit me in my house. Go ahead and raise your hand to me . . . I'll throw you through the window."

Justin, awakened by the commotion, stumbled out of his bedroom.

Afraid for his safety, I pushed Justin into my bedroom. "Just stay in there. Go lie in my bed and wait for me."

Poor sleepy-eyed Justin was so confused that he willingly complied.

I shut the door and turned my attention back to Dad. "Get your things and get out of my house."

Dad tried to work on my sympathy. "I need to use the phone....I need to make a call...You wouldn't put your poor Dad out in the streets without any money, would you?"

I flatly responded, "Yes, I would. Leave."

"Will you at least give me some money?" Dad eyed me suspiciously.

"No." With my arms folded across my chest, I stood watch in the hallway while Dad gathered up his belongings and placed them into his small, blue back pack. He left a jacket and some pants, which I tried to hand to him. He refused to take them.

Abe, warmly snuggled under the covers, awoke to yelling. He raised his head off the pillow and saw the hallway light was on. Surprised that Keith was sleeping through the noise, he nudged him awake.

Abe whispered, "Hey Keith, listen." The shouting lowered several decibels. Abe tried to make out the words. "Your dad said he had to make a phone call, something about money. Amanda told him to leave." No response from Keith. Abe felt uncomfortable. He thought, should I say something? Keith's not getting up to say anything.

In the darkness, Abe peered out over the blanket. He saw me and Dad walking to the front door which was only a few feet away from the sleeper sofa where he and Keith slept.

I unlocked the door and stood by, motioning Dad to step outside.

Standing on the doormat, Dad turned and proclaimed, "You're going to hell."

I raised an eyebrow. "Fine. I'll see you there." I slammed the door in his face, locked it, and whirled around.

Abe and Keith, lying in bed, had their eyes on me.

"I forgot you two were here." I looked at my brother. "Keith, why didn't you do something? Didn't you hear what was going on?"

"Yeah, I heard the yelling back and forth."

"Why didn't you help me?"

"I didn't have to get involved. You took care of it." Keith rubbed his eyes and sat up.

"Oh my God," Abe said. "Is this really happening?"

Keith didn't respond.

"What the fuck is going on?" Abe said. "Amanda just threw her own dad out."

Keith shrugged. "Dad finally pushed his crazy limit. Amanda was pissed because she was trying to help him out."

"And this doesn't bother you at all?"

"I think it's always funny to see people fight."

Abe's jaw dropped.

Concerned, I opened the door and peered down the stairs. I turned to Keith. "How far do you think Dad went?"

"Dunno."

"Should we go after him?"

Keith yawned. "No, it's fine, he's homeless. He's lived on the streets for a long time; he'll be fine." He lay down and closed his eyes.

"Are you okay?" I looked at Abe.

Abe' eyes opened wide. "Uh, I guess so, but that was fucking insane."

"Sorry, I forgot you two were spending the night."

Abe shook his head. "I'm in shock all this is happening. I mean, *nothing* like this has ever happened in my family."

"I guess we've gotten used to it," I said.

Keith lightly snored.

"He's sleeping!" Abe exclaimed. "This is awkward."

"Yeah," I said. "I'm sorry. I'll leave you two alone, so you can go back to sleep, too."

Abe laughed nervously. "I don't think so. There's no way I can go back to sleep now."

I knew I couldn't either. Not with the thought of Dad back on the streets.

CHAPTER FORTY-ONE

2002-2004: BITTER END

AFTER THAT HORRID NIGHT, I apologized to my grandma for my cussing. She conveyed her anguish over Dad's illness. I wanted to help, but friendship was all I could offer.

During our weekly phone calls, I learned more about Dad's childhood and grew closer to Grandma. I played piano for her over the phone. One day, I played two pieces by Beethoven—both of which were my favorites.

Grandma cried.

"Are you okay?" I asked. "What's wrong?"

"*Für Elise* and *The Moonlight Sonata*. Your father used to play those when he was a child."

I empathized with her pain.

Three months later, I received an e-mail from "ginas dad" with the subject line: ***IMPORTANT MESSAGE FROM YOUR FATHER (JUSTIN'S GRANDFATHER) ***. He wrote:

This is your father!!!!!!!

I tried to phone you with my phone card, and I dialed the correct phone number, but you denied being Amanda. I should have identified myself as your father because you sounded very nervous and anxious, even tormented and in great fear. Is someone stalking you? Amanda, I can take you out of all your torments and you and Justin will be safe with me and can get the peace and joy of the Lord in you. Please let me know you got this e-mail.

I am sorry for the last communication being very strong about all the dreams and visions and revelations, but God forbid I don't speak the words that God has put in my mouth.... I am not here to destroy your life; I am here to save it....

Also, please give me the phone number of your mother ... God has given me the gift of healing. If I put my hand on her head in the name of Lord Jesus Christ, the Son of God, she will be healed if she believes in God and the Lord Jesus Christ, Son of the living God, and that I was ordained and sanctified a true prophet of God I love you very much Amanda. Please write as soon as possible. Hold on—help is on the way!

Dad couldn't phone me, because he interposed my phone number with my grandma's. Unaware of his error, his paranoia snowballed. What would have been simply a wrong number to most people became the source of an acute panic attack for Dad.

More importantly, Dad said he loved me, which meant more than it ever had. A part of the dad I cherished was still there, somewhere deep inside.

Communication between us ensued. Dad continually changed his e-mail alias. He moved around from Florida to New York City to Chicago and back. I didn't know how he was getting the money to travel.

One day, Dad confided the emotions he experienced when he became ill in 1999:

It is now 7:20pm in Orlando, Florida. Before being "saved" ("born again"): anxiety, depression, fear of death, living fearfully, easily worried, easily scared, easily provoked, little sleep, problems in soul, mind, body, relationships, led my children to copy my unproductive ways and thoughts which tended to death and the torments of the pit of hell, and the lake of fire and brimstone (don't you know, God and Lord Jesus speak in parables).

After being "saved" ("born again") and I must say the change came slowly...:

I know that I know that I will live forever with everlasting joy with my Lord and Father and... no more death, pain, sorrow, worry, fear, depression, guilt, evil, sin, in this world=the present time=... knowing that death is a promotion (a dead man and a sleeping man know nothing, and dying in Christ is just like sleeping...and I will awake to be with Lord Jesus... and it will be as if no time passed!!!—WOW!!!!!!!) ... free from the fear of evil, sleep and eat and live with great peace and joy—life can be so sweet, on the sunny (with the Son of God) side of the street, not easily provoked ... healed in my soul and mind and heart and body and relationships... and so much more.

Not mo' money: mo' Jesus!!!

God and Lord Jesus and the Holy Ghost told me to tell you to come on over to our side: don't worry, be happy. They'll leave the Light on for you.

Bye! (John 1)

For the first time—it only took him four years—Dad also sent an apology to Hilda:

Tell her I am sorry and regret and repent of discarding her stuff in 1999. That was not right and was not loving your neighbor. And tell her I have prayed that she can get what she needs in God's way, through Christ Jesus, that she may be able to conduct all business and money and travel matters without a problem...

This renewed my hope that the mental illness had not completely taken over his brain. Maybe Dad might still recover.

I emailed him photographs in the hopes of drawing his interest back to the family he had abandoned. He enjoyed the pictures but continued to delete everything because of paranoia.

Dad used calling cards to call me. When it was him the caller ID read "unavailable" or a pay phone number.

Throughout our talks, Dad maintained a sense of humor. We'd share jokes. Nine times out of ten though, Dad's jokes were downright dirty. I'd ask him to stop sharing them.

Although Dad tried to "force" his religion on me, our relationship had improved. I would listen to him, tongue-in-cheek, and would gently tell him when enough was enough ("Dad, I'm tired," or "Dad, sorry, but I have to go now."). He told me how we were all still going to hell unless we heeded his warnings and messages.

Hilda was happy Dad was alive, but heartbroken he wouldn't return. Keith felt ambivalent towards him. After she moved, Jackie didn't let Dad have any of her contact information since his mental state was too unpredictable for her. Dad had lost all sense of boundaries. I maintained an open line of communication with him to keep him company, but sometimes he called and e-mailed me nonstop, and wouldn't get off the phone. It required patience to maintain a relationship.

Grandpa paid for and convinced Dad to move into a studio apartment in Northern Chicago, a few blocks west of Lake Michigan. On the second floor, it had windows overlooking the tree-lined one-way street.

Dad said, "On August 19, 2003, exactly seven years to the date of my operation on August 19, 1996, God has restored me off of the streets. My dad said, 'If it wasn't for your mom, you could've stayed with me in the condo and used the car.' But he doesn't want to hear about religion." He talked to me for hours on end about the squirrels, birds, and cute bunny rabbits he saw from his window.

Things were going well between us until December 10, 2003 when Dad told me to repent, believe his writings, and get baptized to be saved, and maybe God would send me a "saved husband."

Not understanding schizophrenia, anosognosia or severe mental illness, I wrote:

Dad,

Do me a favor and don't mail me anything religious, it makes me turn less religious with every annoying word you write about it.

Who cares about a "saved" husband, I don't need that. Oh, one more thing, you are not a prophet so please quit the delusional lies you are telling yourself and others.

I still love you though and always will because you are still my dad.

Dad cut off communication with me again.

Knowing what I know now, I would not have created a rift between us but would have used our relationship as an asset to possibly get him into treatment. Speaking out of anger and laying blame for things beyond someone's control does not help the situation.

In March 2004, Grandpa suffered a major stroke. I was teaching in my classroom when I got the call. Overwhelmed with the news, I didn't know how to react. Even though Grandma urged us not to worry ourselves, Jackie, Keith, and I booked flights out to Chicago. Hilda flew out from West Virginia to help Grandma until they could find a suitable caretaker for her, since Grandpa had been taking care of her.

Our visit ended up being to the cemetery, not the hospital. Grandpa never regained consciousness and died within days.

I thought of Dad, their only child. I felt sorry Grandpa left this world knowing his son was not the same son he had raised.

Keith and I spoke on the way to our hotel.

"Do you think Dad knows about his dad?" I asked.

"Do you think it would matter to him if he did know?" Keith said.

"He told me that his father was his best-friend, though." I turned to stare at my reflection in the window. I felt older than the child-like image that looked back at me.

For the first time in over ten years, we visited Grandma. Since she was agoraphobic, Grandma never traveled.

She only permitted Jackie, Keith, and me in her condo for a few hours before she said, "I didn't want you children to see me this way."

In actuality, I was a bit surprised to find that her ailing physical condition didn't match her lucid mental condition which I had come to appreciate through our calls.

Grandma woefully mourned the loss of her husband of over sixty years. She lost the will to live and I could tell it in her voice. She didn't want to talk much on the phone anymore.

In early May, Grandma was hospitalized. The doctors estimated she had a few months to live. Without her husband or her son to live for, Grandma constantly tore the IV tubes out of her arms and refused treatment.

On May 15, 2004, she passed away.

Grandma had made up her mind to die.

As Jackie relayed the funeral, flight, hotel, and car arrangements which were already underway, my mind drifted to Dad: did he know his mom was dead, too? I missed Grandma for the both of us. Having gotten the opportunity to develop the close relationship I had with Grandma was probably the only good thing that came out of Dad's illness.

Dad's presence was noticeably missing from both of his parents' funerals in Chicago. Even though Jackie, Keith, and I didn't speak Yiddish, we lead the *kaddish*, a Jewish prayer for the dead, which should have been Dad's duty. What's more, we designed their tombstones, which also should have been Dad's duty.

We later found out that the week before Grandpa's stroke, my grandparents had made an appointment with Dad's cousin Laurie and her husband, both attorneys. My grandparents finally decided that, with Dad's mental state, they needed to take precautions to ensure Dad wouldn't inherit a large sum of money, spend it like he did with his own retirement money, and end up homeless again.

Most of the arrangements for their estate had been settled before Grandpa's death. Unfortunately, there were a few papers that hadn't been signed. Throughout Grandma's stay in the hospital, Laurie kept nudging Grandma to sign. Grandma, unmotivated by life anymore, repeatedly sent her away.

At last, Laurie convinced Grandma it was time to sign the final paperwork regarding her estate. Grandma died hours later.

These signatures prevented Dad from being able to blow through the money overnight. A trust had been set up so that Dad's financial interests would be protected and controlled by a bank. Our grandparents left their personal belongings to us grandkids.

Going through their things, their shelves of antique vases, their walls of collectable paintings, their drawers of rare coins, and their fine china and statuettes was a surreal experience. Sorting through the antiques they had collected, we were unable to find the things we wanted most: photographs. A few black and white photos of Grandpa during his time as a high school science teacher and two photos of Grandpa's parents was all we could find

I wondered if Dad had destroyed the other photos during a visit with his parents.

Throughout the house we found small private notes written between my grandparents. "I'm sorry. I promise I won't give Joey anymore money," was scribbled across one. We found a letter from Dad, informing his parents they could each, "legally gift as much as $10,000 per year without any taxable event occurring."

The more papers we went through, the more we realized Dad had been leeching money from our grandparents for years. My spirit sank.

CHAPTER FORTY-TWO

AUGUST - NOVEMBER 2004:
SAFARI ON THE STREETS

ON AUGUST 5, 2004, DAD contacted me. He used the e-mail alias "yodaddynotyomomma." In his letter, he made no mention of Grandma's death. He did write: "My father, (your grandfather, Justin's great-grandfather) died in March shortly after suffering a stroke."

I knew Dad's cousin Laurie was trying to get hold of him so my grandparents' will could be fully executed and their estate settled. I responded to Dad's e-mail with a request I knew he wouldn't turn down, "I have some information about some money for you." I offered my condolences about Grandpa and gave him my home phone number.

Dad phoned the next day.

Part-way through the call, he said, "You know, both of my parents are dead."

"Yes, I know. It's really sad."

"Dad was hell-bound. I saw him standing there, still in the sky. There was fire in the vision, burning under his feet. It's because he got angry and didn't want to hear about God. I've seen that in my dad, and my mom. The warning sign happened to my dad, but it was too late, he wouldn't accept the sheet of paper."

I was surprised at Dad's callousness. "Did you get to visit them before they died? I hope you didn't say any of that to Grandma."

"I saw my mom in the hospital. Of course I told her. She was too damn stubborn to accept God, so she's damned. And I told her so."

I couldn't believe Dad cursed Grandma on her death bed. I only hoped my grandparents could finally rest in peace. That thought was my only comfort when I heard Dad speak heartlessly about the two people who loved him most in this world and gave up so much for him.

Since coming into some money from his parents, Dad did more traveling, a fact indicated by the postcards I received. A package postmarked August 26th contained a CD of *The Best Worship Songs of the 90s* which I shoved back into the envelope it came in and filed it away under my "Dad" file.

Dad invited Justin and me to visit him. I really missed him but wasn't about to subject Justin to Dad's unpredictable, angry outbursts, so I went alone.

We agreed I would fly to Chicago on the 1st of November. Dad told me we would be visiting New York City and Fort Lauderdale, Florida, as well.

From August through October, Dad sent me numerous packages, letters, and e-mails. He sent me copies of *The Onion*, the Chicago public transportation map, the NYC Subway map, as well as the "Official NYC Guide." I was shocked when Dad mailed a shirt to Justin for his birthday in October. Dad made it clear he wasn't celebrating birthdays or holidays because of his personal religious beliefs, but I knew the shirt was a birthday gift.

On October 13th, he sent me an e-mail which almost ruined things:

I am NOT going to eat (a commandment of God through Lord Jesus via the Holy Ghost) at the IHOP anymore. It is in "boys town." They are all homosexuals = queers = faggots = putos (Spanish) = gays and lesbians = dikes. I let it be known I work for God and Jesus on the streets of the world and did not preach but was loving and friendly and always left a large tip knowing that waiters and waitresses depend on tips and, even with that aren't doing well. But after, with love and without condemnation, I gave them my twelve-page packet, some of their attitudes changed. Generally, they changed to force me to ask for the bill after I was done eating.

The KJV Holy Bible, in Proverbs 23 says not to eat where they give you the evil eye. I was hot inside about this. For love, they return evil, but the worst of it is despising the word of God (see KJV Holy Bible, Luke 10:16). So, I am not to company with those who will not repent or receive the truth or who do not love the word of God and Lord Jesus. I had hoped IHOP stood for "in heaven only peace," and that IS CERTAINLY true of the kingdom of God and Christ. But the Holy Ghost told me a perfect fit for IHOP is "in here only putos." See KJV Holy Bible, 2Corinthians 6:14-18.

God put another 24-hour IHOP before my eyes when riding the bus. I will NOT eat there before you come, but why eat at a corporate place? Let's go to those places not only unique to Chicago, but also a good sampling of the Chicago ethnic culture. So much of Chicago, as well as New York, and Fort Lauderdale and other cities and Toronto and Montreal and even the Arab countries are worse than Sodom and Gomorrah and their other sins are above those in the KJV Holy Bible and they have crossed the line a long time ago and are doing more wickedly each and every day. Help us! Come quickly, Lord Jesus!

I couldn't find a suitable cold weather coat for me at Target or Sears or Marshall Field's or Sportmart. God be willing, I will be led to other places. The weather is getting colder and the building has not yet made heat available. They are not required to until October 15.

When I have sadness and/or heaviness in my heart, God, in the name of Lord Jesus, puts a cute gray or black squirrel before me doing something cute, even a cuddly, gentle bunny rabbit.

In a speech in Colorado the other day, the Democratic vice-presidential running mate of John Kerry, John Edwards, said that the best way to improve the economy is to outsource George W. Bush. I thought that was funny. Did you find that funny?

Hoping to hear from you in writing at your earliest convenience. It is now about 7:30 PM Chicago time on the 13th day of the 10th month of the 4th year of the reign of President George W. Bush. I do not want to use the names for days and months, as they are heathen and derived from the names of false gods that have no breath or life in them and cannot do good and cannot do evil. I do not want to use the heathen year calendar either.

I had to contain my irritation in responding to his email. What could I say to someone as irrational as he?

Dad instructed me to buy a one-way ticket on ATA Airlines and fly from LAX into Midway Airport in downtown Chicago. It felt like a father-daughter relationship again, until he added that the Holy Ghost gave him our itinerary:

1. *Fly into Midway on Monday November 1ˢᵗ.*
2. *Dad will wait for me at the airport. Due to increased security, I should arrive at the airport ticket counter a full <u>four</u> hours before departure.*
3. *We would go to his studio apartment and see stuff, go to nightclubs, and listen to some of his ethnic rhythmic, melodic, & soulful CDs.*
4. *Stay in Chicago on November 1, 2, & 3.*
5. *Leave <u>early</u> on Thursday Nov. 4ᵗʰ from Midway to Ft. Lauderdale, FL.*
6. *On Friday, Nov. 5ᵗʰ, we fly to JFK Airport in NYC*
7. *On Nov. 9ᵗʰ or 10ᵗʰ, I am to fly from NYC-JFK to Long Beach, while Dad is to remain in NYC*
8. *God, via Holy Ghost, in the name of & through His Son, our Lord Jesus Christ says plans subject to change, but we are to meditate on the way!*

In late October, Dad informed me we would not go to Florida, because, as he wrote:

I have been <u>commanded</u> by the Holy Ghost (from God the Father, in the name of His Son, Lord Jesus) to tell you that we will <u>not</u> be going to Florida: <u>only</u> to <u>Chicago</u>, and then to <u>New York City</u>!!

On November 1, tired from the long plane flight, I rubbed my eyes as I exited the plane and followed the signs to baggage claim. I couldn't wait to find Dad. Mental illness or not, he had my love. I still offered him the same respect I gave him when I was younger, even though he wasn't the same.

I scanned the large room for a bald, white guy. All around me were men and women in winter jackets, hats, and scarves. Which one was Dad? I turned back to the carousal littered with mounds of luggage. I yanked my bag off the track. At a tap on my shoulder, I spun around and stared into

Dad's blue eyes. His face, a bit sunburned, had gathered a few more wrinkles since our last encounter in 2002, two years earlier.

Dad didn't say much. I hugged him hello and he motioned for me to follow him. As we neared the door to the outside, I sniffled and wiped underneath my nose with the back of my hand. My hand came away covered in bright red. No sooner had I raised tissue to my face than my nose started inexplicably gushing blood. I dropped my bag and Dad turned to see why I hadn't caught up with him. He went to the restroom to refill my dwindling tissue supply. He handed tissues to me, but showed no reaction to my condition.

This hurt. As hard as I tried to see my dad in this man, I couldn't help but realize how different he was from the dad who rushed me to urgent care over the slightest sore throat or fever when I was a child.

Several minutes later, and after what felt like several liters of blood loss, we stepped outside into the brisk evening air. Cold wind stung my face, whipped my hair into my eyes, and numbed my ears. Dad hailed a cab.

We arrived at the front door of Dad's apartment building and stepped out of the warm cab. Above me, round lights shone down from the building overhang.

Dad smiled and unlocked the lobby door. "At least they finally turned on the heat."

I grinned back through my chattering teeth. As we waited for the rickety elevator, Dad pointed out the mailboxes, the laundry room, and the door to the parking garage—not that he had a car to park.

After the short ride to the second floor, Dad took a right and stopped at the first door on the left. I followed, rolling my large bag behind me. Dad pointed down the hallway. "That's the manager's apartment. He lives there with his wife." He unlocked his door and led me onto the wooden flooring of his studio apartment. The small entryway opened up to a multi-purpose room.

I looked around the entire room—clean and barren, practically devoid of anything.

"Put your bags down," Dad instructed. "Let's go eat."

I couldn't have been happier when I heard those words.

I kept my cashmere coat, gloves, and hat on and wrapped my scarf around my neck as Dad and I stepped back out into the cold. We turned at the street corner and passed the first building. A rustling in the small alleyway between buildings to my right caught my attention. I turned my head in time to see a large rat scurrying alongside a dumpster.

"Dad, look at that huge rat."

Dad shook his head and kept walking.

"Did you see the size of that thing?"

Again, Dad ignored me and kept walking.

"That's not like the cute bunnies and squirrels you told me about on the phone."

Dad hid a smile. After walking several blocks, and taking a bus for part of the way, we found ourselves at an International House of Pancakes. I wondered if this was the same one Dad had written me about.

My feet were sore and I was exhausted by the time we returned to his apartment after 2:30 A.M. Dad had bought a new sleeping bag for me, along with a thin blue foam pad. Even when I camped in the wilderness, I allowed myself thicker padding. That minimal luxury of comfort would apparently not be mine during this visit.

Without any other option, I went to sleep on the floor in the sleeping bag Dad had prepared for me. I was only a few feet from his sleeping bag "bed."

Dawn broke the next day sending pale rays of light through the windows. I turned over, becoming twisted in my sleeping bag which slid easily across the slippery wooden floor. I fell back asleep.

"C'mon," Dad's voice roused me from my dreams.

I groaned.

"Get up. I've already been outside and come back while you're still sleeping."

My hip throbbed. It felt bruised from sleeping on the hard floor. I didn't feel rested at all. My stomach growled, reminding me breakfast was overdue. His kitchen didn't contain a single loaf of bread. I wondered what Dad ate.

"Can we go get breakfast?" I asked.

We left his apartment and he introduced me to his "friends." I met the Asian drycleaners, the Eastern European Internet guys, and the Hungarian girls at the nearby hotel. His Polish barber didn't speak a word of English. Everyone I met seemed to be surprised Dad actually had a real flesh-and-blood relative.

I was mad at myself for not making him stop so I could eat breakfast, but I was also surprised he wasn't feeling any hunger pangs.

We eventually ate lunch at a buffet near the barber. Afterward, he walked me through the stores, and insisted I get a travel toothbrush holder from a little convenience store. He was relieved to know my toothbrush had the proper place to ventilate during my trip.

I spotted a toy store. Inside, a revolving wooden rack held finger puppets. The gray and white fur of the little squirrel stood out. I have always had a "thing" for squirrels. In every state or country I visit, I capture a picture of a squirrel. I bought the puppet.

Dad preached to many people we passed by on the street. He started out commenting on the weather or something trivial. Within minutes, he asked if they were saved and had accepted Jesus as their savior. Most would either ignore him or nod their head to placate him. Dad would go into depth with his beliefs and offer them a sheet of paper, his religious teachings. He demanded they heed his warnings.

I resorted to childish methods to get his attention. As he and I continued down the sidewalk, I took the little squirrel puppet out of the bag and perched him on my finger tip. The squirrel jumped around in front of Dad's face. "Hello. How are you today, sir? Brr...sure is cold out."

Dad cracked a smile.

A few people crossed our path and exchanged strange glances in my direction.

Great. Now, I looked like the insane one.

Later on, we took a trip down memory lane. Dad showed me the apartment he lived in as a child. He walked me down the street to see his old high school where he claimed to have hit a ball on to the top of the roof. He showed me where he rode his bike and where the barking dog behind the fence taunted him as he rode quickly by. The dog was no longer there, but, according to Dad, the brick buildings pretty much looked the same.

On the way to our next stop, we found ourselves on a cold, deserted intersection, waiting for the next bus. Dad paced—either out of nervousness or to keep warm. He mumbled.

"Dad?"

He quieted me with a motion of his hand and continued to move his lips.

"When's the bus coming?" I shivered.

My question was met with silence. Another two minutes passed before I saw the bus at the end of the street heading in our direction.

"It came because I prayed for it to come," Dad said.

The next day, November 3, and two hours of sightseeing later, I still hadn't eaten breakfast, again. I didn't have the guts to stand up to him, partly because I was in a strange town and felt dependent upon his navigation. Every time I reminded Dad of my hunger, he agreed to let me eat and hopped on the next bus or train instead, either forgetting or ignoring my requests. My patience waned as my hunger pangs continued.

He spoke to every passerby donning a half-way friendly glance. No one was spared. A few pretended not to speak English. That didn't stop Dad from attempting to sermonize in whatever language they seemed to speak.

On the bus, Dad turned to face a plump middle-aged man with a bushy mustache.

"Good morning," Dad said.

The man opened up a newspaper and hid behind it. I'm sure he had heard Dad preach to three other people since we had gotten on the bus.

"*¿Hola, como esta?*" Dad asked in Spanish.

The man gave no indication he was listening.

Dad leaned over and squinted, trying to read a few words from the man's newspaper.

"*Guten morgen. Comment allez-vous? Jeden, dwa, trzy.*" Dad said good morning in German, how are you in French, and counted to three in Polish.

The man peered around the edge of his newspaper. With a raised eyebrow, he said, "*Turkce biliyor musun?*"

"Biraz." Dad rocked his head.

The man went back to reading his newspaper.

I leaned over. "What did he say?"

"He asked me if I spoke Turkish. I told him a little."

Dad remained quiet until our stop. I supposed he was irritated he didn't know enough Turkish to convert the man.

We spent the day sightseeing. Dad took me to the Hancock Tower and the Art Institute of Chicago. The stone lions standing guard in front of the building reminded me of my first trip to Chicago when I was only about four years old, when my dad was still my dad.

Everything about the architecture in Chicago was grand: the ornate edging, the statuettes, the sheer detail and massiveness of it all. Dad brought me to his favorite museum: the Museum of Science and Industry. We toured the coal mine, checked out the planes and trains, and enjoyed a dizzying experience inside the IMAX theatre.

By the afternoon, we were both wiped out. Dad directed me along a maze of buses and trains until we ended up at the end of the peninsula by the planetarium. He didn't take me there to observe the stars, but to gain a most breathtaking view of the Chicago skyline. We lay down for a bit on the grassy hillside until the sun crept lower towards the horizon.

After dinner we went to Navy Pier. I spotted a Build-A-Bear shop and coaxed Dad inside. I stuffed a lot of fluff inside a build-a-bear teddy bear to take back home as a souvenir for Justin, while Dad picked out a Chicago Cubs baseball outfit for "Cubby" to wear.

After stopping for a peek underneath a beautiful stone bridge resting atop the Chicago River, we headed back to Dad's apartment. It was almost 11:30 p.m.

Our evening didn't end there. We got into an argument regarding the validity of Dad's "religion."

"Can you please stop preaching to everyone?" I said. "It's really annoying."

"You're annoying." Dad held his manila envelope with his teachings in his hand. "I am a prophet of God. This is what I do."

"You're not a prophet," I said. The day had worn on me. I'd had enough.

Dad's eyes narrowed. He raised his voice and bellowed out some religious nonsense.

I stuck my fingers in my ears in defiance and chanted, "Lalalalala . . . I can't hear you . . . lalalalalala . . . I can't hear you...." And the truth was I couldn't.

Dad yelled back as I continued the charade. He got angrier, then couldn't help it; I was such an immature sight that he eventually broke down laughing.

"Stop it, Amanda. Stop it right now." He chuckled. "You're being childish."

"So are you."

The argument was over.

The next morning we visited Lincoln Park. Gray skies covered us as we perused the Lincoln Park Zoo. Dad led me to his favorite form of free entertainment: the Lincoln Park Conservatory, a heated greenhouse filled with nature's delights. As we meandered along the garden paths, Dad stopped to point out his favorite flowers and plants.

"Oh, look. Amanda, come here and smell this." Dad took off one of his black gloves and reached for a delicate white flower. Leaning in closer to the bush, he lost his balance and tumbled into the planter.

I erupted in laughter, bent down and held out my hand. "Are you okay, Dad?"

Dad took my arm and I pulled him out.

He brushed off his jeans. He bowed his head and walked by. Dad had become far too serious in the last couple of years. When he sat on a bench to rest, I snuggled next to him and took it as a challenge to cajole some good spirit out of him.

"C'mon, Dad. That was hilarious." I stood up, walked back to the bush, and reenacted his fall. "Look, who am I? Look at this pretty flower . . . ah! Help, I've fallen and I can't get up."

Dad shook his head. Tears of laughter filled his eyes. "I...I've lost my glove," Dad said between gasps for air.

I glanced into the planter. There, underneath the bush was his glove. "Look, Dad, it's like O.J. Simpson's black glove. The evidence is still there." I scooped up his glove.

Dad rocked back and forth, trying to suppress the laughter.

On our way out of the flower house, Dad pointed down at the ground. "See that little fern there? Touch it."

I shook my head. "No way. You touch it."

"Amanda, touch it."

"No, Dad. You touch it," I retorted in a juvenile manner. "I don't want to touch some strange fern."

"Amanda, I am telling you to do something. Touch it."

"No." I backed up purposely being silly to annoy him.

Dad lightly touched the edge of the fern and I watched as it curled up. "See, it's a sensitive fern."

"Well, I wouldn't want to hurt its feelings." I saw the tagline below the plant: 'Sensitive Fern.' Oh, Dad was being literal.

For dinner, we headed to another IHOP restaurant on the Southside of Chicago (we had now officially taken every color lines of the Chicago train system). Smaller than the one we had eaten at a couple of nights before, it had the distinct pitched blue roof. As we waited for the waitress to return with the check, the busboy came to clear the table.

"¿Hola, como estas?" Dad inquired.

"Bien, bien." The busboy evidently recognized Dad.

I zoned out and pretended not to hear as Dad lectured the busboy in Spanish. The young man politely nodded and left to the kitchen when the waitress came back. From the looks of things, they were closing up the place.

I sipped the rest of my ice water. Dad took out a handful of quarters from his pocket. He stacked them up and deliberately placed them in the form of a cross.

Cold air snapped at my face when the door opened. Since we had taken a cab there, I figured we would be taking a cab back. I assumed incorrectly. I looked in both directions, but my eyes only found dark emptiness. By now, I realized the pointlessness of harassing Dad over his plans. I followed his lead up the road. The further we got, the closer I walked to him.

"Dad, where are we?" I whispered. "Where are we going?"

Dad shook his head and pretended not to hear me.

Under a bridge, homeless people slept under mounds of dirty blankets on the ground. Some windows of buildings were boarded up; a few had bullet holes in them. I fought off discomfort. The street was eerily quiet. Where were all of the cars and traffic I had become used to seeing in Chicago? I shuddered.

"Dad, my feet hurt and I'm really tired."

Dad shrugged.

I wanted to sit down and sleep, but I felt this area wasn't the safest place to be in the middle of the night.

We came to a street corner with a bit of life. A couple of cars were stopped at the light. I watched in fascination as a haggard-looking man jumped in front of one of the cars with a spray bottle and a rag. He yelled at the driver, offering to clean their windows. The drivers were spared by the green.

Dad and I waited to cross the street, while a man with dirty dreadlocks and seemingly high on drugs harassed us for money.

"Hey, man, spare some money for ya' brother?" He got into Dad's face.

Dad shook his head no, and stared straight ahead.

"Hey man, don't ya got anything here for ya brother, huh?" The stranger got louder and more obnoxious.

I grabbed hold of Dad's arm. The walking sign lit up. We headed across the street.

Belligerent, the man pestered us, keeping time with our steps and jumping about. His request was now a demand. "I said, give me some money, brother. Did ya' hear me? Give me some money brother."

"You're not my brother," Dad said. "I don't have any money, man. Don't you understand? I ain't got nothing, man."

"Don't give me that bullshit. I said give me some fucking money."

I scanned the street for a way out of this escalating situation. I spotted a bar half a block up the street that appeared open. I thought about our chances of racing this would-be mugger. Fifty/fifty? Better than nothing.

Dad was now in an arguing match with this punk as I started speed-walking ahead of them.

Afraid the man might have a weapon, I didn't want to leave Dad behind. In a blur, I turned around to see Dad yelling in the same street language this man was speaking. Like heaven-sent, a cab drove up this lonely street. Dad hailed it. The cabbie promptly pulled to the side. Dad grabbed my arm and whisked me inside, slamming the door shut behind us.

"Drive!" Dad commanded and rattled off his address. The cabbie took off with the lunatic still screaming at us.

"Goddamn mother fucking asshole." The expletives roared out Dad's mouth.

I slunk back in my seat as he continued.

"Fucking mother fucker."

I flinched at his profanity and racial slurs. I looked at our driver and became even more uncomfortable. "Dad, it's okay."

He went right on. "Lazy fucking asshole needs to get a fucking job. I never did that bullshit in all my days on the streets. Never."

I curled into the corner and let my mind drift out the window.

When the cab pulled up to Dad's place, I happily jumped out. Dad had at least gotten it out of his system and remained relatively quiet on the way up the elevator.

Still upset, he left me in his apartment while he went downstairs to do his laundry.

My initial shock of the condition of his place had worn off.

His walk-in closet was empty except for a broom, dustpan, mop, and bucket. A few lonely hangers rested on the closet dowel. Dad had told me earlier not to touch the walls because white specks—of paint?—might come off of them.

In another closet, he kept his towels and sheets in two plastic bags on the floor, which he explained were to keep the bugs out and he was careful not to push them up against the wall. The only clothes I found were a jacket, a grey sweater, and two black turtlenecks. He bought an extra plastic hanger so I could hang up my coat.

The bathroom counter contained only a handful of items: lotion, powder, toothbrush and toothpaste, electric razor, and nail care items. I laughed at seeing Johnson & Johnson Baby Shampoo placed next to his bar of soap. What head of hair was Dad washing? He had already lectured me about cleaning out the drain, because he can't stand long hair clogging it up.

The only two windows were where Dad spent his time watching all the birds and squirrels he'd told me so much about. Bare, the windows lacked any covering other than the unused dingy rolled shades. The wooden floor in the main room only housed his sleeping bag and CDs stacked neatly in a pile next to his 'bed.' Each of the ten short piles lay organized according to genre: Greek, African, Gypsy, etc.

A simple Maplewood TV tray had the task of playing table. Next to that rested a short wooden stool and a two-step stool.

In his kitchen, all of the cabinets and drawers were empty. I opened the refrigerator. Empty space greeted me. I opened the freezer door: the same pristine emptiness. On the counter lay two stacks of manila envelopes— one stack stuffed with his "teachings" and the other stack of empty envelopes awaiting their turn to be stuffed.

On one paper towel-lined shelf, Dad had his socks and underwear; on another, he had extra hand soap, three tools, Windex, and spare rolls of paper towels and toilet paper; below that his Bible was placed on top of an opened ream of white printer paper, a phone book, and neatly stacked rows of quarters for the laundry.

Other than his metro card (bus and train pass), and a few hand-written notes, the rest of the apartment was bare.

I was tired. I squirmed into the nylon bag. I lay on my stomach for a bit before I turned onto my back, which ached after a short while. I settled onto my side. Instead of complaining, I reflected on the homeless years Dad spent sleeping in the cold of night on benches and the ground. My discomfort hardly matched his. I drifted off to sleep, thankful I hadn't gone through what Dad had.

CHAPTER FORTY-THREE

NOVEMBER 5-7, 2004:

PARTING IN NEW YORK CITY

EARLY ON NOVEMBER 5, 2004, with the darkness of night still upon us, Dad woke me.

I rubbed my eyes, trying to focus on his face. I couldn't separate his words from my dreams. "What?"

"Get up and pack your bags," Dad repeated. "We're leaving,"

I wanted to lie back down, but I complied without looking at the time. Half-asleep, I tucked my gloves into my coat pockets, and wheeled my luggage into the hallway.

At the train station, Dad didn't help me as I tried to shove my bag through the turnstile to get onto the L-train. I settled next to him on a plastic seat near the back of the car. My head and arms resting on top of my bag rocked and swayed back and forth with each clicking from the tracks. We switched trains and eventually arrived at O'Hare Airport. Again, I had difficulty maneuvering my luggage as I struggled not to roll over anyone's feet.

"Two one-way tickets to La Guardia," Dad told the agent.

The woman tapped at the keyboard.

Dad handed the agent cash. She gave him back his change and the tickets. We proceeded to the security lane.

I wasn't entirely surprised when Dad and I were directed to a separate screening area. I mean, one-way tickets, paid with cash…of course.

After a thorough screening, I laced up my shoes and followed Dad to our gate.

We landed at LaGuardia Airport in New York City. Since Dad only traveled with his backpack, he appeared a bit miffed at having to wait for my luggage at the baggage claim carousel. I lugged it off the conveyer belt and followed him.

We traveled with metro passes, like we did in Chicago. I used a credit card to purchase mine; Dad used cash as he didn't own a credit card.

One major difference between most Chicago train stations and most New York City train stations we went to: there weren't any escalators or elevators at the NYC stations. Dad's memory failed him momentarily as he led me down a few flights of stairs into a subway station. My bag made a loud thud as it dropped one step at a time. I struggled to keep it from going any faster and rolling me down underneath it.

At the bottom, I stopped to catch my breath.

Dad turned and said, "Uh, this is the wrong station. Go back up." He bounded up the stairs and quickly reached daylight at the top.

I wanted to cry. Instead, I grabbed a tight hold on the handle, and stepped up the stairs, backwards, one slow step at a time. I paused; my fingers felt like they were blistering underneath my gloves from the weight of the load. Switching hands, I continued hauling it up.

Dad looked impatiently down at me. "Hurry up."

Two young black men with bandanas over their heads walked down the stairs. The fellows caught sight of me and stared at this spectacle. Their eyes widened in disbelief as they glanced at Dad and back at me. I mustered an apologetic grin for Dad's rudeness. Evidently impressed at my efforts, they smiled as they passed by. I could hear them whispering to one another, "Damn. Do you see that? Damn. He ain't even helping her." Their laughter faded down into the corridor.

By the time I finally reached the top, I was out of breath. "Dad, why couldn't you help me?" I panted.

"I don't want to hurt my back," he said. "Don't pack so much. Look at me, I only carry this backpack." He smiled.

At that point, I had the desire to punch him.

After checking at the front desks of two hotels, we discovered a sporting event was in town and that most of the rooms were already booked for the night. The hotels with available rooms ridiculously raised prices for the occasion.

I couldn't take it anymore. In front of the large windows of one of the many skyscrapers, I dropped my bag to the ground. "Dad, I'm hungry. And tired. And cold. And my hands hurt from dragging this suitcase up and down subway stairs and in and out of subways."

"Quit whining," he said.

"No. No, I won't. *You* listen to *me*." My voice wavered as I raised it to a near scream.

People continued on their Friday morning walking commute. They tried to ignore our little scene, but I saw more than a few eyes glance curiously in our direction.

"I need to eat," I said. "And I'm sore. I won't keep going. Do you even have *any* idea where we're going?" I slumped onto the ground next to my bag. I felt weak and sick to my stomach. I couldn't understand how Dad was managing to keep going without eating.

By noon, we finally found a hotel, not far from Central Park. No sooner had I dropped off my bag into the room than I found myself sitting in a cab in horrid I-could-walk-faster traffic. Our stop: a Jewish delicatessen for some pastrami on rye. Dad offered me some bitter pickled veggies of some sort. I repeatedly declined.

We walked around police barricades on Central Park West. Apparently the city was preparing for a marathon. All I needed to prepare for was the cold. Dad showed me the view of the castle from Turtle Pond, but I didn't get to see the zoo. I snapped a few shots of Dad in black-and-white and sepia tones. One thing Dad still wasn't aware of: my camera had a flip out screen and camcorder abilities. I used this when he began one of his more unusual recollections as we passed by some beautiful purple, yellow, and red blooms.

"Daddy knows, from being on the street. He learned beautiful things from off the street. He remember the pretty things." He pointed out a formation of stacked boulders. "Look at this, you can walk right on top of this, you can eat a sandwich and bring something to drink."

"Where? Is that where you slept?"

"No, I never slept there. I came here to wash."

"You washed in this lake, over here?" I peered at the darkening reflection of the sky in the lake.

"No, there's a fountain here."

"Where?"

"Someplace here…I brushed my teeth, washed my underarms, took my shirt—"

"Where'd you sleep?"

"By the East River."

Oh my God, I thought. My dad really has been homeless all these years. It amazed me how matter-of-fact he was. His lack of reaction to this hard reality was indicative of his break from reality. His previous self would have never even spoken to a homeless person or someone in my dad's current state of mind.

After watching *The Day After Tomorrow* in the overpriced hotel room, Dad took me on an extended tour through Times Square, Grand Central Station, and by midnight, we were at Ground Zero. The massive pit was all that remained nearly three years after the terrorist attacks had brought down the twin towers.

In the city-that-never-sleeps, I learned it's also the city where you can always eat. At 1:30 a.m., Dad tried to persuade me to join him in enjoying some seasoned meats from a street vendor. I didn't understand how he could walk so far all day without eating and how he could eat so much all night.

By 2 AM, we finally headed back to the hotel. Maybe I'll get some better sleep, I thought to myself. I knew how likely that would be.

On November 6, we found ourselves standing in line behind what appeared to be an Amish tourist group going to the top of the Empire State Building. Once at the observation deck, the wind blew fiercely as I tried to steady the camera for my pictures. Dad told me how only a few weeks earlier, another jumper had fallen to his death. I reflected on this as we headed back down.

For lunch, Dad insisted we go to a restaurant near Spanish Harlem for some pizza with real mozzarella cheese. On the way there and back, I fended off cat calls from the local *Nuyorican* men. I shivered in cold discomfort.

Our next stop was the United Nations building. We stood across the street staring at the flags waving in front. That's when I saw the squirrel. I already had pictures of a few in Chicago, but none in New York. This photogenic furry creature with the bushy tail begged for me to take a photo. I squatted down for the perfect shot and snapped another of the little darling.

"Dad, where are we going next?" No reply. I looked up. "Dad?" Where was he? In a panic, I hopped down the stairs and looked up and down the sidewalk. I glanced across the street, empty at the moment. There he was, in front of the United Nations building, at a bus stop. I turned to the right to see a city bus leading a steady flow of traffic in this direction. Dad wouldn't leave me, would he?

In a split second, I had a decision to make. On the one hand, I had no idea where our hotel was. On the other hand, jaywalking across five or six lanes of traffic can come with dire consequences.

I took my chances and sprinted.

Out of breath, I called out to Dad as he stepped onto the bus, "Were you going to leave me?"

Dad shrugged. "Pay attention and keep up."

I bit my tongue. Who was this stranger?

Later that evening, after touring more of New York City, Dad took me to one of the largest bookstores I had ever seen, multiple stories high. Relieved at the fresh air, I stepped outside. I carried my new piano books in my bag, and held my head down in embarrassment over the argument Dad had gotten in with the cashier. I was surprised security didn't throw us out. Dad, in a failed attempt to evangelize to her, lost his temper, and cussed her out, which I was sure any good prophet would have had the good sense not to do.

Irritated at his little escapade, I whined, "Dad, can we eat now? I'm starving. I've been telling you this for hours." I was shocked his brain wasn't registering hunger pangs.

Dad gave me an ambiguous shrug and rocked his head, still fuming over his encounter.

At long last, I found myself descending steps to an Irish pub below street level. The wait to get a table was long, but with live music to pass the time, we occupied ourselves in the bar/lounge. I sank into an oversized armchair, while Dad sat next to an attractive woman on a couch. He struck up a conversation with her, but religion wasn't on his mind.

He motioned for me to join him on the couch. Unwittingly, I became the bait with which he attempted to reel her in. The woman laughed flirtingly and twisted her manicured nails through her dyed-blonde curls. I couldn't believe my faithful dad, still married to Hilda, was making passes at another woman in front of me. This was so out of character.

By the time we were actually seated, the waiter informed us the kitchen was closed and only appetizers could be ordered.

Dad turned to me sheepishly. "We can have some shrimp cocktail."

"I don't eat seafood," I reminded him. At the urging of my stomach, I settled for some breaded mozzarella sticks I had to choke down with water.

On November 7, Dad and I headed back to the airport. We sat next to each other on a bench in between several airport gates at the terminal.

"Are you sure you don't want to go to Ft. Lauderdale, Florida with me?" he asked.

"I would love to go, but I can't. I have to get back home for Justin. Keith and Abe both have to work tomorrow, and I said I would be home to pick up Justin today."

Dad gripped at his chest and stomach.

"Are you okay?" I asked.

"Heartburn."

"Stop eating that junk in the middle of the night."

He ignored my good advice. "So, you're sure, you don't want to come to Florida with me?"

"Yes, Dad." Florida actually sounded like fun, but I knew I had to go home.

"All right." Dad reached into his back pocket and pulled out his wallet. "Amanda, do you need any money?"

"No, Dad. I'm okay."

Dad pulled three one-hundred dollar bills out and handed them to me. "Here, give this to Keith. I know he isn't doing too well financially. Are you sure you don't need anything?"

"I'm sure." I tucked the cash into my purse. "I know Keith will appreciate this." Dad, you're my old dad, I thought. This momentary glimpse of my old dad was exactly what kept the hope alive that one day, my old dad would return.

I took a few last photos and hugged him goodbye. I watched him disappear through the crowds of people.

I thought about Dad and our little adventure on the streets of Chicago and New York City during the entire flight back to Los Angeles. I never imagined that, only two weeks later, Dad would suffer his first major heart attack. I wouldn't find out about it for another six months.

CHAPTER FORTY-FOUR

NOVEMBER 2004 - MARCH 2005: HEARTACHE

DAD EMAILED ME OFTEN over the next couple of months. Each time I responded, I attached a few photos from our trip together. Dad sent me an email in English and translated into Spanish. He said this was for my Spanish-speaking friends. I'm not sure to whom he was referring.

The holidays came and went. I didn't hear from Dad until the evening of Wednesday, March 16, 2005. Thankfully, I was home when the phone rang.

"Amanda?" a feeble voice sounded on the other end of the line.

"Dad?"

"Amanda, I'm in the hospital and the doctor is making me call you."

Heaven knew what trouble Dad had gotten himself into this time. "What? Why? What happened?"

"I've had another heart attack."

"What are you talking about? When did you have the first?"

"Last year, back on November 16th, 2004, I had my first major heart attack. I could've died. A major artery was blocked. They put a stent in my heart."

I gasped. That meant he had suffered from a heart attack only nine days after we parted in the La Guardia Airport in New York City. I remembered him clasping at his chest.

He coughed. "They put me on medication so it wouldn't be rejected. But I refused to take the drugs because I didn't like the side effects. Last night, I had another heart attack. The doctor wants to do a bypass because one of my arteries in 99% clogged. On the next day, on Friday or possibly on Saturday, all the tubes will be removed. I'll probably be in the hospital for about five days or so, but he says it'll be at least two months of recovery and I'll need home care. This surgery has a high risk, but the doctor says I'll die if I don't do it. At any rate, the doctor wanted me to call and tell you."

"Oh my God, that's horrible, Dad. I can't believe it. Where are you?"

"I'm in CCU, room three. After the surgery, they'll move me to ICU." Dad sounded weak and tired.

"Which hospital are you in?"

"St. Joseph's in Chicago. It's on the north side, on Lake Shore Drive."

"I'll try to fly out there as soon as I can."

"Don't worry." Dad must've been on some sedatives that caused him to drift off. "I'm gonna lie down for a bit now."

"I love you, Dad."

After making calls to the hospital, I confirmed Dad made it through the surgery all right. I contacted Hilda and we both planned to fly out to Chicago on the first available flight. My new boyfriend, Dave, whom I had started dating back in December, agreed to help Keith watch Justin in my absence. Neither Keith nor Jackie could fly out on such short notice.

Hilda and I couldn't get flights until Friday and I had to be home before Monday, which didn't leave me much time.

After traveling across the country, and with darkness upon us, Hilda and I staggered into the hospital on Friday evening. We checked in at the nurses' station in the ICU and waited for them to grant us entry.

The nurse came back. "He says he doesn't want any visitors."

My eyes widened. "What? Are you kidding me? I just flew in from California."

Hilda shook her head.

"I'm sorry," the nurse said.

"I'm his daughter," I said, "and this is his wife. We need to see him."

The nurse nodded and disappeared back into Dad's room, ICU number six. Within moments, she was back in the hallway. "Well, I don't know . . . I don't think it's a good time." I detected an underlying discomfort in her voice.

"Can I talk to you for a minute?" I asked.

The nurse followed me as I walked a few feet down the corridor, out of Dad's earshot.

"I don't know if you or the other nurses have realized my dad is mentally ill," I said. "He has been in a couple of mental hospitals and probably isn't in his right mind. He called me a couple of days ago telling me he was here and that he had a heart attack. If he didn't want to see me, why would he have called me? How else would I know he was here?"

"Oh, that explains a lot. I suspected, but I couldn't know for sure since I don't have all his medical records."

"He might preach to you about God." She feigned a smile as I continued. "Please tell the other nurses about his condition, but it's important Dad doesn't hear you. He will get extremely angry if you mention anything about him being mentally ill or such."

"Okay," she said. "I'll take you two back there. But, if he gets upset, I'll have to ask you to leave. You understand, right?"

I grasped Hilda's hand as we entered his room.

Dad was lying in bed, surrounded by medical contraptions. He weakly blinked in recognition.

Our visit that evening was short. Dad seemed to be friendly enough. Hilda's eyes welled up and she sat quietly in the corner, staring at him. The visit was emotional for her since this was the first time she had laid eyes on her husband since September 1999, five and a half years ago.

On Saturday, Hilda and I went early in the morning to visit Dad. I recounted the whole spiel regarding Dad's mental state with the day shift nurse. This time, much to Hilda's disappointment, Dad refused to see her and only allowed me to come in. She said she'd wait for me in the waiting room.

The doctor wanted Dad to walk.

Dad leaned against me and I supported his weight as we shuffled down the hallways.

"Don't you want to see Hilda?" I asked.

"Absolutely not. Only you, Amanda. Don't bring her here again. I only want to see you."

Dad, tired from exertion, wanted to nap.

Hilda and I spoke to the doctor to find out what aftercare Dad would need. I explained his living arrangement.

"You must get him a bed," the doctor said. "He won't be able to handle the strain of bending up and down to sleep in a sleeping bag on the floor."

Hilda and I hopped into our rental car. We were on a mission to stock Dad's apartment with furniture. Since Dad refused to see Hilda, she arranged a return flight to West Virginia for Sunday. That only left us one day to buy furniture.

"Amandy, how are we going to get into Daddy's apartment? Do you remember where he lives? Can you get him to give you a key?"

Fortunately, I did remember how to get to his apartment which was only a few streets from the hospital. But, I knew getting into his place wouldn't be easy. Dad would never give me the keys.

"I have an idea," I said. "Parking is impossible at his place though. We should leave the car in this parking lot for awhile until we figure out how to get into his apartment. His place isn't a far walk from here."

We headed out into the cold.

Standing in front of his building, I scanned the buzzer list for the apartment manager. I remembered Dad telling me his name several times before. In fact, when I visited Dad back in November, he had introduced me to the manager in the hallway once. Even if I guessed the right button to push, I didn't know if the manager or his wife would be home, or would be willing to let us in.

"Let's hope this works," I told Hilda as I pushed the button. I crossed my fingers and waited. I really didn't have a 'Plan B.'

"Hello?" A gruff voice answered. The man's towering stature was intimidating enough, his eastern European accent only added to his daunting demeanor.

"Hi, this is Joseph's daughter. We met last November. My dad had a heart attack and is in the hospital. I need to get into his apartment and was really hoping you could help me out."

"I'll be right down."

I smiled at Hilda. "Something might go our way today."

On the way up the elevator, I explained dad's background to the manager. He must have appreciated the knowledge because as soon as we were on Dad's floor, he brought his wife out to meet us and to hear Dad's story.

"Please, don't tell him I told you all this," I said. "He'd be angry with me."

"What can we do to help you and Joseph out?"

I explained we needed to get furniture for Dad, thus we would need access to his apartment throughout the day.

"No problem," he said. "I hope Joseph is okay. Here is a key. Just bring it back when you're done."

Our feet sore and our noses cold, Hilda and I walked several blocks up the road to a couple of mattress stores. After going back and forth, begging and pleading with the salespeople, Hilda and I purchased a cheap bed and box springs to be delivered in a couple of hours.

We hurried back to the hospital parking lot. We had a lot of shopping to do before the bed arrived.

As Hilda set up the dishes, cooking utensils, and food in the kitchen, I sat down on Dad's new flimsy dinette set, a card table with chairs, and used my cell phone to call the local phone company. The soonest Dad's phone line could be connected would be sometime next week. Frustrated, I agreed and instructed the company to send all bills to me, in California. I needed to make sure the bills were paid so Dad could contact someone in the event of another emergency. Plus, I wanted the ability to finally get hold of him once in a while to see if he was in good health.

The next morning, Dad was set to be released from the hospital. He had insisted on it, actually. I sat with him in the room while several doctors and nurses paraded through the room. They rattled off instructions for his aftercare: what he could and could not eat—little to no sodium. Sorry Dad, no more greasy junk food in the middle of the night for you—what exercise he could and could not do, what symptoms he needed to watch out for, and what medications he needed to take and how often.

The medication was a sticky issue for Dad. I sat by his side, bemused at the harassment he was giving the nurse and the doctor about the prescriptions.

"Joseph," the doctor said. "Stop reading the inserts with the side effects. You are obsessing about the side effects, even those which are extremely rare. If you don't want to end up back in the hospital, you need to take these as directed."

"Dad," I said. "just listen to the doctor."

Dad bowed his head and agreed to the requests. He cleared his throat and said, "But, what about . . . ."

Dated Thursday, March 31, 2005 at 4:15 PM CST, only 14 days after Dad's open heart surgery, Dad mailed me newspaper clippings from the *Chicago Free Press* in the hope I could use them as topics for Socratic Seminars (classroom discussions) at work. The first article was titled "Gay bashing shakes tranquil Santa Fe, N.M." He underlined key phrases in the text. The second article was titled "Bishop sorry for denying funeral rites to gay man." Dad underlined text that explained this occurred in San Diego, and that the man "died at age 31 of congestive heart failure."

I wondered why Dad had chosen to highlight this. Maybe his heart attacks had shaken him up and he was scared, but couldn't admit it. Maybe Dad was worried about us children and warning us to take care of our health. Maybe he was also trying to mend things with Keith in a roundabout way, from the hollow depths of what remained of his former self.

That familiar part of my old dad was almost gone. It tore me up inside to think about him having normal feelings. That would mean he felt scared and alone.

CHAPTER FORTY-FIVE

MARCH - AUGUST 2005: INTRODUCTIONS

IN MARCH OF 2005, my boyfriend Dave, a tall lanky man with dark hair, proposed to me and I accepted. With this new development, Dave, originally from upstate New York, decided to take root in California. He brought his twelve year-old daughter Sarah out west to live with Justin and me, which meant we needed a larger living space. My two-bedroom, one bath condo was too small. In May, I sold it and bought a house with him. We planned a beach wedding for July 2005 and sent out invitations.

Much to my disbelief, Dad told me he would attend, but soon after, changed his mind. I was crushed.

"At least you won't have to go through what I did," Jackie said.

"But, he was at your wedding," I said. "He walked you down the aisle."

"And I was angry the entire way because of the shit he pulled in the limo with my mom."

I realized Jackie and I were arguing over whose situation was more pitiful. "But, what am I going to do? Dad won't be there."

"Do you remember the Greek dancing we did at the reception? I arranged that for him. I thought maybe it would . . . ." Jackie trailed off. "Dad's not going to get better."

"No," I said. "I don't think that's possible."

"If he took the medicine—"

"He won't." It was painful to admit. "He's too far gone now. All we have is our memories and each other."

Keith walked me down the aisle in Dad's absence.

Having Keith fill the father role was further evidence Dad had permanently changed. In all my childhood, I never imagined Dad refusing to attend my wedding. My thoughts of him were turning bittersweet.

In August, I received a check, a wedding gift from Dad. A few weeks later, I got a strange phone call from Dad.

"Amanda?" Dad said. "I need you to pick me up from the airport in five hours. My flight's boarding now, so I have to hang up."

"You're flying to California?" I asked.

"Yes, I'll be there soon. I decided to come to meet Dave and Sarah. I have to go now. Good bye."

With Dad, there was never was a dull moment.

The sun shone in the summer afternoon. Sarah and Justin chatted in the backseat of my car. They got along well as siblings, perhaps because of the four year age gap and the prospect of instantly losing their only child status. I focused on the ten-lanes-wide freeway and maneuvered through the light weekend traffic.

The last time Justin saw his grandpa when Dad stayed with me in 2002, Justin was five. That was when Dad yelled at Justin and made him cry. Justin was now eight. I wondered how this visit would go.

Dave turned to me. "How long's your dad staying with us?"

"I have no idea," I said.

I pulled to the curb and inched the car forward until I saw him.

Dad told jokes the entire way home and had everyone laughing. I smiled. Maybe this visit would go well.

While I made dinner, Dave took Dad and Sarah to the grocery store. When they returned, Dave told me what happened.

After placing the last item on the conveyer belt, Dad had flirted with the young Asian cashier.

He had smiled and asked, "So, are you married or happy?"

His question was met with a polite laugh. Her cheeks turned red. She avoided looking at him. Dave and Sarah shared in the cashier's discomfort.

In the evening, as Justin prepared the bottom bunk for his grandpa, I had a talk with Dad.

"Tomorrow," I said, "what are you going to do if you wake up before us?"

"Oh, I'll just take a walk around the block."

I eyed him nervously. Dave and I had only moved in about three months ago, and we didn't know many people in the area. "If you get up before us, please don't go out and preach to my neighbors."

"Why not? I'm a prophet. That's my work. I'll take a walk and if I happen to see anyone outside, I'll—"

"Can't you just stay in the house?"

Dad scorned. "I'll do as I see fit, Amanda."

"Okay, but please don't talk to any of my neighbors." I gave him a hug. "I love you. Good night."

The next morning, I awoke to find Dad's backpack by the door. He was dressed and seated on the couch.

"Good morning, Dad." I rubbed the sleep from my eyes. "Did you just get up?"

"No. I've already been out for a walk and back again. When can you drive me to the airport?"

"What are you talking about? You just got here yesterday."

"I came to meet Dave and Sarah. Now, I've met them and I'm ready to fly back."

"So, you're just going to leave? Are you sure?"

Dad smiled politely. "Yes. Thank you for letting me visit."

"I wish you would stay longer. You're welcome here anytime, Dad."

In conversation a few weeks later, Dad confirmed what I had already suspected; he had gone home the following morning because he was offended I wouldn't let him preach to my neighbors.

Maybe his early departure was better for everyone. At least I got to see him again, he met my new family, and he left on relatively good terms, unlike the drama of his last visit.

Remembering Dad's suicide attempts in 1996 and 1997, his disappearance in 1999, his hospitalizations, and homelessness, I came to realize every new visit and every new conversation with Dad was a gift.

* * *

JUNE 24 - JULY 2, 2006: REUNION IN CHICAGO

TWO YEARS HAD PASSED since my grandparents' deaths. Even though it should have been Dad's duty to design their headstones, Jackie, Keith, and I had assumed the responsibility. We gave it much thought and decided on a single long headstone for both. We wanted it to represent our grandparents and what they enjoyed during their lives. For grandpa we chose a microscope since he loved science. For grandma we chose a grand piano to signify her love of music. At the end of the inscription, we signed it "Love, Your Dolls" since Grandma had a way of always referring to us as "Dolls."

Originally, we had hoped to arrange a memorial service to unveil their tombstone at the one-year anniversary of their deaths. Unfortunately, the artist was slow to complete the project. The service was delayed until June of 2006, a little over two years after their passing. With me and the kids out of school, this was an ideal travel time for the whole family.

On Saturday, June 24th, 2006, our plane touched down at Chicago's O'Hare Airport. Dave, Sarah, Justin, and I maneuvered our way over to the baggage claim. Like my Dad had done with me before, I led my family onto El-train. I remembered being about Justin's age when I first rode the El-train with Dad.

After we checked in at the Doubletree Hotel, the agent handed us some warm chocolate cookies which made our weariness melt away. I phoned Dad to let him know we had arrived.

Dad met us in the lobby and suggested we take a stroll. Eventually our long walk ended at Navy Pier. By this time, we were famished.

"I know a good place," Dad said. "Follow me."

I couldn't decide whether the BBQ food or the live Jazz music impressed me more.

"Thanks for bringing us here," I said.

Dad reached for the check. "My treat."

I tried to take the check tray from him. "No, Dad. Thank you, but really, let me pay."

He shook his head and took out his wallet.

Pausing, I said, "Thanks, Dad. That's really nice of you. At least let me pay the tip." I sipped my water and thought about how "fatherly" my dad was being, a glimpse into the past.

Dad stood to leave. I motioned to the kids and they followed Dave outside. Pausing at the door, I turned back to see Dad handing a slip of paper to the waitress along with the bill. I didn't have to ask. I knew all too well the contents of the manila folder that never left his side.

"They have an amazing fireworks display off of the pier," Dad explained as he bounded up a flight of stairs. "But, we better hurry up to get a spot."

Stopping to catch my breath before the next set of steps, I stared in disbelief at my dad.

At the top, he turned his gray-hooded head to us. "See, I'm sixty-two, almost sixty-three and I'm in excellent shape. From all the miles I walk every day, I can beat people half my age. I had heart surgery a year and a half ago, and look at me."

This was the closest Dad had come to smiling all evening. He wouldn't smile for any pictures I snapped that night; he maintained a distant countenance.

Jackie, Neil, and my three-year old niece Mackenzie had alternated their stay between Jackie's mom's and one of Jackie's brother's houses. Because Jackie and Neil didn't own a cell phone, I phoned her mom's.

"Did you still want to see Dad?" I asked.

"Well, I don't want to hear all of his religious crap." She hesitated. "It's been seven years, Amanda."

"I know you haven't seen him in a long time. He looks different now."

"Yes, you've shown me pictures."

"We saw him last night. I told him about our meeting with Laurie on Tuesday to sign the final papers for Grandma and Grandpa's estate. I thought maybe that would be a good day to visit with him since Keith, and you, and I will all be there. Laurie needs Dad to look over a few things anyway. Afterwards, we can all hang out, maybe go downtown. What do you think?"

"It's really hard for me, y'know? I want to see him, of course, but I don't know if I can handle it. Can you at least tell Dad to not fucking preach to us?"

"I'll tell him."

I phoned Dad. Against my better judgment, I relayed Jackie's request. "Dad, Jackie and Keith really want to see you, and I was thinking you could meet us here in the lobby on Tuesday. The only thing they asked is if you can refrain from talk about religion with them since everyone has different beliefs."

Dad became enraged. "Forget it. I don't need to see them. If they want to deny the truth, well, to hell with them."

"We all love you and miss you. It's just hard since everyone follows different religions."

"Amanda, everything's in that writing. They need to read it and believe it to be saved. But if they want to be thick-headed about it, I don't need to waste my time."

"But Laurie needs you to sign some papers." I sat down on the floor. This would be a long phone call.

"I can take the train to her office. There's absolutely no reason why she needs me to be there on Tuesday."

"But I want to see you again. Please, Dad." I twisted the phone cord between my fingers and bit my lip. I knew I shouldn't have done as Jackie requested. I should've known better.

An hour later, I had soothed Dad's ruffled feathers enough for him to tentatively agree to Tuesday's rendezvous.

On Tuesday, June 27th, I headed down to the lobby for the meeting with Laurie. Seated on armchairs and couches around a table, Jackie, Keith, Laurie, and I engaged in small talk.

"Well," Laurie said. "Are you guys prepared to meet your father?"

Keith shrugged. "Doesn't matter to me either way."

I stared at my brother. Even though he hadn't seen Dad since that fateful night nearly four years ago, Keith didn't think much of this encounter. As he had already explained to me, Dad, as Keith knew him during childhood, was gone. When Keith was fifteen and Dad accused him of plotting to kill him, he had unwittingly severed their relationship.

Jackie shut her eyes. "You know, I don't know if this is a good idea, Amanda. I don't know if I can go through with this. I haven't seen Dad since January of 1999," Jackie squirmed on the plush lobby couch. "I still remember that day when Neil and I drove out to Hemet to pick up furniture. Hilda was gone. Dad couldn't care less. I was so uncomfortable during the entire visit….It's been seven years." She tapped her foot. "Laurie, can you go over what we need to sign and do again. I'm having trouble focusing right now."

Laurie started to re-explain.

I spotted him. Wearing jeans, his trademark black leather shoes, and blue shirt tucked in with his black belt, Dad strolled in through the revolving door. I jumped up and rushed over to hug him hello.

Laurie, Keith, and Jackie looked up. Jackie gasped at his appearance. She hadn't seen Dad since he had shaved his head, threw out his glasses, and gained some weight. Her eyes dampened, yet she maintained her composure. Neil introduced Dad to his newest grandchild, Mackenzie.

After signing papers, wrapping up the estate, and saying goodbye to Laurie, we headed outside for a walk.

Jackie didn't say much. Dave, Sarah, and Justin walked behind Neil, who pushed Mackenzie in an umbrella stroller. I was elected to walk and talk with Dad. Even though I couldn't decipher their whispers, I knew Keith was trying his best to comfort Jackie. She maintained a distance, emotionally and physically, from Dad for most of the afternoon. Keith occasionally strode along Dad's side, but all he had to do was listen since Dad didn't pause enough in his speech for Keith to get much of a word in edgewise.

Dad took us on a tour through Lincoln Park. In between Clark Street and Shoreline Drive, we explored the Flower Conservatory. We walked through the park before hopping on a bus south to Michigan Avenue.

I had never been to Millennium Park. Sitting on the concrete wall in front of the water fountain at Millennium Monument, a half-circle of Roman columns across from Wrigley Park, we posed for a few pictures. Dave and Neil took turns with the cameras.

Keith and I sat on either side of Dad. Jackie sat on the edge, beyond the children. Her first reaction to seeing Dad in the lobby was extreme nervousness, anxiety. Here, in front of the fountain, Jackie confided to me she needed to be near Keith and me, for us to protect her. Dad was a stranger to her now. Jackie appeared quiet or shy. Dad seemed not to notice any difference, because he was different.

Passing by the Cloud Gate Sculpture, an enormous jelly-bean shaped chunk of steel, I watched our distorted reflections. Ethereal mirror images of Jackie, Dad, and Keith bounced back at me. Our bodies and faces stretched askew. We appeared as warped as we felt inside.

"Is anybody hungry?" Dad asked. We gathered around; our kids pushed their way to the front. Dad reached into a Whole Foods Market bag and handed us each a banana.

An amazing sight came into view: The Crown Fountain, an architectural work of art. We were all instantly mesmerized by the changing faces projected on the front of two 50-foot glass towers on either side of a reflecting pond. Dad stood by as we stared in awe. For a few minutes apiece, a real-life face was projected onto an LED screen on the front of each tall tower. Two giant faces were looking at one another, yet they appeared to see beyond the other. I stared at the image of a child with a mysterious expression and at the adult with an equally ambiguous expression. The expressions and the faces morphed into new ones. This work of art captured the same attitude Dad had when he communicated with us—as if he were looking through us, focused on something beyond.

"It's getting dark," I said to Dad. "I think the kids are getting hungry. Where do you want to go eat?"

"IHOP," Dad said. "Follow me."

Keith paused. "Dad, I think I'm going to get going."

"Aren't you going to come to dinner with us?" Jackie asked.

"No," Keith said, "Abe is done shopping and I need to meet up with him. Besides, I'm tired." Keith went around and said his good-byes to everyone before ending with Dad. Keith spoke his final, parting words, "It was nice seeing you again." He smiled and gave Dad a hug.

When Keith disappeared around the corner, I sensed that would be the last time Keith would ever see Dad.

By the time we were all seated at a large booth in IHOP, Jackie opened up. She kept stealing glances at Dad as she sipped her soup, especially when Dad preached to the staff. Other than to the waitress and busboy, Dad hardly spoke of religion over dinner.

"Amanda, do you need to go to the restroom?" Jackie asked.

I eyed her strangely. Jackie narrowed her eyes and raised her eyebrows. I got the hint.

"Yeah, let's go," I said. When the door to the restroom shut behind me, I noticed the tears at the corners of my big sister's eyes. "Are you okay?"

Jackie grabbed a paper towel and dabbed them away. "I just feel like Dad is being semi-normal for the first time. I mean, I caught a glimpse of the old Dad." She sniffled. "But, it's so hard. It's making me so sad. I keep having to look away to keep from crying."

My stomach dropped. During the entire day, I had maintained an air of control because I hadn't allowed myself to open up. I kept a divider erected in my mind separating the past and the present. I wasn't about to knock down that wall.

Jackie had always been more sensitive and attuned to her feelings. She felt more and hurt deeper. I stared into Jackie's face. I didn't know what to say. It didn't really matter since she only needed me to listen. I nodded and gave her a hug.

The waitress brought the check as Jackie and I returned to the table.

Dad reached for it.

Jackie, Neil, Dave, and I protested.

"I'm paying the bill," Dad said. "You're my children and you've had to pay to fly out here. I know all of your finances are tight. Let me take care of you."

Jackie and I exchanged a look of surprise. This was our old dad: protective over his kids, and concerned about our finances. We didn't say another word, or our fairytale could dissolve.

We stepped outside. Since we weren't far from his apartment, Dad took us on a tour through his neighborhood.

He pointed upward. "Look at the lightning bugs. It's so pretty here. You don't get this in California."

Justin and Mackenzie scurried around the field, jumping as high as they might, trying to catch one. Each time, the lights slipped through their hands.

CHAPTER FORTY-SIX

JULY 2006: GOODBYES

Back in Dad's apartment, Jackie and I made a beeline for the restroom. She won and went in first. I waited for awhile before she came back out.

"What took so long?" I asked.

"I was snooping." Jackie whispered. "He doesn't have hardly anything in this place. And I can't believe he uses baby shampoo, which I use on Mackenzie's hair."

"He doesn't even have any hair, Jackie."

Jackie walked through his barren place to the kitchen while Dad was busy talking to Neil, Dave, and Sarah. Thirsty, Jackie opened each cabinet in search of cups. Dad only had two. With glass in hand, Jackie flung open the refrigerator to find bottled water. The only things inside were boxes and boxes of baking soda—no food or drinks. Resigned to tap water, she turned toward the sink. As she filled the glass, Jackie pointed at the precise stacks of quarters, for the laundry I assumed. The coins were lined up in perfect rows. Neat pile of manila folders laid exactly on top of one another, and the single stack of photocopies of Dad's handwritten religious papers. He had been stuffing these papers into the envelopes, which is why Dad always had a manila envelope in hand.

Justin and Sarah sat on the edge of Dad's bed looking half-asleep.

"Dad," I said. "I think we're going to head back to the hotel."

Jackie yawned and nodded. "Yeah, we'll probably be heading back to my mom's place, too. It's a long train ride back to the rental car and I've got to get Mackenzie to bed."

Dad turned to me. "How are you getting back?"

"We bought those Metro passes you told us about," I said. "We'll take the bus back."

"Are you sure?"

"Don't worry, Dad. I know how to get back to the hotel."

He turned to Jackie. "What about you? How are all of you getting back to your mom's?"

"We're going to walk back to the El-train and take the blue line out to O'Hare. That's where we parked the rental car. We'll drive back from there."

Dad pursed his lips together and shook his head in disagreement. "Not this late at night you won't. Not by yourselves."

"Joseph," Neil said. "that's the same way we got here. We'll be fine."

"Absolutely not. You don't know your way around here if something were to happen. And you have a small child. I don't want you three to ride the subway at night alone. I'll go with you."

"All the way back?" Jackie asked. She later told me she was secretly glad he still cared.

"Sure. I ride these trains all the time. It's no problem. We'll take a cab to the blue line because it's too far to walk. I'll take you back to your car." Dad's answer was final.

Once outside, Dave, Sarah, Justin, and I said good-bye to the others. Before we walked toward the bus stop, Dad again verified the bus routes with me.

In the cab, Neil, Jackie, and Mackenzie slipped into the backseat while Dad sat in front. On the way to the El-station, Dad yapped the cab driver's ear off. The cab driver even engaged him in a religious discussion. Jackie sat behind him, and squeezed Neil's hand.

They took their seats on the El-train. Mackenzie fell asleep across Neil's lap. Dad handed them a manila folder with his religious literature inside. It quickly became apparent this wouldn't be a peaceful ride back. Jackie scowled. Neil humored Dad, took the envelope, and allowed Dad the freedom to preach.

"It's all there. All you have to do is read it, and believe it. He put me down on the street for three years, but not anymore. God restored me off of the streets in August of 2003, seven years after my prostrate surgery. See, all you gotta do is have faith."

Jackie rolled her eyes and let the noisy sound of traffic and the train tracks drown out Dad's voice. Grandpa had procured an apartment for Dad, not God. She didn't want to hear Dad tell her that God worked through Grandpa, so she kept her mouth shut, turned toward the window and stared into the distance. Coming out of the underground after Logan Square, the blue line continued the rest of the way back to O'Hare Airport along the median of the Kennedy Expressway. Jackie watched the red taillights of the cars.

"You have to want it more than anything else in this world," Dad continued. "See, Neil, the next world is what it's all about."

Jackie moaned. They were a captive audience, trapped here in this train car for the entire ride. She couldn't wait for the train to stop so could exit. Her heart ached because she didn't want to feel that way about Dad. She reflected on the day. During the walk through the city, Dad's demeanor was similar to his old self. He was still making jokes, but now he had to branch off to religion. She shifted in her seat, uncomfortable in her skin. She wished she could tear out of her body and run away.

Jackie stared in her window at Dad's reflection, his empty, lonely eyes. Dad's mouth continued moving as he talked to Neil. Jackie could almost see the "old" Dad's thin brown hair parted to the side, his kind blue eyes behind his gold framed glasses, and a warm smile upon his face. The train started moving again and the vision disappeared. The cars on the road and Dad's reflection flickered before her eyes as the train alternated between the track lights and the cloak of darkness.

The train descended underneath the airport. Mackenzie woke up and held onto Jackie's hand. Neil picked up the umbrella stroller and followed Joseph out. Wavy glass walls lit up in color welcomed them back.

"I'll walk you back to your car," Dad said.

Jackie didn't mind since he had stopped evangelizing for the moment.

Remembering the rest of her travel plans, Jackie turned and asked, "Dad, can we see you again? Mom's going to be taking us all back into downtown to go to the Museum of Science and Industry. How about we catch dinner together afterwards?"

Dad shrugged. "Maybe. How will I get a hold of you?"

Knowing Dad's disrespect for personal boundaries, Jackie didn't want to give him her mom's cell phone. "I'll call you and let you know."

Dad eyed her distrustfully. "Why don't you just give me your mom's number?"

"We are going to be at the museum on Friday. How about if we meet outside at 5 p.m.? Then we can eat dinner."

Dad stared straight ahead. They had reached the airport door leading to the outside.

Before stepping over the threshold, Jackie again asked Dad, "Would you like to meet us for dinner?"

"I don't know. We'll see."

Mackenzie, happy to be outside, ran up and grabbed her daddy's hand. They continued to walk alongside Dad through the parking lot. Jackie slowed a few steps behind them when she heard Dad talking about baptizing Mackenzie. Jackie couldn't bear to hear anymore. When they reached the rental car, she walked around and leaned against the other side. Neil humored Dad and allowed him to place his hand on Mackenzie's head and say a few prayers over his granddaughter. He blessed her.

After buckling Mackenzie in, Jackie embraced Dad. Not wanting to let go, she held back tears long enough to get in the car. No sooner had Dad turned and headed back towards the station, Jackie cried and sobbed. Neil turned the engine and reversed out.

She held her hand against Neil's chest. "Go slow. I want to watch him, until I can't see him anymore." Jackie stared at Dad's figure growing smaller in the distance.

"Do you want me to circle around the lot?" Neil offered.

Jackie was bawling now. "I don't care. I just want to see my dad." Deep inside, something was telling her this would be the last time she would ever see him. Neil edged the car forward. Dad was beyond the reach of their headlights. His gray hooded sweatshirt and blue jeans lit up under the terminal lights. Dad pushed through the revolving door. Jackie could no longer see him.

On Friday, from early morning all the way until late afternoon, Jackie kept borrowing her mom's cell phone and calling Dad's apartment. Since I had bought him an answering machine when I had his phone hooked up, Jackie was able to leave Dad several messages. Either he wasn't home, or he wasn't answering her calls. Jackie tried over and over again to reach him. She kept leaving messages; however, she never left him a return number.

After visiting the museum, she and her family stood on the front steps searching through the crowds of people for Dad. Couples and families walked by. Jackie watched a little girl piggybacking on her dad's back. The child's fingers were tightly grasping her daddy's neck. Jackie remembered doing the same thing.

"Is your father going to show up or what?" LilyAnn asked. "I'm really curious to see what you've been telling me about and what he looks like now."

"I don't know," Jackie said. She closed her eyes. Part of her wanted him to be here, part of her didn't.

They waited nearly half an hour before getting back on the road. When they were almost at LilyAnn's house in the suburbs, Jackie phoned Dad one last time. Miraculously, he picked up the phone.

"Dad, I thought we were going to meet up for dinner. I've been leaving you messages all day."

"Oh, well, you never left me a number to call you back. I couldn't get a hold of you," Dad answered, his voice syrupy sweet.

Jackie had a gut feeling Dad was just toying with her because by not giving him any return phone numbers she had taken the power and control from him.

Steadying her voice, she said, "I'm sorry, this isn't my phone, I can't give you the number."

While Neil was driving, LilyAnn seemed to sense Jackie was getting upset. She gave her a what-the-hell-is-going-on look.

Dad minced his words with double meanings.

Agitated, Jackie pretended to hear phone reception static. "The signal's going out...Oh, we're starting to break up...we're losing the connection...it was nice seeing you, I love you, bye."

Dad didn't have time to react. "Oh, okay, I love you, bye."

That was the last time she heard Dad's voice. Jackie cried the whole way home.

CHAPTER FORTY-SEVEN

JULY 2006 - DECEMBER 2008: DRIFTING AWAY

AFTER WE RETURNED HOME, Dad contacted me on a regular basis. Some people receive magazines every month; I got Dad's religious teachings. Actually, he sent four packets in July and one every month thereafter, both in English and in Spanish. Dad dated them like before, the twenty-ninth day of the twelfth month of the sixth year of the reign of President George W. Bush. In addition to his repetitive religious mandates, Dad reminded me his lease would expire on September 30th and he could depart at any time. He told me, according to God, he could "be any place in the world at any time" and that he "likely will not have a permanent residence or a phone." Because phoning me could be inordinately expensive, he reminded me I would always have his P.O. Box mailing address, which he must maintain lest his needed pension and social security be stopped.

Within a week of Justin's tenth birthday, Dad sent money hidden inside of a letter for him; however, Dad made sure to explain, "God commands us not to honor, celebrate, observe, recognize, or give respect to days, months, times, and years. This is an 'I love you' gift to use as you see fit. You didn't expect it, nor did you ask for it; neither did I promise it to you, nor mention it would or might be forthcoming. This is grace: an unearned and undeserved gift of God." The idea that Dad still loved and cared about his family was the carrot that kept me reaching out to him. But the carrot was always beyond my grasp.

In 2006, Jackie and I became pregnant, each with a second child. Her daughter was due in April 2007, my son in July.

2007 started out like the previous year. Dad still professed to be a prophet of God. Hilda continued to send him cards and gifts on holidays and letters and cards throughout the year, which she had done every year since he abandoned her in 1999. Dad never acknowledged nor responded to any of her communication, yet never returned anything to her as undeliverable.

Early in 2007, my husband's dad passed away at a hospital in upstate New York, the night before his scheduled heart surgery. Days earlier, I had encouraged Dave to fly out to see his dad and to be there for the surgery, which he did. He had spent the entire day at his dad's house and told him our baby boy would be named after him, David. His dad had smiled at the news.

As Dave mourned, I consoled him. "I'm sorry about your dad's passing. I understand how you feel. Back in 2002 when my entire family believed my dad was dead, I felt horrible at not being able to say good-bye. At least you were able to share the last day with your dad and tell him how much you loved him. So many people don't get that opportunity."

In April, Jackie gave birth to Rebecca. During her pregnancy, she had e-mailed me ultrasound pictures, a few of which I forwarded to Dad at her request.

"Did Dad see the pictures?" Jackie asked me one day.

"Yes," I said.

"Well, did he say anything? Did he say anything about the granddaughter he probably won't ever even meet?" Jackie sounded bitter.

"No, he didn't really say anything. But I send him pictures all the time and he doesn't say much. I sent him ultrasounds of my baby, too."

Jackie dropped the issue. I didn't want to have to tell her Dad said it looked like she had a demon inside her, which I promptly made him apologize for saying. He'd been irritated because he'd asked for Keith's and Jackie's contact information and they still refused to allow him to have their addresses or phone numbers. When Jackie mailed a card to Dad's P.O. Box, she wouldn't even put a return address on it. I think that hurt him, but considering his unpredictable behavior and irrational angry outbursts, I completely understood why they felt the necessity to withhold information.

In July, I gave birth to my second son. He was born on Keith's birthday—coincidental because Hilda and I share a birthday, too. There weren't any complications with the delivery, and I immediately fell in love with him. We gave the newest addition to our family Dave's dad's first name and my Grandpa's middle name. I remembered the day Justin was born—my dad, with a vacant look in his eyes, held his first grandchild. Dad wouldn't be there to hold baby David, or his granddaughter Rebecca.

Later in the evening, while my angelic baby soundly slept in the hospital glass-sided bassinet, I lay in the hospital bed, staring out the little window. Fireworks exploded in the distance. I watched the colors sprinkling down out of the sky. My thoughts again wandered back to Dad.

I emailed photos of my newest son to Dad. He responded sweetly and commented on "how precious are the photos of little David Jonathan!!! As it is written, all the angels in heaven behold the face of a child before their Father."

I was thrilled and surprised he signed it "Dad," not the "Prophet of God."

The year 2008 was similar to the previous years. Dad settled into a fairly predictable pattern: he would mostly spend the warm months in Chicago, the cool ones in Ft. Lauderdale. How was he living—on the streets, in shelters, in cheap motels? He wouldn't tell me, so I had no idea unless, by chance, he stayed at a motel whose number showed up on my caller ID.

Occasionally during phone conversations, Dad related a story from his childhood. I capitalized on these moments, trying to get him to elaborate, trying to bring back the "old" Dad. It didn't work. He would snap back into his current self and change the topic to religion.

I grew tired of hearing about his desires for a new wife 'which God would be sending him at any time.' To me, this meant Dad was lonely. I couldn't allow myself to imagine what he was going through. He would tell me about various women he met whom he felt might be his next wife. Inadvertently, they would try to take advantage of Dad in some way and he was forced—at least in his mind—to change his e-mail identity again and again: Ari Neshama, Leone Di Leon, Michael Carlucci, Your Dad, John Delamunte, BillyFromPhilly, atrueprophetofGod, and so forth.

On June 15, 2008, Dad sent me a copy of his profile on an online dating website. I couldn't believe he had the audacity to search for another wife while still legally married to Hilda. I felt terribly sad for him and for Hilda as I read his tagline: "Praying to God, in the name of His Son Lord Jesus, for my predestinated wife." In disbelief, I read through the ad he created:

About me: *I am divorced of God (and will be married by God, and not by man's paperwork or laws), I have been to/worked in many countries in the world, and will continue to do so as commanded by God.*

I'm looking for: *My wife will be in complete agreement on the one correct doctrine of our faith. She, as have I, must forsake everything, everyone and everyplace, and not look back. Giving others the words leading to everlasting life, helping and comforting them in this world, and confirming our love for them, on the street, planes, trains, public transportation, in museums, restaurants, nightclubs, anywhere, anytime, Like Jesus, we'll live together, die together, be resurrected from the dead together, and ascend up to heaven together. Amen.*

My Basics
Ethnicity: *White/Caucasian*
I am an Ashkenazi Jew by heritage (tribe of Reuben), and somewhat by culture, but a born again = saved Christian by faith.
Religion: *Christian/Other - Jesus is my boss, and God is Jesus' boss.*
Occupation: *Retired. I tell others how to live forever in paradise*

Dad started to end our phone calls and some e-mails with, "Now, this may be the last time you ever hear from me again." The first time I heard him say this, I believed it and became distressed. After hearing it so often though, I no longer took the threat seriously.

In the fall of 2008, Dad shared more of his visions and dreams with me. I took notes on as much as I could. He told me about his visions, his travels abroad, and his prophecy. If it weren't for the postcards postmarked from around the world, I would've had serious difficulty believing any of it. Because of the evidence, I was left trying to separate reality from his distorted reality. I gave up trying.

On November 1, 2008, I received what would be the last written communication from Dad for several years. His email was filled with the usual religious messages

I didn't know how to respond. Turns out I didn't have to—Dad immediately deleted his e-mail address.

I couldn't dwell on it with three kids at home, a husband, and a full-time job—I had to go about my life. Besides, he had disappeared before. I would simply have to wait it out a few weeks or months before he would contact me again.

Or at least that's what I assumed.

CHAPTER FORTY-EIGHT

DECEMBER 2008 – DECEMBER 2009:
THE GREAT DISAPPEARING ACT

I RECEIVED AN URGENT phone call from Dad on December 23, 2008.

I picked up the phone to hear his weakened voice. "Dad? What's wrong?"

"I'm sick. I'm worried because I've been waking up with chills, shaking, heart racing, and strange dreams. I can't sleep more than one and a half hours at a time."

"It sounds like you have the flu. The flu causes all of those things to happen."

"Even the strange dreams?"

"Sure. Especially if you have a fever and haven't been sleeping."

Dad sounded relieved. "Oh, good. I was starting to get really worried. But, I don't know what's wrong with me."

I felt Dad wanted someone to take care of him. Being a mom now myself, I took on that role. "Can you get to the store? Are you staying in a motel?"

"Yes, I'm staying at a place in Tampa, Florida. Yes, I can take the bus."

"Well, I think you need to buy some chicken noodle soup, saltine-crackers, and apple juice."

"But, I'm concerned about my sodium and sugar intake. I've also been having chest pains."

I became alarmed at hearing this. I didn't want to worry Dad though, especially with his paranoia. On the other hand, I was surprised to hear him say he cared about what he ate. I knew Dad had terrible eating habits. His healthy diets were always short-lived. "What have you been eating lately?"

"I ate a burger the other day, and had some Greek food. I haven't eaten anything today."

Just as I suspected. Still, I worried about the chest pains. "Don't you have Medicare since you turned 65? Why don't you go to the doctor?"

"I can't afford the co-pays."

I remembered he was on a fixed income between his pension and social-security, which he only just qualified for in July. I had no idea about what had become of any money my grandparents left for him in the trust.

"God told me to call you," he said.

"Okay. Since you haven't eaten, I want you to get some low-sodium chicken noodle soup and low-sodium saltine crackers or sodium-free crackers."

Like a child, Dad repeated the instructions back and had me say them again, followed by him repeating them one last time before he agreed to hang up and go to the store.

"I hope you feel better," I said.

The next morning, the day before Christmas, Dad called me at 11:15 a.m., Florida time.

"I'm worse." Dad grumbled. "I've only had two hours of sleep. I gave all the food away to a food pantry."

I remembered how every time one of us helped Dad—be it by getting him clothes, a jacket, furniture—he would eventually give it all away. In this way, he never allowed anyone to help him.

Dad sounded terrible as he continued. "God told me not to eat. I will be healed with faith. I'm not to eat for two days, only fast and drink water."

Whatever thought I ever had of normalcy flew away with Dad's admission God was still "talking" to him. He usually meant this in the literal sense. I said, "Dad, you really shouldn't be around others when you're sick. You need to stay in the room and get better. You need to eat something healthy."

"What you told me to do didn't work. I felt worse because what you said wasn't right." As if he could sense my irritation, he went on to say, "But, your love was right, in God. You've always shared with others like when I was on the streets. You know, because you've been without before…you are able to show that mercy." His thoughts branched out in different directions. "The King James Bible—the others distort the Word of God—in Philippians, chapter two, it says, 'Yet I supposed it necessary to send you.' It almost makes me cry—I love the word of God so much. I go out, even when sick, to preach the Word of God to show I am a good Christian." He hardly took a breath as he continued. "God put me on the streets from New York, to Florida, to California. I've had to walk fifty-three miles…on the street from 2000-2003. In Hebrews, chapter 10, verses 30-31: 'Call to remembrance' . . . what little I had was taken away. It's like in Psalm 103. I was crucified by her."

"Who?" I was confused.

"My mom," Dad said, "I was born again and saved. None of the organized religions are right; the devil has infiltrated them because they ask for money. They promise heaven, deliver hell. I never asked for money. When you're homeless, people look at you like you're no good, trash."

I paused to think about that statement. People do judge the homeless, in the belief they're all lazy, and if they had only made better choices in life, they wouldn't be there. If only people realized how far from the truth they might be.

Dad rambled on, "In Romans 14: 'there is nothing unclean in and of itself.' If I eat food because it's 'good for me,' that's a sin. After my heart attack, you were there in my dream, Amanda."

I wondered if Dad remembered me visiting him in the hospital room, after his surgery, when he was still under anesthesia.

"'Sugar is what caused your heart attack,' the surgeon told me. I woke up shaking. The surgeon was right. I shouldn't eat hot dogs because they are from mixed meat." Dad coughed. "This is the Word of God. Do the writing now. You've finished school, bought a condo, and have a good job—all on your own. Look how God has blessed you—husband, house, kids—because you have compassion for the poor and needy. You are the only one. I forgive you for putting me out. God loves you for how much you ministered to me; I want you to know that."

It was the first time in the past twelve years that Dad ever expressed these sentiments: his pride, his love, his understanding. It meant more to me than anyone could imagine. Dad—my Dad—must still be in there, lost deep down in this man's psyche, yet he couldn't regain control of his mind. Heat rose to my cheeks and I held back the tears.

Dad coughed. "God tells me I'm talking too much . . . children are always your children. Look at me, I don't work, God provides for me."

That's not a fair statement, I thought. There are plenty of other homeless people without anything. Dad had a pension, social security, and my grandparents' good grace. I shook it off and listened to Dad go on.

"God rebuked me for eating and told me to donate it and to spread the word of God. I show my faith through my work, shown by love. This may be the last time I talk to you. I don't want you to be sad. Because I go where God calls me, I can be any place in the world at any time. So, there will be no more contact from me, no visits, no phone calls, no email, no letters. Amanda, don't be sad about this. If and when you do this writing, you will see and hear the way I do; you will understand and rejoice." Dad continued coughing. "I have to go. I love you."

I got a sinking feeling in my stomach that somehow Dad meant these words in a way he never had. Perhaps all the other times were merely to prepare me for today.

"I love you too, Dad," I said. I wanted Dad to hear the love in my voice and know he would be missed.

February, March, April, and May passed by without any word. I had an unsettled feeling about this current communication break. In the past, Dad only cut off communication after we fought, except for 2000-2002 when he first left the United States. Without any way to contact him and with no one else to turn to, since he only kept in contact with me, I phoned his cousin Laurie.

"Have you heard from Dad?" I asked.

"No, I'm sorry, Amanda. I haven't. When was the last time you talked with him?"

"Back in December, five months ago."

"Oh, really? But, hasn't he disappeared for that amount of time before?"

"Yes," I admitted. "But he usually contacts me around birthdays and holidays. My birthday came and went. Jackie's birthday came and went. Mackenzie and Rebecca's birthdays came and went. Besides, this time, it's different. I have this feeling. The last conversation I had with him sounded so final. I was left with the impression it really would be the last time I would ever hear from him. Plus, he had been complaining about chest pain the day before. I know Dad doesn't take his medication, nor has he improved his eating habits since his last heart attack. Hilda and I are worried about him, but I have no way of contacting him. I mean, if something were to happen to him."

"Well, doesn't he have an e-mail address or something?"

"Not right now. When he did, he never kept it for long because he'd get paranoid and delete it." I remembered why I had called her. "Laurie, I know you handled my grandparents' estate and set up the trust for Dad. I know he has been getting his pension and social security checks deposited into his account. Is there any way you can contact the bank where the trust is set up—I don't even remember the name of it—and see if Dad has withdrawn any money?"

"I don't think they'll release that type of information without a court order."

"Could you at least try? I mean, we don't need to know his balance or how much he is withdrawing. I just want to know if there's been any activity on his account at all. Maybe if you speak with the manager and explain the situation. They gotta know you are the one who set up the trust in the first place."

"I'll try and see what I can do. I'll give them a call, but I don't think I'll find out much. Didn't your Dad have a P.O. Box?"

"Yes, he does, in Chicago. He told me he needed to maintain it so that he could get mailings from social security and his pension company. He told me he only had to check his mail once every six months to keep it active."

"Hasn't it nearly been that long? Maybe you should try to contact the post office and see if they can give you any information."

Finally, I could do something. "That's a good idea. Will you still try to call the bank? Hilda's worried we would never know if he ended up in a hospital. I told her we'd be able to find out, but I'm not so sure. I just didn't want Hilda to stress any more than she is already. She still loves him and hangs on to the hope he may come back to her, so she might be able to help him. Laurie, I'm worried that even if Dad died, we might never find out about it if he has no identification on him. Neither the hospital nor the police would know his identity."

"I'll check. It's been really busy here at the office, so give me until next week."

A week later, Laurie confirmed what she had suspected: no personal information could be given without a court order.

I searching online for the post office I Dad took me to during my visit five years earlier.

I know people complain about the Department of Motor Vehicles and the post office with all their bureaucratic red tape. I can now personally attest to the problem. Even though I figured out which post office branch I wanted, I couldn't find the right phone number. I dialed many numbers listed for that post office. Either I got a machine or I got a main call center. The operators gave me the branch number where no one would answer the phone. It rang and rang. No machine picked up. I kept searching the Internet for other numbers to dial. Each time, I was at the same dead end. Finally, I somehow got hold of a shipping warehouse phone operator at the branch. Eventually, on my second or third time calling that man, I was given a phone number that actually worked.

Relieved to hear the woman's mid-western accent on the other line, I related my story to the sympathetic woman, who got her supervisor on the phone.

"Hi, ma'am," the second voice greeted me. "I understand how difficult your situation is. In fact, believe it or not, I had a man in here the other day with a similar situation. As I told him, because of the privacy laws, I am unable to release any information to you. I'm really sorry."

Sorry wasn't good enough. It wasn't their fault, but I had to keep trying, for Dad. "I understand. But, I'm not really looking for what kind of mail he's getting or his information. I know his P.O. Box number. I only need a single yes or no answer. Has he checked his mail?" I remembered what Dad told me and added, "He said he has to check his box every six months for it to remain open. Could you tell me if it's still active?"

"No, I can't tell you that. I'm sorry. We don't have any requirement as to how often someone needs to check their box. Some customers pay for their box six months or twelve months in advance. It sounds like he was telling you he pays every six months."

"What happens if he doesn't pay?"

"We close the P.O. Box and after ten days, we can reissue it to someone else."

"If that happens, what do you do with any mail sent to him at that P.O. Box?"

"We would return it to you."

An idea was forming in my mind. "So, if I were to mail him a letter every month, I could assume he was still checking it and paying for it, unless the letter was returned to me?"

"Yes, that's right," the manager replied.

Even though I didn't have any answers, I felt better. The two women were kind, but the law had their hands tied. I knew what I had to do next. On June 6, 2009, I mailed Dad a letter with the usual niceties and told him I missed him. I also related that when I took my family to a Greek festival a few weeks ago, I ran into an old Greek dancing friend of Dad's, Joel, and that I taught Sarah how to do Greek dances, which she enjoyed immensely. In the end, I said, "I'd love it if you would call me to say hi. I do miss hearing your voice." I sat back and hoped for the best.

I updated Hilda on my plan. She mailed Dad a card that requested he call his children (which would be me). We waited.

In July, I made plans to take Justin and David to Jackie's house for the weekend. Dave and Sarah couldn't come because of college and work, but that was the only weekend Jackie had available. Besides which, we hadn't gotten together in awhile. During the drive, at 7 PM on Thursday, July 16, 2009, I received a cell phone call from Sarah.

"Amanda," Sarah said, "Your dad just called. In fact, my dad's talking to him on the home phone right now."

What bad luck. The one time Dad calls and I'm not home. "Tell him I'll be back on Monday and ask him to call back."

"Okay." Sarah relayed the message to Dave.

"Sarah, can you do me a favor?" I asked. "Can you please write down whatever you can remember him saying. I haven't heard from him in nearly six months and I really want to know how he's doing. See if you can find out where he is."

"The caller ID said Riverside Hotel. I already wrote everything down."

I smiled at her quick thinking.

"He was talking fast like normal. He had a lot of breaks in his speech . . . flustered maybe? Almost a stutter, but not quite. He didn't mention God at all which was unusual. The first thing he asked was, 'Where's Amanda?' I said you were driving to visit Aunt Jackie. He asked about David and Justin and where they were and I said with you. He asked when you'd be back, but he didn't say the typical God, your Savior and stuff." Sarah interrupted her train of thought to say, "Dad just hung up the phone. Do you want to talk to him?"

"Yes, please."

Dave got on the line.

"Hi, Dave. What did my Dad say to you?"

"I don't remember everything. He said he's in Ft. Lauderdale, Florida. He told me he's growing a beard to look like Jesus and that women tell him he looks 40. He said his life is like James Bond's and he can't stay in one place. I asked him, 'Where have you been and what have you been through?' He said he can't explain it to me because I'm not at a higher level with God and I won't understand. He said that he'd been to 45 of the 50 states in America, North and South Africa, and the Mediterranean. He also said something about six month days and six month nights in Scandinavia. I don't remember much else."

What were the odds that he would've called the one weekend out of the year when I had gone out of town? "Did you ask him to call me back on Monday?"

"Yes I did, but he said he didn't need to and it wasn't important. He also said something about God."

I hung up and phoned Hilda. She sounded relieved he was alive, but asked where he was, or how we could find him. I reminded her I recently sent her a packet from the Outpost for Hope organization that shows families like ours how to file a missing persons report with the police.

"Oh, I've tried that before," Hilda said. "The police wouldn't help me. Nobody would help me. People don't understand. If only Daddy had taken his medicine. I don't know." Hilda sighed. The years of pain showed in her voice. "Nothing helped. Oh, how many times I cried, asking God, 'Why? Why that happened to him?' I don't know, dear, what's in his mind; hopefully, it won't be too late. He was the most wonderful person in my life. I never met anyone like him; he was the only person I loved. But, that's the way it is, life is that way. It's sad."

As I listened to Hilda relate what she'd gone through, I realized how little I initially understood. Every family member had a small piece of the puzzle and, after thirteen years, we put the pieces together.

"I know it's horrible. It's not your fault though. You didn't cause his illness. We need to focus on ourselves, too. We need to move on with our own lives. Try not to be sad for him—he knows no better, now. He believes he is a prophet and he is happy with that. It's important we find happiness in life, too."

"Amanda, do you know that after he left in 1999, I was living in West Virginia by myself, alone. Nobody was around me. I would walk by the river and scream and cry. Sitting by the river at night, I would scream, 'God, help me! Let me get out of this place! Lord, help me!'"

I couldn't imagine living through that. "How did you get through it?" I asked."Have you tried talking to a psychologist?"

"What are doctors going to do for me? Give me medication? I am going to do this for myself, by myself. I did it myself, without any doctors. I didn't get depressed or anxious. I was hurt though. It felt like a jungle out there in West Virginia—no houses around. But I pray every single day, even up until this day. Before I get out of bed every morning, I read the Bible for 30 minutes every day, and pray for everyone. I say, 'Please God, don't let Joseph be alone.'" Hilda took a breath. She continued, "That's the only reason I am alive today. I found wonderful people, like my family. Mary, the friend I made when your Dad first left me here in West Virginia, is more than a sister to me. Besides, the psychologists are going to make me more crazy."

The line went silent. I didn't push the issue. Each of us had to find our own way of dealing with the situation. It had been over ten years since Dad flipped out. Yet, if I mention this to Jackie, she says it feels like only yesterday. To watch a loved one fade away is worse than death. Jackie's tried clairvoyant readings, spiritual healings, and different meditation practices like yoga to deal with this. She's explored spiritual practices like Zen Buddhism, Tibetan Buddhism, chanting, Center for Spiritual Healing, a church of religious science. And although she denounces organized religion, she's constantly seeking spiritual well-being. I ask myself why? Why does Jackie have to go through all this to come to peace?

Keith has moved on with his life; he doesn't live in the past. He doesn't dwell on things he can't change, and we can't change what's happened. Some people say his lack of emotions isn't healthy, but who's to say? Maybe he's got it right, and everyone else is needlessly suffering. Why keep hoping Dad will get better? Keith's right; it isn't going to happen. Dad is gone. The Dad we all knew and loved will never come back to us.

"Ai-yi-yi," Hilda said. "Your daddy. I hope he is okay. I still worry about him."

"Me, too," I said. "But you know how Dad is. He's smart and he's taken care of himself on the streets before. Who knows? He's probably in Florida right now. I'm sure he's fine."

After ending the call, I thought about Dad the rest of the way to Jackie's house. I hoped maybe Dave was wrong, maybe Dad would call back.

AFTERWORD

SHOULD I BLAME DAD for wanting to believe he was something grander than he was: a loving husband, a devoted father of three, and an intelligent, educated man with a stable job? Perhaps life was too mundane for him and yet, he seemed happy.

Maybe he *was* happy, but when he was diagnosed with cancer, he became so afraid of losing everything he cherished that his fears became a self-fulfilling prophecy. Was it because of the stress of the prostate cancer, or side effects of the general anesthesia, or some medical mistake, of which we were unable to get any information about without a court order, thanks to an overreaching Health Insurance Portability and Accountability Act's (HIPAA) stringent guidelines? Was it an imbalance of hormones? Or was it being an only child to two neurotic parents, along with a possible genetic predisposition? What was the cause for Dad's drastic personality change? I'll probably never know. I'm not a psychiatrist or psychologist; I'm simply his daughter.

I remember a college paper once assigned to me. I had to answer: *What is the meaning of life?* Life is what we make of it. I've accepted I don't have all the answers.

Whether or not my dad is still alive doesn't change the problem. Within a single year, my dad, the "prophet", stranded his wife across the country, traveled to over thirty countries on several continents, and spent his life savings along the way. According to Dad, people in Africa hailed him as a prophet for bringing rain, he was arrested in Israel for intervening between his Palestinian taxi driver and a Jewish police officer, and he preached to a lower level Mafioso son in Italy.

Not long after in Chicago, Dad preached to the wrong people. Drug dealers broke his nose, stole his wallet, and drove off in his car. Oddly enough, this car would be confiscated by the Chicago Police Department after being used in drug runs for several years, and later sold off to Hilda's friends from West Virginia who would purchase it at a police auction in Florida.

Were they grandiose delusions? Was all of this a figment of his imagination? I don't think so. What about all of the other graphic visions and hallucinations that plagued Dad? Were they creations of his paranoid brain? Maybe. But, the fact there is evidence to support much of his claims, including letters postmarked from around the world and hospital records, lends credence to his claims. They were real to him.

Some people turn paranoid and delusional because of drugs; my dad didn't have a history of drug or alcohol abuse. According the National Institute of Mental Health, most cases of paranoid schizophrenia—which is what he was once diagnosed with—become apparent when a person is in their late-teens or early-twenties; late onset of the disorder is much more unusual, especially in cases as severe as my father's. What makes Dad's condition especially frustrating is that he gives the appearance of being sane and normal at times; many would only consider him a religious zealot.

Besides Dad's short involuntary confinements in mental institutions, successful treatment has been impossible, thanks in large part to the American mental health laws. Much to our family's horror, we found the laws worked to keep people mentally insane as opposed to helping them to heal, to be healthy and happy, and to become functioning members of society.

Prior to the legal changes that led to deinstitutionalization in 1969 in California (and other states) with the implementation of the Lanterman-Petris-Short (LPS) Act, the mentally ill were purportedly abused and mistreated. Controversial psychiatric treatments such as shock therapy and even more horrific methods such as lobotomies had been occasionally used to "heal" individuals against their wishes. Some patients were wrongly locked away in mental institutions, never allowed to rejoin society.

There was a societal backlash to the abuse; state hospitals were shut down and patients were discharged, but patients were given minimal follow-up care in their communities. The enactment of mental health deinstitutionalization laws during the mid-twentieth century had horrific and unintended consequences: the prison and homeless populations swelled by people with mental illness. Some people praised the legal changes, while others saw the problems with the patients' newfound legal protections. It effectively tied doctors' hands, preventing them from treating those obviously in need, until too late. Basically, people who suffer from Anosognosia, a lack of insight into their illness (different from denial) must try to kill themselves or someone else before being treated.

The Treatment Advocacy Center is one organization trying to resolve this; they are fighting for legal changes that can fix the systematic abuse and neglect of the mentally ill. This includes assisted outpatient treatment (AOT) for those in medical need and court-ordered treatment for individuals with severe mental illnesses who have a history of medication noncompliance, as a condition of remaining in the community. Sadly, my dad was never offered this medical option. This treatment mechanism is used until a person is well enough to maintain his or her own treatment regime. It is a less restrictive and less costly alternative to inpatient hospitalization, and even more importantly, it is effective at reducing negative outcomes including homelessness, incarceration and arrests.

In 2002, California—where Dad lived when he first became ill—passed Laura's law, which is modeled after New York's highly successful Kendra's Law (In 1999, New York legislation enacted Kendra's Law in response to the horrific death of Kendra Webdale. A local man, with an untreated severe mental illness, pushed her in front of a New York City subway train to her death). Two separate independent studies over 10 years proved Kendra's Law:

- Helps the mentally ill by reducing homelessness (74%); suicide attempts (55%); and substance abuse (48%)
- Keeps the public safer by reducing physical harm to others (47%) and property destruction (43%)
- Saves money by reducing hospitalization (77%); arrests (83%); and incarceration (87%)

In May 2007, California's Department of Mental Health confirmed that Nevada County saved $1.81 for every $1.00 spent on assisted outpatient treatment by reducing costs to other county systems, such as emergency departments, ambulance, law enforcement, and the courts.

Some people, remembering the horrors of the past, have feared Kendra's Law would lead to a roundup of mentally ill individuals and force them into treatment. The truth is Kendra's Law's narrowly-focused eligibility criteria, stringent multi-layer administrative requirements, independent judicial review and strong due process protections protect against misuse. The law has strict eligibility criteria and numerous consumer protections. A patient may be placed in assisted outpatient treatment only if, after a hearing, the court finds ALL of the following criteria have been met. The consumer must:

- be eighteen years of age or older; and
- suffer from a mental illness; and
- be unlikely to survive safely in the community without supervision, based on a clinical determination; and
- have a history of non-compliance with treatment that has:
  1. been a significant factor in his or her being in a hospital, prison or jail at least twice within the last thirty-six months or;
  2. resulted in one or more acts, attempts or threats of serious violent behavior toward self or others within the last forty-eight months; and
- be unlikely to voluntarily participate in treatment; and
- be, in view of his or her treatment history and current behavior, in need of assisted outpatient treatment in order to prevent a relapse or deterioration which would be likely to result in:
  1. a substantial risk of physical harm to the consumer as manifested by threats of or attempts at suicide or serious bodily harm or conduct demonstrating that the consumer is dangerous to himself or herself, or
  2. a substantial risk of physical harm to other persons as manifested by homicidal or other violent behavior by which others are placed in reasonable fear of serious physical harm; and
- be likely to benefit from assisted outpatient treatment; and
- if the consumer has a health care proxy, any directions in it will be taken into account by the court in determining the written treatment plan.

However, nothing precludes a person with a health care proxy from being eligible for assisted outpatient treatment.

Under these narrow conditions, my dad would have most likely qualified for help had this law been in place at the onset of his illness.

Unfortunately in California, it is up to each individual county to pass a resolution to implement AB 1421 (Laura's Law), which was named after Laura Wilcox who, along with two other people, was killed by a mental health patient who had resisted treatment which his concerned family had sought out, prior to the murders. As of 2012, only two out of fifty-eight California counties have implemented this life-saving law. In large part this is due to the public's lack of awareness of the benefits of the law. In 2012, the state law was renewed.

There is hard evidence of the fiscal and societal benefits of keeping more people out of mental hospitals, preventing the revolving door of hospitalization and/or jailing, and preventing the needless tragedies that occur when mental illnesses go untreated, namely homelessness, victimization, death from untreated illness, murders and suicides.

We are in the midst of a mental illness crisis.

People with mental illness are victimized by laws that only allow treatment based on danger. Currently, in most places, they have a legal right to be mentally ill, even when incapable of making that decision. Families, on the other hand, have no rights to help their disabled loved ones. So the afflicted can wreak havoc upon their family and remain ill, even when they have lost the ability to reason or to make any sound judgment in their best interest.

Unbelievably, I have heard people argue it is better to be homeless and/or suffering from severe mental illnesses than to be forced into treatment. People of sound mind disagree. If a child's parents "medically neglect" their child by refusing treatment for a curable disease, society says this amounts to child abuse. The court system can and has ordered treatment for "medically neglected" children. Laws are in place to prevent child abuse and to uphold compulsory education. This is all good, but who is looking out for the disabled and vulnerable adults suffering from severe mental illnesses? Families torn apart by a loved one's severe mental illness cannot help their loved one and are instead stuck in a corner with no way out of the darkness, which is exactly where my family ended up, face to face at a dead end.

It may be too late for my dad, but not for others. Although most people have been fortunate enough to enjoy mental stability, this doesn't change the uncomfortable truth: mental illness is everyone's problem. Kendra and Laura and other innocent victims are evidence of this fact.

SOURCES

2011-2012 Nevada County Grand Jury. *Laura's Law in Nevada County: A Model for Action – Saving Money and Lives.* Superior Court of California Country of Nevada. 2012. PDF on Web. 16 August 2012.

A Guide to Laura's Law. Treatment Advocacy Center. 21 Nov. 2002. Web. 6 May 2013.

Amador, Xavier. *I Am Not Sick, I Don't Need Help!* New York: Vida Press, 2012. Print.

"Deinstitutionalization: A Psychiatric Titanic." *Frontline on Public Broadcasting Service.* WGBH Educational Foundation. 10 May 2005. Web. 9 May 2010.

Fact Sheet: Myths about Kendra's Law. Treatment Advocacy Center. 2009. Web. 9 May 2010.

NAMI.com. National Alliance on Mental Illness. 2013. Web. 6 May 2013.

"Schizophrenia." *National Institute of Mental Health.* U.S. Department of Health and Human Services. 7 May 2010. Web. 9 May 2010.

RESOURCES

1. LEAP Institute
   Learn about Dr. Xavier Amador's LEAP Method for improving communication. www.LEAPinstitute.org
2. National Alliance of Mental Illness (NAMI)
   Find information about your local affiliate. They are an excellent resource and their family-to-family program is outstanding. www.nami.org
3. National Institute of Mental Health (NIMH)
   Read more information about mental disorders. www.NIMH.gov
4. Outpost for Hope
   The missing, missing and how to help the forgotten victims of homelessness. www.outpostforhope.org
5. Treatment Advocacy Center (TAC)
   Find information about the mental health laws in your state. www.tac.org

AUTHOR'S STATEMENT

THIS BOOK CAME ABOUT after numerous interviews and extensive research. Every effort has been made to insure the accuracy of the information in this text. Unfortunately, while under tremendous stress, individuals' memories can occasionally distort reality. In a few cases, details of actual events have been determined based on a melding of different people's recollections and points-of-view. However, the physical evidence to support the claims made in this book is abundant and well-documented through postcards, letters, e-mails, photos, videos, and medical records. Actual names have been changed in order to protect the privacy of the individuals   involved.

INTERVIEWS: WHAT WE HAVE LEARNED

AMANDA

I HAVE LEARNED STIGMA can prevent families from openly communicating about a brain disease. Communication and cooperation among family members is critical. A united front is the best way to help.

Get educated. NAMI's Family to Family program is an excellent start. Speak about it. Don't be afraid to ask others for help; you can't shoulder the burden alone. Anosognosia is real. Instead of blaming a person for denying they are ill, take the time to understand their brain may be making it impossible for them to comprehend their illness. If your loved one suffers from anosognosia, focus on the benefits of treatment, instead of trying to convince the person he/she is ill. Read Dr. Xavier Amador's book *I am Not Sick, I Don't Need Help*.

Laugh. A sense of humor will carry you through the tough times. Keep hope alive. Advocate for your loved one. If this isn't possible, advocate for others. Don't complain about the system, change it. Lastly, send mail until it gets returned if your loved one has an address.

HILDA

YOU HAVE TO DEAL with it day by day. Try to find some help. You need support.

When I took my husband to the doctors, everyone said he was okay. Even the psychiatrists couldn't obligate him into treatment if he didn't want to willingly. I was in limbo. It was so sad to not be able to find help for him. Nobody could do anything.

This has to change. Doctors and hospitals need to help. I support assisted outpatient treatment because it is not right to let family members refuse treatment, to become homeless, to be taken advantage of, or to be hurt. It's hard to leave a family member out in the streets but the law was against us. The law didn't let us help our family member who's ill.

The patient privacy laws are too extreme. When everything is confidential, how can a family deal with the person who is ill, when the doctors won't even tell the spouse anything? How can that be okay? Doctors and families need to be able to work together to help patients.

Psychiatrists need to spend more than half an hour or hour with patients. Doctors and nurses need to educate family members. I never thought mental illness would happen to my family. I wasn't prepared for it and didn't know what to do. Somebody should have told me.

If your loved one becomes sick, first try to relax and talk with your ill family member. Say, "I think it would be a good idea to see a doctor. [Don't say the word psychologist]. We can try to figure out what's going on. Something isn't right with your medication." You can't be mad at or mean to your loved one. That makes it worse.

At some point, if they refuse help, you will get angry. It's hard. Try to find help. Your family, friends, doctors, sometimes church, can help.

Stigma affects people. At times, coworkers, friends, people from church didn't want to look at us, like they didn't understand what was wrong or know what to say. They didn't want to upset us, so they said nothing. They were polite, not wanting to hurt our feelings. They would talk to my husband, but I could feel the tension and knew what they were thinking. They should have been more honest with me, but not judge us.

After he became sick, we couldn't spend time with friends anymore, which only made it harder for me to not have that support. I would push him out of the house, so I could talk to people. My family was trying to help him. When we went to Argentina, my family took him everywhere. He was entertained and seemed happier. But when we returned to America, it was the same thing.

The only thing I could do was to pray to God for help. I told myself I have to do things on my own, I have to make new friends, I have to keep living. People always ask me how I've handled this and how I'm such a strong person. I say, I told myself I have to survive, to keep going with my life. At the time, the church was a very good support for me. It was hard for me, but what could I do? After he abandoned me, I used to sit by the river, crying, screaming, and praying. Being by myself and going through that helped. I didn't go to church after that, because I feel church is business, and God is with me. Now, I listen to pastors on television or radio. I enjoy listening to their programs, which makes me happy. Reading the bible and praying for help and for my husband has helped.

Ultimately, the family needs to support, needs to help, and needs to share the problems.

JACKIE

IN MY MIND, I no longer have a father. For a long time, I thought that Dad's "condition" would just go away on its own and I'd have my father back. After time passed, however, I realized he was never going to be the same, never going to get better. There is a deep hole in my heart, a kind of void that has never healed. I think it would be easier for me to come to a final sense of closure if he was dead. I feel like I'm grieving for a walking dead person/ for the living dead. Not knowing where in the world he is, if he's dead or alive, that is much harder to deal with.

I have found myself drawn to older fatherly-type men, especially those with similar facial features as my dad as if they were some sort of replacement for him. A piece of my childhood, a big sense of safety, security, and my identify is forever lost except in my memories. My children will never have a "grandpa" to love and bond with like I had.

The support of my husband and my mom, and the shared grieving experience with my siblings and stepmom has kept me going. Although I've always been close to my sister and brother, their presence has been a constant source of stability and safety for me and serves as a reminder of who I am when I feel lost and unsafe in the world.

For me, the best way I've dealt with my loss has been to pretend it doesn't exist, to ignore the pain, to just remember the good times, what I want to remember. However, when that protective wall starts to crumble and I find myself curled up in the fetal position crying uncontrollably, then the loving, warm embrace of my husband, with his protective arms around me, or a phone call to my sister helps pull me through.

I don't know what advice I have to offer others in similar situations, except to nourish/ maintain the close relationships that you do have—they will be a source of strength for you.

KEITH

WHAT I HAVE LEARNED through this process is acceptance. You have to realize that things just will not be the same as they were before and someone whose has a mental illness will never be the same person you knew before. You cannot change this, it is a losing battle. You have to accept the reality of how things are now in order to be able to move forward with your life and not allow it to consume you. There will be good days and bad days, just as there are with any illness. Finding support with family and friends, and talking openly about it can make it easier.

It doesn't have to be the white elephant in the room. I chose to move on with my life, and take it for what it is. This does not mean I don't care, it means I am not letting it stop my life from moving forward. Don't let someone else's illness define who you are as a person, do what you can to support those around you who are also dealing with it.

Mental illness is just that, an illness…although an invisible one. The person suffering may accept help when you try, and many times they may not. Either way, you will need to be able to accept the new reality in order to move on yourself.

READING DISCUSSION QUESTIONS

1. What is the theme of *Losing Dad*? Besides mental illness, how can this theme relate to life and the world? In what ways can you relate to this story's message?
2. What was the cause of Joseph's transformation? What evidence is there to support your opinion?
3. Considering the family's different reactions, is there a right way to deal with mental illness? Evaluate each character's reactions. Consider possible cultural bias.
4. What part might social stigma have played in the story? How might stigma be reduced?
5. What role did mental health laws play in the story? What are the laws in your state or country? Are these adequate? What, if anything, would you change? How?
6. Anosognosia, a term coined by neurobiologists, means lack of insight. If the family members had been aware of Joseph's anosognosia early on, do you think this story may have ended differently? How so?
7. If you were Amanda, Hilda, Jackie, or Keith, how would you feel now? What more could you do for Joseph? For each other?
8. Communication is important in a family. Think about the communication in your family. How well would your family be equipped to handle the onset of a severe mental illness?
9. How has mental illness affected your life, if at all? How has mental illness affected our society?
10. There are many other losses which people can experience such as death, disease, substance abuse, disabilities, war, trauma, births, job losses, financial loss, bullying or harassment. What stages of grief do you think are healthy for people to go through? What is not healthy? When should someone seek help?

ACKNOWLEDGEMENTS

OKAY, THIS IS GOING to read a little like the long academy award acceptance speeches.

I would like to thank: Hilda, without you, none of this would be possible. I am forever grateful and only wish I could do more to ease your suffering. You have the strength of Penelope, which I admire; Dad: I love you more than you know and wish you were still in our lives. I have learned to accept you for who you are now, but will always remember you for who you really were; my grandparents: I love you and am sorry you had to lose your only son. I can only imagine how difficult Dad's illness was for you. This is for you and for all parents suffering like you did; Jackie, Ms. Grammar Queen, for your help; Neil, for another bit of the puzzle; Keith, for finally freakin' opening up to me, about damn time. It was worth the wait; Mom, for sharing private moments and being so supportive the entire way; Debbie Patinkin, for your help and guidance through the hard times with Dad. I know my grandparents would thank you, too; IraLee, your sense of humor and willingness to share has been fantastic; Abe Nieves, for your humorous take on the situation; my wonderful editor, Jean Jenkins, for your editing expertise and invaluable career advice; Ingrid Ricks, for your encouragement and guidance; Hyla Molander, for your advice with Scribd.com; Saddleback Writers' Guild (Mel Zimmerman, Jacquelyn Hanson, & David Eugene Andrews), for your tireless assistance, honest criticism, and friendly banter; Doug Ordunio, for pushing me forward in the beginning of my writing journey; Duy Le and Ken Elliott, for your enthusiasm, support, and specific suggestions; Bonnie, your early encouragement was Price-less; Southern California Writers' Conference, for the wonderful workshops and connections; Robert Yehling, for your belief in this book; Lisa Park, for suffering through the beginning of my learning curve with kindness; all the LQ Ladies for advice and friendship; Nelda, for your support; Nicole Trinh for helping me get things together in the end;

Jill Elaine Hughes, for your suggestions during the editing process; Sara Clay, one of my first readers, for your encouragement; Yvonne Mendez, for lending an ear when I needed it; Lynn Camp, for knowing me so well that you knew when others wouldn't; National Alliance on Mental Illness, Orange County Affiliate (NAMI-OC), for the helpful education, what a wonderful resource. I wish I'd taken the classes sooner; Brian & Carla Jacobs, for empowering me to advocate; Treatment Advocacy Center, including Dorothy Fuller, for your tireless advocacy on behalf of the most vulnerable members of society; and last, but not least, my printer, for being so dependable. You've taken a lot of abuse.

ABOUT THE AUTHOR

BECAUSE OF HER FAMILY'S experience, Amanda LaPera is a vocal advocate for individuals and families affected by severe mental illness. She serves on the Board of Directors for the Orange County affiliate of the National Alliance on Mental Illness (NAMI-OC). With her book, *Losing Dad*, she hopes to raise awareness, eliminate stigma, and offer hope.

Her writing has appeared in numerous anthologies, newspapers, and websites. She maintains a blog where the topics range from writing to mental health to life in general.

She lives with her children and two dogs in California, where she teaches English. In addition to reading and writing, she finds joy in music, art, and nature, which she learned from her dad.

To request Amanda LaPera for speaking engagements, contact her through her publisher on the web at www.adamopress.com. For more information, visit www.losingdad.com.

CPSIA information can be obtained at www.ICGtesting.com
Printed in the USA
LVOW08s1952041013

355418LV00002B/4/P